Knowledge, Innovation and Economic Growth

Knowledge, Innovation and Economic Growth

The Theory and Practice of Learning Regions

Edited by

Frans Boekema

Professor of Economic Geography, Catholic University Nijmegen and Associate Professor of Regional Economics and Spatial Sciences, Tilburg University, The Netherlands

Kevin Morgan

Professor of European Regional Development, University Wales, Cardiff, UK

Silvia Bakkers

Assistant Professor of Regional Economics, Tilburg University, The Netherlands

Roel Rutten

PhD Student in the Department of Policy and Organization Studies, Tilburg University, The Netherlands

Edward Elgar

Cheltenham, UK ● Northampton, MA, USA

Published by
Edward Elgar Publishing Limited
Glensanda House
Montpellier Parade
Cheltenham
Glos GL50 1UA
UK

Edward Elgar Publishing, Inc.
136 West Street
Suite 202
Northampton
Massachusetts 01060
USA

A catalogue record for this book
is available from the British Library

Library of Congress Cataloguing in Publication Data
Knowledge, innovation and economic growth : the theory and practice of learning regions / edited by Frans Boekema . . . [et al.]
    (Includes bibliographical references.)
    1. Economic development – Effect of education on. 2. Knowledge – Economic aspects. 3. Learning – Economic aspects. 4. Information society. I. Boekema, Frans.
HD75.7   K59 2000
338.9 – dc21   99–059120
ISBN 1 84064 215 7

Printed and bound in Great Britain by MPG Books Ltd, Bodmin, Cornwall

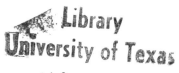

Contents

Figures

Tables

Contributors

Silvia Bakkers is Assistant Professor of Regional Economics in the Economics Department of Tilburg University in the Netherlands (see below for full biography).

Nicola Bellini is Senior Lecturer at the Scuola Superiore Santa-Anna in Pisa, Italy.

Frans Boekema is Professor of Economic Geography in the Department of Human Geography of the Faculty of Policy Sciences at Nijmegen University, and Associate Professor of Regional Economics in the Economics Department of Tilburg University in the Netherlands (see below for full biography).

Jan Cobbenhagen is Senior Researcher at the Maastricht Economic Research Institute on Innovation and Technology, MERIT.

Ben Dankbaar is Professor at the Nijmegen Business School of Nijmegen University in the Netherlands.

Jules van Dijck is Emeritus Professor in Policy and Organization Studies at Tilburg University in the Netherlands.

Marina van Geenhuizen is Assistant Professor in the Department of Technology, Policy and Management of the Technical University of Delft in the Netherlands.

Arnoud Lagendijk is Post-Doc in the Department of Spatial Planning of the Faculty of Policy Sciences of Nijmegen University in the Netherlands.

Jan Lambooy is Professor of Economic Geography in the Department of Spatial Sciences of the University of Utrecht, and Professor of Regional Economics in the Faculty of Economics of the University of Amsterdam.

Mikel Landabaso is Senior Researcher of DG 16 (CSM2 3/63) at the European Commission, Brussels.

Marius Meeus is Associate Professor in the Department of Technology Management at the Technical University Eindhoven in the Netherlands.

Kevin Morgan is Professor of Regional Economics at Cardiff University, Wales, UK.

Peter Nijkamp is Professor of Spatial Economics in the Economics Department of the Free University of Amsterdam in the Netherlands.

Leon Oerlemans is Assistant Professor in the Department of Technology Management of the Technical University Eindhoven in the Netherlands.

Päivi Oinas is Assistant Professor of Economic Geography in the Faculty of Economics of Erasmus University in Rotterdam, the Netherlands.

Roel Rutten is PhD student at Tilburg University and consultant of ERAC (European Regional Affairs Consultants) in Boxtel, the Netherlands (see below for full biography).

The editors

Frans Boekema (1949) graduated in Regional Economics in 1977 from Tilburg University. In 1978 he started his career as Assistant Professor of Regional Economics and Economic Geography at the same university. In 1986 he completed his dissertation on Local initiatives and regional development. In 1990 he was appointed as Associate Professor of Regional Economics and Economic Geography. In 1995 he became a part-time professor in Economic Geography at the Faculty of Policy Sciences of Nijmegen University. In the meantime he was also working as manager of the Regional Economic Department of the Economic Institute Tilburg, a research and consultancy institute. His main fields of research activities are: local and regional development, innovation and technological development and regions, border-regions and border crossing activities, learning regions, and regional developments in Europe.

Silvia Bakkers (1974) graduated in Regional Economics from Tilburg University in 1997. She started as junior researcher and consultant at Buck Consultants International in Nijmegen in the Netherlands. Since 1998 she has been Assistant Professor of Regional Economics and Economic Geography at the Economic Faculty of Tilburg University in the Netherlands. In addition, she is one of the project managers for educational innovations at this institute. She was also one of the organizers of the international seminar on The Learning Region, from which this publication is one of the results. She has visited several universities and other organizations around Europe to supply intensive courses on spatial economics. In 1999 she was also one of the organizers of another international seminar on the role of universities and knowledge-infrastructure for regional development. Her main fields of interest are locational behaviour and the role of telematica, sustainable development and local economic policy.

Roel Rutten (1971) graduated in Policy and Organizational Sciences from Tilburg University in 1995. He is working part-time as consultant and research fellow at ERAC, European Regional Affairs Consultants, in Boxtel in the Netherlands. He is also a PhD student working on regional innovation systems and clusters. For this research project he gained experience with many empirical regional projects in several countries of the European Union.

He was also one of the members of the organizing committees for the international seminars on Learning Regions and the role of Universities for regional development. His main fields of research are technologic development and innovation, clustering, industrial districts, and regional technology plans.

Kevin Morgan is Professor of Regional Economics, Department of City and Regional Planning, Cardiff University, Wales, UK.

Preface

In recent years many articles on topics like innovation, technology transfer, knowledge infrastructure and learning regions have been published in journals. It is striking that not only scientists are interested in these topics, but also politicians, policy makers and even business people turn out to be on top of the involved themes. The attention paid to these contributions makes it clear that regions are becoming more and more the focal points where knowledge creation and learning are concerned in the new age of global, knowledge-intensive capitalism. From several case studies which deal with the learning region approach one might conclude that these regions function as collectors and repositories of knowledge and ideas, and that at the same time they are providing the underlying environment or infrastructure which facilitates the flow of learning, knowledge and ideas. Although in some publications we can read about the end of geography and the death of distance, the learning region approach proves that regions, on the other hand, are becoming more important modes of economic and technical organization on the national and international scale.

There is another reason why the idea of the learning region is a hot item these days. Universities and other knowledge-intensive institutions have to compete with several other knowledge brokers. Due to the fact that the editors as well as most of the authors are all working at universities, we are highly involved in the never ending debate about the role of universities in the future. In other words, how should universities and the knowledge infrastructure deal with the growing need for (applied) research and consultancy from society in general and from the regions in particular?

From the above-mentioned backgrounds Tilburg University did a good job in organizing an international seminar 'The Learning Region, Theory, Policy and Practice' on 27 March 1998. The organizers succeeded in attracting very well-known participants from the scientific world as well as from the policy and political world. In this way the seminar was an interesting mix of theoretical papers on the one hand and empirical and practical contributions on the other.

In this book the papers that have been presented at the seminar are brought together. We are delighted that so many speakers were willing to contribute. In addition to those papers some very interesting external authors were asked to join in, which they fortunately did. The result of all this co-operation, the efforts of the editing team and last but not least the enormous lay-out technical support by Ms Roos Pijpers in my opinion is a very interesting book!

I am convinced that this book will be very useful for many (spatial) economic researchers as well as for those who are interested in the role of knowledge in an economy in general and in the learning region paradigm in particular.

Professor Kevin Morgan
Cardiff University

PART ONE

The Learning Region Paradigm Explained

1. Introduction to Learning Regions: a New Issue for Analysis?

Frans Boekema, Kevin Morgan, Silvia Bakkers and Roel Rutten

In recent years a steady stream of literature has appeared on learning regions, but the interest in learning regions has not been confined to academia alone. Many regions throughout the European Union, for example, are working on the development of regional innovation strategies in an effort, supported by the European Commission, to further learning processes in regions.

There is no simple definition of the learning region. It is too complex an issue to be captured in one phrase. The learning region is the physical expression of the understanding which has grown, particularly during the last decade and a half, that economic growth is dependent on innovation, and innovation, in turn, is dependent on the creation, dissemination and application of knowledge. The latter is usually referred to as learning, and learning processes are generally believed to be connected with space. Hence learning regions. But neither of these issues is in itself very new. Space, innovation, knowledge and related issues have been studied for a long time – both separately and in relation to each other, and not just from the perspective of a single discipline. Why, then, this publication on learning regions? The reason is as obvious as it is trivial. After reading a library of publications on learning regions and related issues and after attending innumerable seminars and lectures on the subject, we still do not have the answers to many of the fundamental questions. And because our investigation of the learning region continues every day, our understanding of this phenomenon is continuing to grow. But each step we advance raises new questions. The aim of this book, therefore, is to show the rich diversity of research approaches to the learning region. We shall give some answers and we shall inevitably ask new questions.

1.1 THE LEARNING REGION PARADIGM

As we review the considerable volume of literature on the learning region, we cannot feel but overwhelmed by the wealth and diversity of insights and angles of research associated with this concept. This is both a weakness and a strength. It is a weakness in that the diversity of the concept prevents it from developing into a consistent theory, but this diversity is also a strength in that it sheds light on the connections between the various elements that constitute learning regions: knowledge, learning, innovation, networks, institutions and space. In this volume, we will concentrate on these strengths. We shall do so by referring to the learning region as a paradigm rather than a concept or a theory. A concept or a theory is a set of consistent and accepted, if not proven, statements. Hypotheses, which can be tested, can be derived from these statements. This is much less the case with a paradigm, which is described as a 'pattern' in Webster's dictionary. Because of its diversity, the 'learning region' has more resemblance to a paradigm than to a theory. The learning region has foundations in a multiplicity of theories which have in common that they focus on the learning process. 'Learning' is the pattern in the learning region paradigm. The focus on learning is rooted in the conviction that the nature of the economy has shifted from a labour and capital-based economy to a knowledge-based one, where knowledge is the most important resource and learning the most important process. The processes at work here have already been described by Schumpeter when he described economic development as the outcome of what he called new combinations. In his view, making use of new knowledge, or making use of old knowledge in new ways, contributes to innovations which, in turn, lead to economic development (Schumpeter, 1926). Current research has only underlined Schumpeter's findings, hence the title of this volume: 'Knowledge, Innovation and Economic Growth'.

As its title suggests, the aim of this volume is to discuss some key elements of the learning region paradigm. We do so by adopting a multidisciplinary approach. We consider the theoretical diversity of the learning region paradigm to be a strength, as it allows us to look beyond traditional horizons. It also explains the question mark in the title of this chapter. Knowledge, innovation and economic growth have been studied before and so they are not new issues for analysis. But the fact that they are now studied from the perspective of learning, which makes their interconnectedness even clearer, is the merit of this new paradigm: the learning region. Looking at knowledge, learning and innovation from the perspective of learning has indeed raised some new questions. The fact that we are now on our way to becoming an increasingly globalized and knowledge-intensive economy urges us to rethink the nature of competition, particularly in relation to learning. Following the lines of the learning region paradigm, we must find answers to the question of how knowledge creation and learning lead to competitive advantage. We also have to take into account that 'networks' and the 'factor space' play a different role when perceived through the learning region paradigm. It leads us to redefine these concepts and the connections between them. Finally, we have to consider the policy implications of the learning region paradigm. Thus, rather than posing a new issue for analysis, the learning region paradigm raises new questions. In what follows we will highlight some of the issues and related questions in order to set the stage for the discussions in this book.

1.2 COMPETITION IN THE KNOWLEDGE-BASED ECONOMY

In their recent book, Maskell *et al.* (1998) explain that the globalization of the economy has given rise to a new knowledge-based economy through a process which they call 'ubiquitification'. Their argument is that many competitive advantages have been eroded because the knowledge and technologies on which they were based are now available on a global scale and successful practices of firms have been copied elsewhere. Firms in low-cost countries, in particular, have benefited from this process, posing a formidable threat to western firms (p. 19). In other words, formerly localized inputs have been converted to 'ubiquities' through the globalization of the economy. This means that they can no longer be used as a source of sustain-able competitive advantage, since they are available to competitors worldwide (p. 22).

Following a similar line of thinking, Porter (1990) has differentiated between higher-order and lower-order competitive advantages. Lower-order advantages, for example, labour costs, availability of raw materials, economies of scale, use of technologies, are easy for competitors to imitate, duplicate, or nullify (pp. 49–50), particularly in an international economy, where transport costs are negligible and markets are increasingly global. 'Higher-order advantages, such as proprietary process technology, product differentiation based on unique products or services, brand reputation ..., customer relationships protected by high customer costs of switching vendors, are more durable' (p. 50). Higher-order advantages, according to Porter, have several characteristics which make them more durable: 1) they require more advanced skills and capabilities to achieve them, 2) they depend on 'sustained and cumulative investments in physical facilities and specialized and often risky learning, research and development, or marketing', and 3) a combination of larger investments with a superior performance of the activities involved (p. 50).

These higher-order advantages are less susceptible to ubiquitification; they also require more effort to create them. But, once in place, they create the dynamic economic processes which Schumpeter envisaged when he described the kind of competition that was based on 'new combinations', the kind of competition which surpasses price competition and initiates a process of creative destruction. To maintain their competitiveness, therefore, firms must invest in the creation of more stable advantages, an activity which is closely related to the creation of enhanced knowledge used for the development of firm-specific competences. This process has led to the gradual materialization of a knowledge-based economy 'where the competitive edge of many firms has shifted from static price competition towards dynamic improvement, favouring those who can create knowledge faster than their competitors' (Maskell *et al.*, 1998, p. 24). In short, the creation of competitive advantage is an act of innovation through which firms develop new and better ways of competing. Innovation encompasses much more than technology, as Porter (1990) recognizes in his definition of innovation.

> Innovation here is defined broadly, to include both improvements in technology and better methods or ways of doing things. It can be manifested in product changes, process changes, new approaches to marketing, new forms of distribution, and new conceptions of scope .... Much innovation, in practice, is rather mundane and incremental rather than radical. ... It results from organizational learning as much as from formal R&D. It always involves investment in developing skills and knowledge. (p. 45)

Porter's definition points at knowledge and learning, which are key concepts in the knowledge-based economy. Firms derive their competitiveness from firm-specific competences which they develop through the combination of tangible and intangible resources. Firm-specific competences enable firms to do things that their competitors cannot imitate or duplicate, at least not in the short term (Maskell *et al.*, 1998). Developing intangible resources requires investment in a wide variety of factors, such as human skills, organizational capacities, distribution and logistics, advertising, image, design, reputation, etc. These factors attribute immaterial qualities to (material) products and these are increasingly important for our appreciation of these products (den Hartog *et al.*, 1997; Jacobs, 1996).

Intangibles are embedded in human knowledge, skills and experiences, and in organizational routines which must be mobilized in new and creative ways (cf. Schumpeter's new combinations) in order to produce innovations. The paradox of our increasingly technological society is that technology is no longer a decisive factor for the creation of competitiveness, since it is available worldwide. Instead, human skills and knowledge now make the difference. This is good news for firms, as skills and knowledge are highly personal. It opens the door to the creation of firm-specific competences – if personal knowledge and skills are embedded in an organizational context and are transformed into firm-specific practices and routines. The prospects for creating firm-specific competences become even better when we realize that personal skills, knowledge, organizational routines, and practices belong to the realms of what has become known as tacit knowledge. This means that they cannot easily be disseminated to, or copied by, other firms. In short, tacit knowledge embedded in an organizational context is the key to competitiveness in the knowledge-based economy (cf. Jacobs, 1996; Maskell, *et al.*, 1998; Morgan, 1997; Nonaka and Takeuchi, 1995).

1.3 KNOWLEDGE CREATION, LEARNING AND COMPETITIVE ADVANTAGE

As we stated above, knowledge is the most important resource in the knowledge-based economy and learning is the most important process (Morgan, 1997). Knowledge is crucial to create firm-specific competences and learning is the process through which firms create and acquire knowledge. A successful attempt to explain the process of knowledge creation and learning within firms was made by Nonaka and Takeuchi (1995). In their view, innovation is more than just the internal processing of outside information in order to solve problems. Rather, innovation is about the creation of new knowledge and information in order to recreate the environment. Knowledge can be divided into tacit knowledge and codified knowledge, the former being difficult to transfer, as it cannot be removed from its human and social context. The two types of knowledge, Nonaka and Takeuchi state, are complementary. The creation of knowledge is a process in which tacit knowledge is converted into codified knowledge and vice versa. The logic behind this is that new knowledge which an organization may want to absorb is often tacit and must first be codified to make it transferable. This new knowledge must then be internalized, i.e. people in the organization must learn to use it, which means that the new knowledge must become a part of their, and their organization's, pool of tacit knowledge. Codified and tacit knowledge are constantly in interaction with each other, thus creating a dynamic spiral of knowledge conversion leading to innovation.

Maskell *et al.* (1998) hold a slightly different opinion about the codification of tacit knowledge. They state that, although most knowledge will eventually become more codified, not all forms of knowledge can be codified. But without codification, transfer of knowledge will be difficult and can take place only by demonstration. Codification, therefore, is important, since it 'implies a lasting reduction in the otherwise recurrent costs of communicating knowledge from one individual, department or organization to another' (p. 37). Codification of knowledge does not mean that the receiver of the knowledge can use it immediately and without incurring costs. The effect of codification is that little has to be invested in the relation between the owner and receiver of the knowledge in order to convey its content. Another effect of codification is that the knowledge will eventually become diffused on a wider scale, which makes it impossible to use that knowledge as a basis for sustainable competitive advantage. In fact, because most knowledge will eventually become more codified and be diffused in the many interactions within a firm, the best way for a firm to preserve its competitive advantage is to constantly create new knowledge.

Let us follow for a moment the arguments of Nonaka and Takeuchi (1995) about knowledge creation in firms. They state that the creation of new knowledge takes place through the constant interaction between tacit and codified forms of knowledge. This interaction and creation of knowledge occurs at the level of the individual, not the organization. However, if the knowledge is not shared with others and if it is not sustained in groups or departments, a continuous process of knowledge creation will not be established. Such a process is necessary to enable organizations to internalize new knowledge and to be able to make use of it. Organizations therefore have a very important role in creating the right conditions to support knowledge creation. Knowledge at the level of the organization activates knowledge at the level of the individual. Through interaction with their environment (the organizational context), the knowledge of individuals will become part of the organizational knowledge pool. This interactive creation of knowledge cannot flourish in a rigid top-down and hierarchical approach to management, as such an approach is not particularly suited to dealing with tacit knowledge. Neither can knowledge creation flourish in a predominantly top-down and task force approach to management, because such structures have difficulties in dealing with codified knowledge. A combination of both management approaches – in which the middle level, in particular, plays an important intermediary role between the strategies and concepts from the top and the practices and more 'pedestrian forms of knowledge' (Morgan, 1997) from the bottom – is most conducive to knowledge creation. This dynamic and inter-active process of knowledge creation is the key to innovation. Its outcomes will materialize in the form of new products, services, processes, etc.

Nonaka and Takeuchi focus their attention exclusively on firms. We believe, however, that the processes they describe are equally applicable at the inter-firm level. This means that, in our view, networks must facilitate the interactive creation of knowledge between members of different organiza-tions. In this way, knowledge from one organization can be transferred to another organization and vice versa. And, more importantly, the combination of knowledge from several organizations will lead to the creation of previously unthought of new knowledge. The actual exchange of knowledge between organizations will often take place in task forces composed of members from the various organizations involved. Often withdrawn from direct hierarchical control, these task forces seem an ideal compromise between a top-down and a bottom-up style of management.

1.4 INNOVATION AND NETWORKS

Competitiveness is also strongly related to specialization. Firms cannot be successful in everything, which means that they have to choose the market and industry in which they want to compete (Porter, 1990). Others (Best, 1990; Scott, 1988; Storper 1992) have argued in relation to this that technological developments are now proceeding so quickly that firms cannot stay abreast in every field. They have to specialize in activities and technologies which form the basis of their core competences. Only in those areas can they hope to create sufficient firm-specific competences to develop a sustainable competitive advantage. Other authors, such as Håkansson and Johanson (1993), have reached similar conclusions from another perspective, that of resources. The resource-based perspective argues that networks are important for innovation, since no single firm controls sufficient resources itself. Thus innovation requires the mobilization of both internal and external resources, and external resources are mobilized through network relations. Networks, in this perspective, 'consist of actors and the relations among them, and of activities/resources and the dependencies between them' (Håkansson and Johanson, 1993, p. 36).

The consequence of both the specialization and the resource-based perspectives is the need for flexible networks. In order to seize opportunities, firms must be able to combine various specializations, resources, strengths and skills which are outside their own area of control. Firms increasingly depend on other firms for these inputs. The knowledge-based economy is thus a network economy where innovations are created on an inter-firm level. Clearly, this makes the learning region paradigm a strong argument in favour of the embeddedness approach of socio-economic inquiry. Given the many interdependencies between actors – without which learning is not possible – actors and interactions cannot be studied in isolation. Embeddedness is a key element of the learning region paradigm.

Networks, however, do not automatically enhance learning and produce innovation and competitive advantage. A high degree of trust and commitment among people and organizations is essential. Trust is defined as 'the confidence that parties will work for mutual gain and refrain from [Williamsonian] opportunistic behaviour. ... [Trust] cannot be bought; rather it has to be earned. ... [It is] one of those rare assets, like loyalty and goodwill, which have value but no price' (Morgan, 1997, p. 30). Trust must be earned and reinforced and, as such, it is a by-product of, rather than a precondition for, successful collaboration. Low-trust relationships severely inhibit interaction and collaboration, while trust-based relationships offer

> at least three major benefits on participants who have taken the time and trouble to develop these relational assets: 1) they are able to economise on time and effort because it is extremely efficient to be able to rely on the word of one's partner; 2) they are better placed to cope with uncertainty because, while it does not eliminate risk, trust reduces risk and dissolves possibilities for action which would have been unattractive otherwise; and 3) they have greater capacity for learning because they are party to thicker and richer flows of information (Morgan, 1997, pp. 30–31).

1.5   THE FACTOR OF SPACE

Another key element in the learning region paradigm is the factor of space. By itself, this term already suggests that distances matter in relation to learning. A general assumption underlying the learning region paradigm is that of the geography of knowledge. This assumption elaborates on the distinction between codified and tacit, or embedded, knowledge. Codified knowledge can easily be transferred on a global scale, for example, through the use of the Internet. Tacit knowledge, on the other hand, requires a lot of intensive face-to-face communication to transfer not only the content, but also the context, of the knowledge. In order to be able to absorb and to use tacit knowledge, the receiver will have to (learn to) understand the context in which the knowledge is embedded. Intensive face-to-face communication gains from proximity. Thus, in the case of tacit knowledge, proximity – although not essential – greatly assists the process of knowledge transfer. Various case studies of successful regions seem to support this assumption of the geography of knowledge. In the well-known regions often used as examples – such as Emilia-Romagna and Silicon Valley – the actors understand the social codes, the routines, etc. They are a community and their interactions are characterized by a considerable amount of trust. This gives the insiders of such a regional community an advantage over outsiders when it comes to the transfer of tacit (embedded) knowledge.

It is clear from the above that proximity is only one part of the explanation of the impact of 'space' on learning in networks. Institutional factors also play a crucial role, as Maskell *et al.* (1998) have explained where they point to the advantages of territorially embedded networks; networks that are 'strongly rooted in the specific social and institutional setting of place, region or country' (p. 49). They go on to argue that 'the tacitness of the knowledge created in settings where localised, inter-organisational assets are important, prevents dissemination to outsiders' (p. 49). This allows territorially embedded networks to develop unique, localized capabilities; combinations of institutional endowments, built structures, natural resources and the knowledge and skills in a region from which firms draw competitive advantages (Maskell *et al.*, 1998, p. 53). These competitive advantages are difficult for firms (networks) in other regions to copy. Note that 'localised capabilities' can also include more traditional kinds of agglomeration economies. In particular, built structures and institutional endowments are affected by agglomeration economies. The differences between central and peripheral regions can be deduced from the fact that agglomeration economies in central regions have created more and better conditions for learning. Authorities have tried for decades to create agglomeration economies in peripheral regions, with varying success. We have seen a steady stream of new initiatives based on the learning region paradigm, and this brings us to our next issue, that of regional policy.

1.6 REGIONAL POLICY

The question arises whether learning regions can be promoted. Or perhaps it is better to speak of regional learning, as that is what is actually taking place: various regional actors are engaged in exchange relations through which they learn. We shall return to the issue of learning regions versus regional learning later, but first we shall look at the policy aspects of the learning region paradigm. The first question to be asked is whether regions are an appropriate level for innovation policy,[1] and this does seem to be the case. The reason for this is that regional innovation policy is targeted mainly at SMEs and there is a 'natural fit' between the regional orientation of the majority of SMEs and the policy level of regional authorities and other regional actors involved in innovation support. The regional level – if embedded in a national and European structure – is best suited to identifying regional needs, strengths, issues, etc. and developing a focused strategy that accounts for the 'couleur locale' of a region (cf. European Commission, 1995, 1998 and AWT, 1995).

The learning region paradigm has notably affected regional innovation policy, one of the most striking examples being the RTP initiative of the European Commission.[2] Regional policy has been a key issue for the European Commission for a long time. Traditionally, however, innovation policy was not a concern of regional policy makers in the Commission. This situation changed in the early 1990s and resulted in the RTP and related initiatives, where the 'learning region' is explicitly used as a policy metaphor. The aim of these initiatives is to develop a regional innovation strategy through a joint effort of all the regional partners: the business community, intermediary organizations, research and education centres and regional authorities. Without exception, these strategies focus on furthering the exchange of knowledge between firms and between firms and other players in the region. In other words, these strategies promote learning among regional actors – without, of course, ignoring the non-regional relations. But inter-actions between regional partners are also improved at an institutional level. Their common effort, i.e. the development of a regional innovation strategy, does not stop once this strategy has reached its objective. Instead, the RTP and similar initiatives promote the creation of durable structures and platforms for regional players to continue to exchange information and develop a common vision. This leads to the institutionalization of exchange relations between regional players. Several policy fields, such as SME support, education and research policy, and so on, can thus be integrated and made more effective. Ideally, the regional players will develop a kind of co-ordinative network which supports the development of their region.

This brings us back to the distinction between regional learning and learning regions. When actors engage in regionally-based exchange relations through which they learn, we may speak of regional learning. If, however, the actors in a region – the business community, intermediary organizations, research and education centres and regional authorities – collaborate closely with each other on an institutional level in order to develop and implement regional innovation strategies, we may speak of learning regions. Thus learning regions can be the outcome of regional innovation policy, but in order to avoid an unproductive discussion on what is or is not a 'learning region', we prefer to continue to use learning regions as a metaphor for policy makers – and in this sense it has proved to be very useful. Except for the contribution of Oinas in Chapter 4, this volume will use the (now common) term 'learning regions' to cover both learning regions and regional learning.

1.7   OUTLINE OF THE BOOK

The discussion of some of the key elements of the theories underlying the learning region paradigm cannot be exhaustive. It can only show the diversity of our subject. The issues raised in this introduction are discussed in greater detail in the following chapters. In this outline of the book each chapter is discussed briefly. From this discussion, the relations between the chapters and the key elements of the learning region paradigm which have been discussed above, will become clear. In Part One of this volume – The Learning Region Paradigm Explained – the theoretical basis of the learning region paradigm is explored. In Chapter 2, Lambooy argues that regions that benefit from agglomeration economies and, hence, from a diversified economic structure, have a wide access to one of the main sources of economic growth:

knowledge. He introduces the concept of 'institutional–technological infrastructure' – indicating both economic actors and institutions. Regions with a diversified knowledge base as part of their institutional–technological infrastructure have better prospects of economic growth, because institutions play a vital role in the learning process. Lambooy distinguishes three aspects of learning: the cognitive, the institutional and the spatial. Furthermore, he focuses on the connection between the following four concepts: knowledge, innovation, learning regions and agglomeration economies. He makes clear that larger, diversified agglomerations can support the networks and institutional structures that are necessary to nurture learning and innovation.

The central question in the third chapter focuses on the learning capability of regions and how this capability can be improved through regional policy. Taking a conceptual perspective, van Geenhuizen and Nijkamp look at the learning capabilities of regions as their ability to create, attract, absorb and act upon new knowledge. The learning capability of regions is based on skills which have to be co-ordinated, preserved and, of course, renewed. The chapter goes on to discuss the complexities of regional learning capabilities which have to be dealt with at the policy level. The authors draw attention to the multi-actor and multi-layer setting of knowledge creation, which makes complexity and diversity key issues of regional learning.

Chapter 4 considers the importance of non-local relations in the process of learning. Referring to the global–local debate, Oinas stresses in this chapter that we are in danger of overemphasizing the importance of proximity. He argues that, while local relations are important, it needs to be increasingly emphasized that the creation and maintenance of non-local connections also play a significant role in sustaining competitiveness. Such relationships allow for the incorporation centrally of new ideas into a specific process of technological learning. Even in a process of localized learning the importance of non-local relations cannot be overlooked.

Part Two of this volume discusses the policy and practice of learning regions. These two elements come together in the EU policy on innovation and regional development, which is discussed by Landabaso in Chapter 5. He distinguishes between two types of conditions that have to be taken into account in regional innovation policy: 1) the necessary conditions, i.e. the basic physical infrastructure and human resources with a minimum level of training, and 2) the sufficient conditions, i.e. the intangibles, which assumes the existence of regional strengths, such as the capacity of regional firms to innovate, the availability of business services, transfer of technology, and so on. Effective regional policy must create both types of conditions, but the sufficient conditions are becoming increasingly important, as they trigger learning processes in the regional economy. The chapter shows how EU policy is shifting towards improving the sufficient conditions, particularly in disadvantaged regions.

In Chapter 6, Bellini discusses the role of regional governments in economic development from the perspective of the learning region paradigm. Based on the examples of the regions Emilia-Romagna and Tuscany, he argues that learning and building learning capacity play an increasingly important role in regional policy in Italy. The policy problems in these regions is not new, but the requirements in terms of policy styles and capabilities are unmistakably different from the past and provide an exemplary case of the more general reshaping of industry–state relations. Focusing on 'regional planning' (as collective exercises) and on 'plans' (the design of the learning region), this chapter is not just another case study of the Third Italy; it also shows that reference to learning processes should lead to a reappraisal of regional economic policies.

Chapter 7 is a case study of technology transfer and innovation policy in Flanders. Dankbaar and Cobbenhagen discuss how Flanders copes with an 'embarrassment of choices' of technology transfer institutions and intermediaries aiming to support SMEs. After conducting a series of interviews, Dankbaar and Cobbenhagen discovered that intermediary organizations and enterprises in Flanders have almost completely opposite ideas of the priorities for the support of SMEs. Moreover, policy and innovation support organizations seem to be focused mainly on technical innovation, while SMEs are in need of support for economic innovation (e.g. managerial skills). Flanders seems therefore to suffer from a technology-centred approach which is far removed from the everyday concerns of the Flemish SMEs.

Part Three of this volume draws attention to firms, networks and learning in practice. A complaint against the learning region paradigm is the lack of empirical research to support its assertions. In this part several case studies are discussed which provide some much-needed empirical support for the learning region paradigm. In Chapter 8, Oerlemans, Meeus and Boekema discuss the results of empirical research which they have carried out in the Dutch region of North Brabant. They question the importance of regional embeddedness of firms in relation to innovation. This is an issue which, as Oinas shows in Chapter 4, has become perceived wisdom in much of the literature on learning regions. The authors of this chapter argue from empirical evidence that the embeddedness perspective should not be taken for granted.

In Chapter 9, Lagendijk discusses learning in non-core regions with particular attention to the connections between policy and business in regional learning. This chapter presents the results of a study on innovative forms of regional support to SME development in non-core regions, inspired by the 'cluster concept'. Lagendijk argues that learning takes place at various levels and it is the intertwining of business learning and policy learning that triggers regional development. Clusters are often presented as the appropriate vehicle for this intertwining. But regional actors in non-core regions often need to fight hard to align the interest of firms with that of the region.

Meeus, Oerlemans and van Dijck draw attention in Chapter 10 to the empirical specification of learning processes. They focus on questions about the patterns of interaction between various actors at the regional level; the influence on, and the contribution to, learning processes; and the differences between transaction-level and innovation-level interactions. Their discussion is based on empirical research into manufacturing industry in the Dutch region of North Brabant. Their findings suggest that there are considerable differences between the various actors and their interactions in relation to learning processes.

In Chapter 11, Rutten discusses a case study of inter-firm collaboration on product development. Several years ago Océ, a manufacturer of copiers and printers in Venlo, the Netherlands, launched its KIC project (knowledge industry clustering), under which several regional suppliers work closely together with Océ on the engineering of subassemblies for Océ. Suppliers were originally involved only in the engineering of separate parts. Under the KIC project, however, they learned to work in multidisciplinary teams on the development of complete subassemblies, consisting of several parts. This case study discusses the motivations behind the KIC project, the lessons learned and the results of KIC, from the perspective of both Océ and the suppliers.

The final part of this volume, Part Four, consists of only one chapter, in which the editors try to place the previous chapters in a broader perspective, reflecting on what scholars and practitioners have done so far and where further research should be directed. The previous storm of discussions will be placed against a coherent background, that of the learning region paradigm.

NOTES

1. Promoting innovation is essentially a case of promoting learning, following this chapter's definition of innovation. This makes 'innovation policy' the proper term to describe policy initiatives that follow the lines of the learning region paradigm.
2. The RTP (Regional Technology Plan) initiative was launched in 1994, soon to be replaced by the RIS (Regional Innovation Strategy) and RITTS (Regional Innovation and Technology Transfer Strategies and infrastructures) initiatives.

REFERENCES

AWT (Dutch Advisory Council for Science and Technology Policy) (1995), *Regionaal technologiebeleid* [regional technology policy], The Hague: SDU Drukkerij.

Best, M. (1990), *The new competition: institutions of industrial restructuring,*

Cambridge, Mass.: Polity Press.

European Commission (1995), *Green paper on innovation*, Brussels.

European Commission (1998), *Reinforcing cohesion and competitiveness through RTD and innovation policies*, Brussels.

Håkansson, H. and J. Johanson (1993), 'The network as a governance structure: interfirm cooperation beyond markets and hierarchies', in: G. Grabher (ed.), *The embedded firm: on the socioeconomics of industrial networks*, London: Routledge.

Hartog, P. den et al. (1997), 'Intangibles: the soft side of innovation', in *Futures*, **29** (1), pp. 33–45.

Jacobs, D. (1996), *Het kennisoffensief: slim concurreren in de kenniseconomie* [the knowledge offensive: smart competition in the knowledge economy], Alphen aan den Rijn: Samson.

Maskell, P. (1998), *Competitiveness, localised learning and regional development: specialisation and prosperity in small open economies*, London: Routledge.

Morgan, K. (1997), 'The learning region: institutions, innovation and regional renewal', in: *Regional Studies*, **31**, (5), pp. 491–503.

Nonaka, I. and K. Takeuchi (1995), *The knowledge-creating company: how Japanese companies create the dynamics of innovation*, Oxford: Oxford University Press.

Porter, M. (1990), *The competitive advantage of nations*, London: The Macmillan Press.

Schumpeter, J. (1926), *Theorie der wirtschaftlichen Entwicklung: eine Untersuchung über Unternehmengewinn, Kapital, Kredit, Zins und den Konjunkturzyklus*, München und Leipzig: Duncker & Humbolt.

Scott, A. (1988), 'Flexible production systems and regional development: the rise of new industrial spaces in North America and Western Europe', in *International Journal of Urban and Regional Research*, **12** (2), pp. 171–185.

Storper, M. (1992), 'The limits to globalization: technology districts and international trade', in *Economic Geography*, **68**, pp. 60–93.

2. Learning and Agglomeration Economies: Adapting to Differentiating Economic Structures

Jan Lambooy*

2.1 INTRODUCTION

New social and economic structures are becoming increasingly heterogeneous and complex. Learning, adaptation and flexibility are becoming more and more important attributes for people and systems. National and regional innovation systems have to be developed with a high degree of freedom for the development of new ideas. In this process, regions with an open adaptive culture and economic structure have an advantage. This is one of the reasons – another one is the size of the economy – for agglomeration economies. Agglomerations are worlds of variables with complexity and chance as an underlying structure. In this environment, individuals are constantly undergoing new experiences and consequently have to adapt their perceptions by a cognitive process of scanning the set of heterogeneous new variables from the environment.

In this chapter, we contend that regions with a diversified knowledge base as part of their 'institutional–technological infrastructure' – indicating economic actors (individual persons and organizations) and institutions – have better prospects of growth and survival in an evolutionary process of economic competition. The concept of 'institutional–technological infrastructure' has a wider meaning than that of Feldman and Florida (1994, p. 211), who use 'technological infrastructure', which they define with reference to the following four indicators:

1. firms in related industries;
2. university R&D;
3. industrial R&D;
4. business-service firms.

*The author is grateful to Professor Kevin O'Connor of Monash University in Australia for his comments on an earlier version.

In their approach, knowledge and knowledge development is restricted to R&D, but a region's knowledge base can be associated with broader characteristics. We contend that regions with 'agglomeration economies' and, hence, with a diversified economic structure, have a wide access to one of the main sources of economic growth: knowledge. Knowledge is a main resource in the process of economic growth. Resources are both tangible and intangible entities that are available to people, firms and countries (or populations) and enable them to produce and consume efficiently or effectively (Hunt, 1997, p. 60).

In this chapter, we will consider how the 'learning' of individuals, organizations, institutions and regions means coping with the need to adapt to a continually changing and complex environment. This requires innovation, Schumpeter's concept, with which he indicated that certain persons, entrepreneurs, were the dynamic element in the process of reconfiguration of economic structures (sometimes called 'creative destruction', because of the associated loss of many 'outmoded' technologies). In our approach to learning we distinguish three aspects: the cognitive, the institutional and the spatial aspects of this process. We also focus on the connections between the four concepts of 'knowledge', 'innovation', 'learning regions' and 'agglomeration economies'.

2.2 LEARNING CAPABILITIES AND ORGANIZATIONAL LEARNING

Knowledge and information are not identical. It is useful to distinguish three concepts of information: 'data', 'information' and 'knowledge'. 'Data' means unstructured information, whereas structured information (tables, articles, books) can be called 'information'. 'Knowledge' encompasses the use of both data and information through the personal capacity of judgement. Data and information can easily be transmitted in many impersonal ways, whereas the transfer of knowledge requires more personal contacts. Knowledge also refers to the capacities for problem-definition and problem-solving. Workers in professional services, headquarter functions and R&D labs can be called 'knowledge workers'. They are the carriers of knowledge production. Advanced producer services, or knowledge-intensive services, play an important role in the development of knowledge, in facilitating the use of knowledge and, hence, in overall economic change and adjustment. These higher-order services – more particularly finance, real estate, law and the professional service workers in all kinds of headquarters – are highly concentrated in metropolitan areas.

The Process of Learning

Learning is a cognitive process of acquiring new capabilities that enable a person or organization to deal more effectively with the social, economic and physical environment. In response to the various degrees of environmental complexity, a variety of forms of learning and capabilities exist. They can be classified according to different principles or theories. Nelson and Winter (1982) have classified activities into 'routines' and 'search' to cope with different degrees of complexity. A distinction can also be made between the acquisition of 'tacit' (Polanyi, 1966) and 'explicit' knowledge. This distinction rests on the rules of accessing the memory and on the possibility of formalizing and routinizing the procedures. Tacit knowledge was described by Polanyi as the knowledge we possess but 'cannot tell'. It is more or less similar to 'intuition', the knowledge we have without 'access-rules' to our memory. Through our experiences we learn and thus accumulate tacit knowledge, which can be used for a variety of activities. An example is the ability to drive a car without using the manuals for its engine and other components. We drive on our intuition, or tacit knowledge. Another example is the decision made by a chess grandmaster in a complicated position. He does not decide purely by calculating the various possibilities; he uses his tacit knowledge, or intuition, to access his memory in order to find similar positions (configurations) in prior games on which he can fall back in his judgement.

The second kind of knowledge, 'explicit knowledge', is where we know the 'access-rules' to our personal memory and to its written or electronic storage. In the first stage of its development, this kind of knowledge is personal, but after a certain period of time it generally turns into 'information', because it can be routinized, codified and formalized. This makes access still easier, as is the case with written media or computerized databases. The distinction between the two kinds of knowledge has important implications for the organization of knowledge production. Tacit knowledge is strictly personal, while explicit knowledge, although it may have many personal aspects in the first stages of its development, can later be codified, stored and transmitted. Consequently, making people with essential tacit knowledge redundant – as frequently happens in an attempt to create 'lean companies' – may prove to be a crucial error.

Learning is primarily an individual process, but it can develop better in interactive configurations, as in organizations and producer–consumer relations. This is the reason why 'organizational learning' is receiving more and more attention (De Geus, 1997; Senge, 1990). Learning, therefore, can also be considered as an interactive process of team members (as in the case of a team of professional researchers) and a social process (because it favours the construction of networks of people sharing 'social capital'), resulting in knowledge-building and a 'collective memory' of organizations. Knowledge-building is a multifaceted endeavour. It requires a combination of technological and social actions (Earl, 1994). Organizations are also important because of their ability to arrange the conditions for learning and to use the results of that process. Firms and other organizations vary widely in their capacity to learn and use the many kinds of competencies developed through learning (De Geus, 1997).

An organization is a structured set of personal relations, with a formalized and common goal. Institutions and regions are different in this regard. They are not 'actors'. Regions are territorially defined sets of populations, cultures, jurisdictions and economic structures, which may show a certain level of integration, but this does not necessarily have to be the case. Institutions are 'sets of rules', collective memories of the routines and values which people use when they act. These can be 'tacit' (as in family or corporate cultures) or 'explicit' (as in laws and church rules). The capability to learn is not only a matter of people, but is also associated with the efficiency of the organizations which accumulate information and knowledge and mediate between the participants. Organizations have an active role in the economic process, while institutions may be seen as guardians of trust, certainty and security. Through economic growth with a concomitantly larger complexity, organizations and institutions are continually challenged to adapt.

Learning results in new capabilities which enable people to work at a more sophisticated level of activities, which means being able to deal with a higher level of complexity. This is particularly important for newer activities in an economy. Old activities are often already 'routinized', in the sense of being organized into simpler routines and procedures, with a strong emphasis on physical capital. New activities have not yet been converted into reproducible production techniques and, hence, need a higher input of expertise or professional judgement. However, we have to bear in mind that professional expertise is also needed in activities which may be 'old' as a category, but which are intricately complex, like some large-scale industries (e.g. steel) and certain government activities, the management of large organizations and creative activities (art, design).

Levels of Learning

To augment our understanding of the cognitive process of learning, it is useful to construct a hierarchy of the complexity of learning and knowledge-building for three kinds of actors. The first level is the individual person, the second level is the social network in which people participate when they learn, and the third level is the organization (firm, school, government). Networks are more difficult to define than organizations; they are sets of loosely connected relations between individual persons and organizations (firms), with attributes of both kinds of relations, often without the formalized structures of organizations. Williamson calls them 'hybrid organizations' (Williamson, 1985). The concept of network is used in many disciplines, but with different objectives (Lambooy, 1987). Genosko (1997, p. 285) contends: 'the network concept is "enigmatic" and appears in many shapes and forms. It is sometimes so varied as to fall into the "whatever-you-like" category. In economics synonyms for networks are "strategic alliances", "joint ventures", "round tables" and such nomenclature.'

In sociological and geographical literature the network is used with the – sometimes hidden – goal of evading economics and replacing the market, expressed in prices and quantities, as the vehicle of relations. However, many relations described as networks can be perceived as market relations: either between individuals or between organizations. The economic synonyms for networks emphasize this aspect. The words used suggest that the element of an alliance or joint venture is combined with contracts between partners, resulting in agreements about the division of labour in R&D, production and the division of costs and benefits. Networks are created by individuals or organizations to augment the benefits of their activities, whether in the market or in other parts of social life. If economic networks are more or less permanent, they can be likened to organizations, but if they are casual with their activities priced, they rather resemble common market relations. One basic assumption in the network model is that firms depend on other firms and that co-operation is a necessary condition for gaining access to strategic resources. Another assumption is that firms have strategic positions depending on their access to resources. Market relations can be described as sets of interconnected exchange relationships; the competitive position of a firm depends on the extent to which a firm extracts value from the relationship (Van Houtum, 1998). Networks are often instrumental in the imitation and diffusion of knowledge. Imitation is a lower-cost solution for acquiring new knowledge, instead of investment in R&D by the firm itself.

Learning is not only the acquisition of new knowledge, but also its production (Lambooy, 1997). It takes organization, time and investment. If knowledge is the product of more or less coherent groups, it is the result of 'social learning' and may be called 'organizational knowledge'. This is more than just the personal expertise of knowledge-workers in that it may encompass a combination of technical and organizational elements. As Morgan (1992, p. 166) argues, in the context of innovation and the networked economy: 'At both levels – the corporate and the regional – it seems that innovation is increasingly being recognized for what it is, namely, a collective social endeavour.' This kind of development of knowledge and innovation is especially important in markets with a high degree of complexity and uncertainty (Mintzberg, 1979).

One possible way for organizations to reduce complexity is to restructure knowledge in a simpler, codified way. This enables the knowledge to be more widely used even when users do not understand the 'scientific' basis as, for example, with cars and computers. Codified knowledge lowers production costs and is an asset in itself. When knowledge can be codified and if it becomes proprietary information, it can be transmitted, primarily to other persons or departments of the organization. It becomes a set of capabilities or an organizational asset, with procedures and routines in production, administration and financial directives and data-sets on which a firm can base its market strategy. This is one reason why ever more organizations are developing 'knowledge management' programmes. This new specialization deals with the management of the three distinct forms of information (data, information and knowledge). Knowledge managers consider not only the production and distribution of knowledge, but also its development and management.

2.3   DIFFERENTIATION AND COMPLEXITY OF STRUCTURES

Economic theory is based mainly on concepts developed in a world where the production of goods was the predominant activity. Goldfinger (1994) contends that, in our time, a revolution has occurred which has resulted in the dominance of the production of intangibles. Information on the 'real' economy becomes more and more difficult to acquire. Production in a 'knowledge economy', however, is still strongly dependent on a division of labour, probably even more than before.

Adam Smith used his concept of 'division of labour' to explain its impact on increasing the productivity and growth of a firm. Although initially used to show how a firm's internal division of labour could lead to a rise in the productivity per worker, the concept can also be applied to the inter-firm division of labour. If the increasing division of labour is so important at the firm level, why should it not form the basis for other dimensions of economic growth as well? It leads to a further differentiation of the economic structure, to new investment, new employment and to the development of new demand and supply. The result is that not only may productivity rise, but complexity will also increase (Lambooy, 1991). It becomes more difficult to co-ordinate the economy, so that transaction costs rise. The need for information will become so large in this complex world that the increases in the transaction costs of co-ordination will no longer be covered by the benefits of the increasing division of labour. However, there are two sides to rising costs. First, the financial costs associated with increasing complexity and, secondly, and more pleasantly, many new firms can be established, leading to the production of more information and co-ordination activities, mainly professional producer services. The markets, as the major mechanism for co-ordination, will become more complex and, consequently, will require more expertise to be used effectively. The rising complexity may also lead to an expansion of government, because rules have to be set and implemented in order to ensure an orderly functioning market. Although costs may rise, one of the effects will be that GDP will increase, because these costs will be counted as wealth-creating activities and not as costs. An example is the comparatively extreme rise of the costs of lawyers in the USA, leading to an increasing GDP. The differentiation of the economic structure and, concomitantly, its increased complexity, can be connected – or even equated – with economic growth (Warsh, 1984).

Differentiation can also be related to the necessity for learning. The rapidly changing and increasingly complex economic environment needs more data, information and knowledge. In modern society, information and knowledge-production are crucial for economic growth and for the successful co-ordination of the economy. Apart from the market mechanism, organizations and institutions are necessary to co-ordinate the disparate decisions of the economic actors. Differentiation of economic activities and a more complex economic structure result in a lower degree of certainty and the need to complement the market mechanism with other mechanisms (organization, institutions). This explains why, in an uncertain and complex environment, learning is one of the most important capabilities of a society. This is true for firms, persons, organizations, institutions, regions and countries alike. Learning is a process which enables people to cope with a constantly changing and increasingly complex environment. Complexity means that the components of a structure are becoming more numerous and differentiated. Not only a firm, a market, or an industry, but also the economy of a region or a nation, can all be regarded as structures. Although the common definitions of 'structure' in dictionaries express a certain stability of the configuration of its elements, even structures alter. For economic actors this means that they must continuously monitor the changes in the environment. Failure to do so could lead to the loss of an organization's economic strength and, ultimately, to its disappearance. Because of ever changing structures, the need to learn will always exist.

Baranzani and Scazzieri (1990, p. 1) distinguish two kinds of structure that are commonly used in economic theory:

> On the one hand, 'structure' is conceived as the network of interpersonal relationships on which the fabric of society is founded. Such relationships describe the social rules and personal and collective beliefs that provide the framework for the collective action of economic agents. Institutions provide an important example of the way in which this notion of structure can be used in economic analysis ... On

the other hand, 'structure' is conceived as a set of relationships among economic magnitudes such as sectoral outputs, population and technology. Such relationships describe in the first instance the outcome, not the motivations, of agents' aggregate behaviour.

Spatial structure might be conceived as part of the second kind of structure distinguished by Baranzani and Scazzierri, because it shows the spatial composition, or spatial pattern, of the location of economic activities, infrastructure and buildings. In fact, however, spatial structure is very different from the second kind of structure distinguished by these authors, because it has too many specific non-economic attributes. That is why we have to distinguish spatial structure from the two structures described by Baranzani and Scazzieri. Market structure, too, is something different; it is neither an institution, nor a set of relationships of economic magnitudes in an aggregate form. 'Market structure' can be defined as the set of conditions and rules which influence the behaviour of the actors in a certain market, and it further denotes the degree of concentration, the conditions for and the dynamics of entry, as well as the power positions of certain market parties. A market structure is not static, but always dynamic, viz. it develops under the pressure of external conditions, more in particular, technology and institutional developments, as well as of internal factors like scale and organization. Since enterprises and non-market organizations are very basic entities in economic theory, and even more so in economic practice, it is remarkable that neither Krugman nor Baranzani and Scazzieri pay any attention to the 'organization' as an economic structure. Many economic actors work in enterprises or similar organizations and are thus part of one of the most significant economic structures. Organizations are the 'context' of many economic actors.

We therefore conclude from the above that we can distinguish at least five kinds of 'structure' which are all very common in economic theory. If we compare the attention paid to structure in economic theory with that paid to behaviour, we observe a strong difference in approach. In micro-economic theory, the term 'behaviour' is commonly used to describe the actions of rational man – not the individual of 'real life' (whatever that may be), but a statistical concept of man as a part of a certain class of people who possess an identical set of properties, such as the 'representative firm' or the 'representative consumer'. Often the preference function, or the utility function, is standardized. The production function shows 'constant returns to scale'. The budget, or the income, and the external environment of the individual are assumed to be given and more or less stable. There is no 'feedback': the individual does not influence the structural environment; individuals do not have to learn, because of the presupposed stability of the 'structure'. The common assumptions are that the economic agent has full information and that production factors are mobile for all applications, but again, within the structure. These and other assumptions result in a theory which is elegant, but often not useful in the field of spatial economics, where increasing returns exist and environments are highly unstable.

We can distinguish between the changes within economic structures and the changes of economic structures. In mainstream economics the emphasis is on the first category, but in other theoretical approaches, like institutional and evolutionary economics, the second kind of change is emphasized (Lambooy, 1996).

2.4   KNOWLEDGE AND INNOVATION

Knowledge ('expertise') is primarily an attribute of persons and teams, more particularly, of professionals, in all kinds of economic activities. The major concentration of professionals ('knowledge workers') can be found in the advanced producer services. The growth in the number of professionals reflects the increasing complexity of the economic structure (Lambooy, 1988).

Professionals can be integrated within organizations or their knowledge can be purchased from other firms. This choice is very important, because firms, like any other organization, have to generate and maintain a certain specialization of their knowledge-base (Tordoir, 1993; Garnsworthy and O'Connor, 1997). Just relying on the knowledge of others is a strategy which may be permissible only for markets with a high degree of certainty. If a firm is active in a market with much uncertainty and a high degree of complexity, it would need to develop its own knowledge-base, not only including knowledge on 'how-to-produce' (know-how), but also on 'how-to-organize' and 'how-to-market' (Cornish, 1997). Some of this knowledge may be routinized – that is, become current practice – but it will be necessary to upgrade the knowledge-base continually. Only firms in very simple, stable markets can survive without new investments in knowledge. This relates to the firm's possibilities for innovation. A firm's capacity to innovate by generating new knowledge or by monitoring the new developments of other knowledge-producers (firms, universities or government-subsidized institutions) is often limited because of the high costs associated with in-house monitoring of the market and R&D. This explains the necessity to choose between: (1) emulation, (2) purchasing knowledge, or (3) co-operation in R&D. The two latter options can be found in many organizational forms: within an organization (firm) or within networks of different shapes. This suggests that the boundary of the firm is related not only to the ownership of 'old' production factors (capital, labour) and to the production of goods and services, but also to the property rights of knowledge. Co-operation in markets where the boundaries of firms are very important will often result in vertical or horizontal integration, but networks can also be used for this goal. The choice will depend on the market structure and the need to safeguard new knowledge from imitation, in order to benefit from previous investments (Lambooy, 1997) In regions where knowledge is shared between enterprises co-operating in networks, for example, those of regions like the 'Third Italy' and Baden-Württemberg, the outcome of R&D will be shared across the networks, whereas the results in expensive and highly competitive pharmacological R&D will be kept in-house by the large oligopolistic corporations.

It is not only the market structure that may be decisive, the spatial structure is also important (Camagni, 1991; Krugman, 1995; Manshanden, 1996; Henderson, 1997; Simmie, 1997). Cornish (1997, p. 162) argues:

> There is evidence that the size and number of similar, related, and supporting industries in a particular milieu has an effect on the types of new products that originate there. Long before a new product is conceived of, the knowledge and experience that are available in the local economy both inform and limit the product opportunities that are possible for entrepreneurs in that location to pursue. Proximity between product developers and potential users probably counts most prior to product innovation, during the creative process in which the idea for a new product is first identified.

Learning, as the capability to generate new knowledge, can result in more innovation, which means entering the market with products or services based on new knowledge. This concept was – as we said before – introduced by Schumpeter, to indicate the 'new combination' of production factors created by an entrepreneur to introduce products and production processes to the market. New knowledge is not the only base of innovation. Innovations can also be based on imitation from elsewhere (other regions or other industries). Schumpeter distinguished five kinds of innovation: new products, new production processes, new materials, new organizations and new markets. In his earlier work, the person of the entrepreneur played a large role in his theory. Later, he came to recognize the enormous potential of organized knowledge development in large corporations as a base for innovation (Schumpeter, 1943). With that personal evolution, Schumpeter recognized that the economy and markets did not rest only on decentralized decision-making, as the Austrian School (Hayek, Mieses, and Demsetz) had contended (Wegner, 1997). Organizations and institutions, as well as individual entrepreneurs and managers, are important for decision-making, learning and the generation of knowledge. These entities (organizations and institutions) are expressions of the search for certainty and continuity, but also the mechanisms of collective action. They have a common collective memory; people in organizations also share certain cultural values.

Although innovation is often associated with individual actors, e.g. the entrepreneur of a small or medium-sized firm (SME), the increasing complexity of markets and the costs of research explain why the picture is more complicated. Innovation is a social process, based on perceived problems, technological opportunities and individual and social needs. Innovators do not work in a vacuum, they are 'embedded' in networks of social relations, in regions in which they have received their education, and they are dependent on the available knowledge-base of the organizations in which they work, or on professional workers (for example, scientists) whom they happen to know.

2.5   AGGLOMERATION ECONOMIES AND LEARNING

Regions are places that comprise a very different set of persons, organizations and institutions. However, the concept of 'learning regions' presupposes that a certain unity exists which is more than the 'unity of a container'. At least some regions may possess certain organizational and institutional configurations which result in a kind of uniqueness in an economic, spatial and cultural sense. The concept of 'learning regions' can disclose a process of increasing integration of the actors in a certain territory, and it can also be used as a concept pointing towards the social aspects of the learning processes in a region with clearly idiosyncratic – region-specific – characteristics, not only of the economic structure, but also of the organizations, institutions and culture involved.

A Marshallian View

The learning processes and the development of specific knowledge are often associated with the institutional–technological environment, usually the specific characteristics of regions. We contend that regions with agglomeration economies have better opportunities for developing a strong knowledge-base and for nurturing new growth opportunities.

The concept of agglomeration economies, and the related concept of 'external economies', have developed from strictly technical into more encompassing concepts. Malmberg and Maskell (1997, p. 32) contend:

> There seems currently to be a tendency to assume that the mechanisms leading to agglomeration are more subtle and of a 'socio-cultural' rather than purely economic nature, and that the key to explaining the sustained existence of agglomerations of

related industries lies in their superior ability to enhance learning, creativity and innovations, defined in a broad sense.

In this and the following section, we will discuss this point and argue that agglomeration economies have to be connected with the 'socio-economic infrastructure' of a region and with the behavioural options of people in their – sometimes adverse – regional environment. The advantages of this spatial structure are connected with the five central concepts used in the theory of agglomeration economies: scale, differentiation (in connection with specialization), information, organization and dynamic external effects.

Paul Krugman emphasizes the central importance of agglomeration economies and 'increasing returns to scale' for economic development (Krugman, 1991; 1995). He argues that these concepts need to be connected with that of 'market structure': 'In spatial economics ... you really cannot get started at all without finding a way to deal with scale economies and oligopolistic firms' (Krugman, 1995, p. 35). His arguments are connected with the positive effects of the increasing market size and firm size, with the differentiation and specialization of production and products and increasing productivity. This relates to the theory of externalities (or external economies) developed by Marshall (1890) based on his experience as a close observer of the local economy in the London neighbourhoods of his time. The basic idea is that economic agents cannot capture all the benefits of their activities in the prices on the market. He noticed that many craftsmen and tradesmen of the same sector occupied locations where they could see what others were doing and where they could emulate the successful entrepreneurs without having invested in basic research or in the costs of experiments. Proximity to the other entrepreneurs was regarded as an economic asset offering comparative advantages ('external economies') in the process of what we would like to call 'collective learning'. These locations also offered opportunities for prospective and new entrepreneurs to gain experience from a number of learning processes, initially by working within a firm and, subsequently, by observing what other entrepreneurs do. At the same time, they could save on acquiring information as well as on purchasing and transport costs. This spatial structure, with producers located in an 'Industrial District', thus enabled them to produce more efficiently there than in other locations, because of the advantages resulting from the spatial proximity (Visser, 1996).

Marshall argued that these advantages are the result of the spatial proximity of producers and the specific atmosphere beneficial to the exchange and emulation of knowledge, to learning effects and trust. He emphasized that the specific environment of a firm could be crucial for its survival. The common denominator is that these effects are outside the control of the firm, but they do influence an entrepreneur's capacity to compete, because they influence his cost function or his quality level. Marshall pointed out the effect of external economies of scale arising from the presence of many firms of a similar industry or trade in one area. According to Marshall, these advantages accrue to the firm because of three factors:

1. the pooling of a local labour market for experienced workers;
2. the provision of intermediate inputs in a great variety and at low cost; and
3. the local information flows, which enable ideas to spread through learning and then cumulate in that area.

A Contemporary View

Marshallian external effects are, at least partially, connected with the process of learning in networks of entrepreneurs with both market and non-market relations. Marshall connected this approach with Adam Smith's idea of the positive effects of differentiation through increased scale and the division of labour in markets. It is important to observe that Marshall used his concept of external economies in a dynamic way, in which learning effects in non-market relations were very important. In later studies of the neoclassical school, this dynamic aspect disappeared, to be rediscovered only recently by economists like Paul Romer (1987) and Paul Krugman (1995).

According to Krugman, the main reason why mainstream economics ignored the dynamics was the focus on the mathematical problems associated with the use of increasing returns to scale. The basic concept of neoclassical theory is general equilibrium, which is possible only when constant returns are assumed to be a general property of the production functions (Krugman, 1995; Arthur, 1996). Arthur (1996) emphasizes that increasing returns are associated with innovations and technological developments and, consequently, with sometimes radical changes of structures. These changes continually unsettle the market equilibria, and temporarily create monopolistic characteristics and Schumpeterian 'creative destruction' in many markets. In those parts of the economy where these 'disturbances' in the market structure are usual (as in the entertainment sector, and in the pharmaceutical and electronics industries), firms need a different kind of organization and management than in sectors with traditional activities with constant returns. Many investigations of the past decade show that, even today, these dynamic external economies are still important, not only in areas with crafts (Visser, 1996), but also in regions with the newest industries, like those in Silicon Valley and the Boston Metropolitan Area (Saxenian, 1994; Feldman and Audretsch, 1995; Henderson, 1997). However, one needs to emphasize that the concept of 'dynamic' is used in the restrictive sense of effects within a given structure, not in the broader sense of changes of structures.

Various authors have published papers on the phenomenon of agglomeration economies, but emphasizing different aspects. Whereas Marshall emphasizes the advantages for entrepreneurs of similar industries or trades of being located within the same region (what is currently called 'localization economies'), the urban economist Jane Jacobs (1968; 1984) emphasizes differentiation and specialization as the basic processes of agglomeration economies (which can be likened to 'urbanization economies'). Krugman argues that scale and market structure are the central issues. He emphasizes 'Marshallian externalities' more than 'Jacobs externalities'. He also pays less attention to the organization of enterprises and the dynamics of changing structures, which he includes only via path-dependency and cumulative causation, not as a fundamental change due to technological factors and increased complexity, as Pasinetti (1993) and Saviotti (1996) do. Many recent studies emphasize the key role of knowledge workers in attracting and reinforcing new economic developments (Guilhon *et al.*, 1997). They reinforce the 'urbanization economies' and accompany the 'Jacobs externalities'. In general, authors who are occupied with these concepts do not pay attention to individual qualities and to behavioural aspects. The crucial question is whether entrepreneurs can survive successfully only in favourable environments or agglomerations, or whether they can find ways and means of overcoming their problems in regions with adverse characteristics. This issue is related to the theory of access to strategic resources.

2.6   BEHAVIOUR AND THE ECONOMIC ENVIRONMENT

Recently, Vaessen (1993) and many others have emphasized the fact that both entrepreneurs and consumers act and react in an environment ('structure') which is not 'given' or static, but is continuously changing. People are 'embedded' in a dynamic environment which is made up of physical and social elements. They act in a 'context-dependent' and 'path-dependent' manner. People do not behave as if history and the environment are of no importance and these, in turn, influence their environment. Feedback mechanisms are more common than is acknowledged by mainstream economists. It is fair to assume that, in a sense, learning and the accumulation of knowledge are connected with behaviour in space. Learning shows the characteristics of 'contextual rationality' (March, 1988, p. 38): people adjust their goals and their behaviour, depending on their context and past experiences. Or, as March put it:

> Ideas of contextual rationality emphasize the extent to which choice behaviour is embedded in a complex of other claims on the attention of actors and other

structures of social and cognitive relations. ... They focus on the way in which choice behaviour in a particular situation is affected by the opportunity costs of attending to that situation and by the apparent tendency for people, problems, solutions, and choices to be joined by the relatively arbitrary accidents of their simultaneity rather than by their prima facie relevance to each other.

The goals of learning are only 'given' for a limited number of cases, and then only for relatively simple cases and for the short term. They develop interactively in relation to systematic and stochastic changes in the environment. People are social beings in their cognitive activities. They respond to intended and non-intended information from others, they develop networks, sets of relations which derive actions not solely from egoism and economic rationality. The 'embeddedness' of people's behaviour is related to the existence of spatial patterns as a special kind of 'context'. Within certain spaces (neighbourhoods, cities, regions), social and economic relations have a higher density. This offers opportunities for unplanned meetings and for sustained and structured relationships. New means of transport and telecommunication have blurred this clear spatial pattern, yet most relations are still more intensely developed in spatial proximity. This means that the division of labour, with the differentiation and specialization it entails, will develop first within high-density areas and, more particularly, within urban regions (Jacobs, 1984). In an urban environment with uncertainty and asymmetrical information, economic agents try to minimize uncertainty either by creating uncertainty-reducing institutions and organizations, or by uncertainty and risk-avoiding behaviour. One strategy which aims at reducing uncertainty for both producers and consumers is the choice of a location in an urbanized region. This offers them a structured network of suppliers and buyers. The preferred strategy will depend on personal capacities and on the market structure.

Scott (1988) emphasized that smaller and weaker businesses can survive in highly developed agglomerations because of the differentiation and specialization associated with a well-developed system of outsourcing, with the concomitant opportunities for vertical disintegration. This offers SMEs the opportunity to find a 'niche' in the market, where specialization can help them to survive. The process of continuous differentiation creates new products and services, but it also intensifies competition and creates a need for other forms of co-ordination than the market, such as networks. Thus, the choice of a 'niche' has to be made very carefully: either to cut costs and compete on prices, or to create an advantage based on location and quality. The strategy of getting a place in the market depends on the quality of the entrepreneur and his professional advisers (professional services). The opportunities offered by the environment can be very confusing. One possible reaction is 'trial and error', other possibilities are emulation and co-operation in networks. An interesting point is that, in regions with a certain specialization (as in Silicon Valley), there is a relatively low entry-level to the market for new entrepreneurs, due to their previous experience with other firms, their learning processes and their social networks.

Vaessen (1993) shows that entrepreneurs located in regions further away from the economic core region of a country encounter more difficulties in their struggle to survive. But such locations may at the same time be the explanation for his conclusion that these regions, besides having their fair share of weak firms, often prove to have more strong firms than might have been expected if the negative structure of the peripheral location were indeed a decisive factor in a firm's survival. These successful entrepreneurs have to be more alert and more aware of what is going on, and they have to perform better than similar firms located in an agglomeration. The weaker firms in the diversified economy of a city region have more external advantages, so entrepreneurs in other regions have to design a strategy to overcome their disadvantages. Vaessen (1993, p. 179) argues:

> But even if non-central areas prove to accommodate low percentages of growth-inducing activities, the absolute number of firms may still be considerable. Their presence poses a challenge to prevailing theoretical insights about the importance of territorial conditions for innovation and competitiveness. ... [Firms] revealed a considerable ability to overcome the constraints of the production environment. They did so by manipulating external resource conditions, by immunizing themselves against them, or by adapting to them. ... The second basic source of ... thriving market access is the organization the entrepreneurs came from. ... It is quite clear that the entrepreneurs developed their wide outlook and linkage network in the organizations where they worked before starting their own business. These incubator or parent organizations all operated on a national or international scale. ... This suggests that regional science might be able to supplement the prevailing ecological perspective with an economic heredity aproach.

Vaessen and Keeble (1995) have made a comparison between firms in the South East of England and firms on the periphery (Wales, Northern England and Merseyside) as to their R&D activities. They conclude:

> Overall, an important and perhaps paradoxical finding is that despite a somewhat inferior occupational and skill structure, relatively large numbers of peripheral SMEs have apparently been able to achieve considerable size and growth. One possible hypothesis to explain this is that entrepreneurs faced with regional labour market inadequacies adopt deliberate strategies to counterbalance these deficiencies through in-service training (Vaessen & Keeble, 1995, p. 503).

Enterprises with an 'inferior' location can thus carry the associated extra costs by working harder and performing better to compete successfully. Vaessen and Keeble continue (p. 503): '... many SMEs do not remain passive towards external pressures and constraints imposed by their regional environment. Instead, enterprises in peripheral regions may actively and even successfully work to develop strategies to overcome these constraints'. This argument, which rests on the observation of personal capabilities of devising strategies in adverse circumstances, is valid for existing firms and for firms which have survived competitive forces, but is most probably not enough to explain the development of regions. The general development patterns in large agglomerations and in regions with specialized and differentiated economic activities, like Silicon Valley and the Boston Route 128 area, show that it is important to have certain favourable 'structural' conditions. To develop successful regions or successful clusters of economic activity, one would have to consider the quality of the context: the characteristics of the other firms, schools, infrastructure, as well as the availability of and easy access to information.

Although the success of regions is not solely dependent on 'structures' and 'environments', a focus on the behaviour of entrepreneurs, professional workers and government officials does not provide an adequate explanation. But the difference is one of degree. Schmidt (1997, p. 18) argues that individual actors can create organizational structures for resolving market failures which are more effective than government intervention. This is the reason why economic development 'from below' can succeed, even without government help. Schmidt (p.20) further contends that two conditions are necessary: the mobilization of unused local resources (financial and human) and the effective use of these resources. This can be achieved through the special strategies of individual entrepreneurs (Vaessen, 1993), or through organizational arrangements (joint action or networking) and spatial clustering. Schmidt concludes (p. 21):

> the argument is that clustering facilitates the mobilisation of financial and human resources, that it breaks down investment into small risky steps, that the enterprise of one creates a foothold for the other, that ladders are constructed which enable small enterprise to climb up and grow. It is a process in which enterprises create for each other - often unwittingly, sometimes intentionally - possibilities for accumulating capital and skill.

2.7 KNOWLEDGE BASE AND 'LEARNING REGIONS'

The difference between learning regions and learning organizations is that the latter have a stronger and more formalized coherence, with a common goal and a central governance, whilst regions, even metropolitan regions, often have no central authority. A region with a government of its own can be compared with an economic organization, but has a different kind of goal-setting procedure. In both kinds of region, the process of knowledge-building requires the presence of economic activities to nurture the process of differentiation of existing and new activities. Persons who can learn and develop skills and knowledge, both tacit and explicit, are the basic elements in this process. Organizations and regions need to invest in these persons, organizations and processes. A basic element here is the development of channels of communication to transmit knowledge to other persons and organizations (Hassink, 1997). Organizations and networks are like channels. These channels, however, are not always accessible to non-members. Easy access to the basic resource of knowledge is a necessary precondition for growth. Regional authorities can ensure that knowledge is diffused to persons and organizations, such as SMEs, which have difficulties in accessing knowledge. In many European countries, efforts are made to ensure that government-based organizations are created which subsume the role of 'brokers' in these processes (Morgan, 1997). These organizations are often regionalized offices of central government-based structures, often called Regional Innovation Centres, or Regional Incubation Centres, purporting to nurture regional innovation initiatives. They are primarily focused on SMEs (Asheim and Isaksen, 1997; Genosko, 1997).

The persons with the most sophisticated knowledge are the professional 'knowledge workers'. They can assist governments and other organizations to build and manage a regional knowledge base. Much tacit and explicit knowledge develops, however, not through conscious policy but through a large number of 'unintended' actions. Individuals, organizations (including 'hybrid' organizations, or networks) and institutions, are all partners in the process of developing a region's 'set of capabilities'. That is why the 'institutional–technological infrastructure' rather than the 'technological infrastructure', to which we referred earlier, is to be regarded as the correct concept. The process of knowledge-building and its management is 'embedded' in a region's fabric of actors and institutions. The uniqueness of the region's set of capabilities lies largely in the relations developed by individuals and organizations. These relations are important for gaining access to the decisive elements of the knowledge base.

2.8 CONCLUSIONS

In institutional economics (with authors like Williamson and Nobel prize-winner Douglas North) much attention is devoted to the impact of the institutional configuration of countries on growth. Comparative studies show that an important effect does indeed exist. Institutional configurations are difficult to change, however, because they entail many tacit elements which are based on learning processes in families, at school and in employment. It has become clear that the success of an economy is interrelated with the institutional configuration of the country involved. As such, it is interesting to observe that many cross-border mergers or takeovers fail because of cultural differences.

'Learning regions' depend on learning persons and learning organizations, such as firms and networks, within institutional structures that can nurture new developments. The best opportunities for this process are to be found in larger diversified agglomerations. Because learning is an interactive process, the opportunities for learning and innovation are widely available in those regions. In regions with adverse environments, economic growth depends more on the innovative behaviour of individual entrepreneurs and on the strategies of local organizations. In general, the increasingly complex economy needs more knowledge to resolve development problems. 'Learning regions' need the development of an integrated 'institutional–technological infrastructure'.

REFERENCES

Arthur, W.B. (1996), 'Increasing returns and the new world of business', *Harvard Business Review*, July/August, 100–109.

Asheim, B.T. and A. Isaksen (1997), 'Location, agglomeration and innovation: towards regional innovation systems in Norway?', *European Planning Studies*, **5** (3), pp. 299–330.

Baranzani, M. and R. Scazzieri (1990), *The Economic Theory of Structure and Change*, Cambridge: Cambridge University Press.

Camagni, R. (ed.) (1991), *Innovation Networks: Spatial Perspectives*, London: Belhaven Press.

Cornish, S.L. (1997), 'Product innovation and spatial dynamics of market intelligence: does proximity to markets matter?', in *Economic Geography*, **73** (2), pp. 143-65.

Dunford, M. and G. Kafkalis (1992), *Cities and Regions in the New Europe*, London: Belhaven Press.

Earl, M.J. (1994), 'Knowledge as strategy', in C. Ciborra and T. Jelassi (eds), *Strategic Information Systems*, New York: John Wiley.

Feldman, M.P. and D.B. Audretsch (1995), 'Science-based diversity, specialization, localized competition and innovation', Paper presented at the Tinbergen Institute, Amsterdam.

Feldman, M.P. and R. Florida (1994), 'The geographic sources of innovation: technological infrastructure and product innovation in the United States', *Annals of the Association of American Geographers*, **84** (2), pp. 210–229.

Garnsworthy, A. and K. O'Connor (1997), 'Knowledge-based manufacturing and regional change', in P. Droege (ed.), *Intelligent Environments*, Amsterdam: North-Holland, pp. 87-97.

Genosko, J. (1997), 'Innovative milieux and globalisation', in *European Planning Studies*, **5** (3), pp. 283-97.

Geus, A. de (1997), *The Living Company*, London: Longview.

Goldfinger, Ch. (1994), *L'Utile et le Futile*, Brussels: Editions Odile Jacob.

Guilhon, B., P. Huard, M. Orillard and J.B Zimmermann (1997), *Economie de la connaissance et organisations*, Paris: L' Harmattan.

Hassink, R. (1997) 'Localized industrial learning and innovation policies. Editorial: globalization, regional and local knowledge transfer', *Special Issue of European Planning Studies*, **5** (3), pp. 279-82.

Henderson, V. (1997), 'Externalities and industrial development', *Journal of Urban Economics*, **42**, pp. 449-70.

Houtum, H. van (1998), Doctoral dissertation. To be published at KUB (Tilburg).

Hunt, S. (1997), 'Resource-advantage theory', *Journal of Economic Issues*, **31** (1), pp. 59-78.

Jacobs, J. (1968), *The Economy of Cities*, London: Weidenfeld.

Jacobs, J. (1984), *Cities and the Wealth of Nations*, New York: Random House.

Kogut, B. and U. Zander (1992). 'Knowledge of the firm', in *Organizational Science*, **3** (3), pp. 383-97.

Krugman, P. (1991), *Trade and Geography*, Cambridge, Mass.: MIT Press.

Krugman, P. (1995), *Development, Geography and Economic Theory*, Cambridge, Mass.: MIT Press.

Lambooy, J.G. (1986), 'Locational decisions and regional structure', in J.H.P. Paelinck (ed.) *Human Behaviour in Geographical Space*, London: Gower, pp. 149-65.

Lambooy, J.G. (1987), 'Information and internationalisation', *Revue d'Economie Regionale et Urbaine*, **5**, pp. 719-31.

Lambooy, J.G. (1988), 'Intermediaire dienstverlening en economische complexiteit', *Economisch en Sociaal Tijdschrift*, **42** (5), pp. 617-29.

Lambooy, J.G. (1991), 'Complexity, formations and networks', in M. de Smidt and E. Wever (eds), *Complexes, Formations and Networks*, Utrecht: Nederlandse Geografische Studies, nr. 132, pp.15-23.

Lambooy, J.G. (1996), 'Knowledge production, organisation and agglomeration economies', Amsterdam, Tinbergen Institute discussion paper.

Lambooy, J.G. (1997), 'Knowledge production, organisation and agglomeration economies', *GeoJournal*, **41** (4), pp. 293-300.

Malmberg, A. and P. Maskell (1997), 'Towards an explanation of regional specialization and industry agglomeration', in *European Planning Studies*, **5** (1), pp. 25-41.

Manshanden, W. (1996), *Zakelijke Diensten en Regionaal-economische Ontwikkeling; de economie van nabijheid*, Utrecht/Amsterdam: KNAG/FEE-UvA (*Nederlandse Geografische Studies*, nr. 205).

March, J.G. (1988), 'Bounded rationality, ambiguity, and the engineering of choice', in D.E. Bell, H. Raiffa and A. Tversky (eds), *Decision Making*, Cambridge: Cambridge University Press, pp. 33-58.

Marshall, A. (1890), *Principles of Economics*, London: Macmillan.

Martin, R. and P. Sunley (1996), 'Paul Krugman's geographical economics and its implications for regional development theory: a critical assessment', *Economic Geography*, **72** (3), pp. 259-92.

Mintzberg, H. (1979), *The Structuring of Organisations*, New York: Prentice Hall.

Morgan, K. (1992), 'Innovating by networking: new models of corporate and regional development', in M. Dunford and G. Kafkalis (eds), op cit.

Morgan, K. (1997), 'The learning region: institutions, innovation and regional renewal', *Regional Studies*, **31** (5), pp. 491-503.

Nelson, R.R. and S.G. Winter (1982), *An Evolutionary Theory of Economic Change*, Cambridge, Mass.: Belknap Press.

Pasinetti, L. (1993), *Structural Economic Dynamics*, Cambridge: Cambridge University Press.

Polanyi, K. (1966), *The Tacit Dimension*, New York: Bantam Doubleday Dell Publishing Group.

Romer, P. (1987), 'Growth based on increasing returns due to specialization', *American Economic Review*, **77**, pp. 56-62.

Saviotti, P.P. (1996), *Technological Evolution, Variety and the Economy*, Cheltenham: Edward Elgar.

Saxenian, A. (1994), *The Regional Advantage*, Cambridge, Mass.: MIT Press.

Schmidt, H. (1997), *Collective Efficiency and Increasing Returns*, Sussex: Institute of Development Studies, Working Paper no. 50.

Schumpeter, J.A. (1943), *Capitalism, Socialism and Democracy*, Allen & Unwin.

Scott, A.J. (1988), 'Flexible production systems and regional development', *International Journal of Urban and Regional Research Policy*, (12), pp. 171-85.

Senge, P. (1990), *The Fifth Discipline*, New York: Doubleday.

Simmie, J. (ed.) (1997), *Innovation, Networks and Learning Regions?*, London: Jessica Kingsley Publishers.

Tordoir, P. (1993), *The Professional Knowledge Economy*, Amsterdam: Dissertation for Master's degree, University of Amsterdam.

Vaessen, P. (1993), *Small business growth in contrasting environments*. Nijmegen: Catholic University / *Netherlands Geographical Studies*, no. 165.

Vaessen, P. and D. Keeble (1995), 'Growth-oriented SMEs in unfavourable environments', *Regional Studies*, **29** (6), pp. 489-505.

Visser, E.J. (1996), *Local Sources of Competitiveness; Spatial Clustering and Organisational Dynamics in Small-Scale Clothing in Lima, Peru*, Amsterdam: Tinbergen Institute.

Warsh, D. (1984), *The Economic Theory of Complexity*, Bloomington (Ind): Univ of Indiana Press.

Wegner, G. (1997), 'Economic policy from an evolutionary perspective: a new approach', in *Journal of Institutional and Theoretical Economics*, **153**, pp. 485-509.

Williamson, O.E. (1985), *The Economic Institutions of Capitalism*, New York: The Free Press.

Williamson, O.E. (1990), *Industrial Organization*, Cheltenham: Edward Elgar.

3. The Learning Capabilities of Regions: Conceptual Policies and Patterns

**Marina van Geenhuizen and
Peter Nijkamp**

3.1 INTRODUCTION

With the increased territorial openness, factor mobility, and the weakening of national protective measures, regions are growing in importance as the spatial framework for economic competition. It is now recognized that knowledge – with learning as the most important process – constitutes one of the few important sources of competitiveness (cf. Camagni, 1991; Knight, 1995; Kuklinski, 1996; Lambooy, 1997; Morgan, 1997). The awareness of the social embeddedness of economic interaction (Grabher, 1993) has given a further impetus to the recognition of the region as a main territorial framework for learning and knowledge-based economic growth. The core argument is that tacit knowledge – with its crucial role in innovation – is highly territorial-specific because of its embodiment in individuals, its social and cultural context and, therefore, its need for proximity.

At the same time, the speed and complexity of knowledge development is higher than ever before. For example, there is a constant shortening of the life cycles of products and time to market and an increase in the integration of products and services, in hybrid technologies, in functionality and in the number of product variants (customizing) (den Hertog and Huizenga, 1997). These developments make it even more urgent to devote attention to learning and knowledge-based growth.

Over the past two decades, research has concentrated overwhelmingly on innovation, with shifts in focus from innovation in its own right to innovation embedded in socio-cultural processes, institutions and networks. At the same time, there has been a move from a static to a dynamic approach to innovation (cf. Amin and Thrift, 1994; Bertuglia *et al.*, 1997; Ratti *et al.*, 1997). The recent 'passion' for learning regions may be seen as a further step in an attempt to uncover the basic processes underlying the dynamics of innovation and regional economic growth.

The fact that the study of learning regions is relatively new explains the lack of a proper definition of learning regions as an analytical and testable concept. Associated with this is a shortage of cross-comparative research using a similar analytical framework leading to generic insights into learning regions. This chapter is an attempt to shed light on various underexposed conceptual and empirical issues, paying particular attention to policy and empirical implications.

The chapter is structured as follows. First, there is a brief conceptual exploration of learning regions and the learning involved, as well as of the conditions that facilitate learning (Section 3.2). This section is rather short, as Chapter 1 also partly deals with these issues. In order to avoid too much overlap, the description is only brief. In order to stress diversity in learning, the chapter continues with a discussion of different learning patterns associated with particular product types (Section 3.3). An empirical study conducted in various European cities serves to underline this diversity. This can be found in Appendix 1, at the end of the chapter. Section 3.4 explores the inherent complexity of learning regions in the light of policies to improve their performance. The findings in this section form the input for a discussion of appropriate policy approaches and of the research needed for a problem diagnosis (Section 3.5). The final section of the chapter 3.6 draws some conclusions.

3.2 CONCEPTUAL EXPLORATION

The concept of a learning region has two connotations. First, it refers to areas which have a body of knowledge (incorporated in research institutes and laboratories, higher education facilities) through which they can augment their productivity. Secondly, the concept refers to areas which use this body of knowledge to try to achieve a better performance through active and comprehensive learning. This section explores important notions associated with learning regions, derived from the literature. It focuses first on the purpose of learning, learning actors and learning networks, and the type of knowledge involved. There follows an exploration of the notion of learning capability.

The concept of learning regions is often associated with the need for improved competitiveness in global markets. Thus, learning is not an aim in itself, but serves to improve the actors' performance, although it is not always clear what this improved performance implies. It may refer to innovation and profitability, sustainability, or merely efficiency. The same vagueness holds for competition, where there is vagueness about which regions are being competed with, about the dimensions of competition and the level of ambition (for example, catching up, defeating) and, hence, the amount of learning effort needed. There is no doubt that part of the competitive strength of a region is determined by its natural, physical conditions, but part is contingent on indigenous managerial and learning skills. For example, regions can capitalize on their 'main port' function, and can even outperform others by exploiting their 'brain port' potential.

With regard to the actors involved, learning certainly refers to regional firms, but there are two reasons for including other categories of regional actors. First, learning for innovation is increasingly taking place in different networks. Secondly, part of the learning is rooted in the region, which points to local authorities and supporting organizations as participants in learning. Learning therefore takes place at different levels. When we explore what is being learned, it is necessary to distinguish between two types of knowledge: explicit knowledge, embodied in machines, patents, documents, computer programmes, etc., and implicit knowledge, embodied in human beings. The former is also called formal, codified knowledge and the latter tacit knowledge (Nonaka and Takeuchi, 1995). Tacit knowledge is rooted in practice and experience, and transmitted by apprenticeship and training through 'watching and doing' forms of learning, strongly 'coloured' by the social and cultural setting. It cannot be readily articulated and is therefore not easily communicable or tradable. Because of its wholly personal embodied nature, it can be traded only through the labour market.

An area of tacit knowledge – connected with creativity and intuition – is now widely regarded as making the most important contribution to new combinations and new applications in product innovation. This is also referred to as serendipity (den Hertog and Huizenga, 1997). Unexpected events, failure and chance play an important role here. The awareness of the role of tacit knowledge forms the basis for the articulation of the need for spatial proximity in innovation, and provides the ground for the need to study regions as an important spatial framework for learning (Morgan, 1997).

It should be emphasized that a different area of tacit knowledge produces routines. These are forms of rule-guided behaviour in which incremental adjustments are made to preexisting patterns. There is a danger, however, that routines blind actors to new developments in the external environment, so that decision-making tends to rely on old success stories and well-known solutions, even where the environment is changing rapidly. In evolutionary approaches to the subject, this phenomenon is known as path dependence (Arthur, 1994; Boschma and Lambooy, 1998; van Geenhuizen, 1998). In a situation of path dependence it is difficult to abandon technologies or product-markets, etc. once they have been selected, because of an accumulation of experience, routines, and capital in the past. In other words, the increasing returns from a previously selected behaviour makes a withdrawal from this behaviour less likely. The above observations point to at least two basic types of learning, namely, one leading to tacit knowledge, which produces new combinations and applications, and one leading to the removal of obsolete routines (de-learning).

Regional learning capability may be conceived of as a set of conditions that allow regional actors to learn and improve their performance. Various preconditions can be identified for the adoption of an integrated approach:

1. *Consensus* among the regional actors involved. Learning as a collective action needs to be accepted as a meaningful strategy. In addition, a certain level of trust is necessary, so that the benefits of learning are also contingent on its acceptance (Morgan, 1997; Nooteboom, 1996).
2. *Networking to promote knowledge creation and flow.* Innovation is an interactive process within firms, between firms (suppliers, contractors), and between firms and various institutions. Accordingly, networking is important to enhance serendipity.
3. *Transformation of knowledge.* Because of differences in vocabulary and frameworks, knowledge cannot always flow smoothly (Kamann, 1994; Williams and Gibson, 1990). Thus, transformation is necessary, for example, in flows between basic and applied knowledge, and between different disciplines.
4. *Management of human capital.* This concerns the resident population and the work force in local firms. There needs to be sufficient investment in skills for learning and skills for management, and for learning itself in art and science at different levels, in different combinations, and through formal as well as informal education.
5. *Management of public stocks of knowledge.* This includes the updating of archives, libraries, etc., and providing access to them.
6. *Identification of new learning and knowledge needs.* This precondition is concerned with the monitoring of needs while anticipating new developments. Producing early warning signals is important here.

A key condition at a higher level is the self-organizing power to co-ordinate, preserve and renew the above preconditions (cf. Amin and Thrift, 1994; Camagni, 1991; Ratti *et al.*, 1997; Storper, 1996). This ability can develop only if there is a certain social and cultural coherence in the region and sets of common aims and conventions (routines) directing socio-economic behaviour. The common aims cover a wide range of interrelated fields, reflecting the multi-faceted nature and setting of learning networks, i.e. ranging from culture and education to the labour and housing markets (Knight, 1995). Such circumstances develop spontaneously in certain regions, but in other regions there seems to be a need for system integrators, such as a key person (natural leader) or a public–private agency (Bramanti and Senn, 1997).

Networking has been identified as an important precondition for learning. Networking means here an intentional participation by regional actors in networks, the formation of new networks and the dissolution of old ones. Learning networks can be defined as sets of connected exchange relationships among actors involved in learning (cf. Cook, 1982; Håkansson, 1989). Network behaviour may be both co-operative and competitive. As with many other networks, a structural approach allows a number of components and aspects to be distinguished. Networking is therefore about establishing linkages in order to acquire strategic resources for learning, such as human capital and finance for R&D, and information about the external environment. Active networks undertake activities such as R&D, brainstorming in group sessions, or simply working together and learning-by-doing. Networks can become active learning networks only if there is access to facilities (or channels) to promote learning interaction. Good examples of these are access to the Internet and to data banks. The interaction within and between networks is defined by the type of relationship involved, for example, simple and complex, symmetrical and asymmetrical, horizontal and vertical relationships. Power is an important aspect of networks, in view of steering. Power differs within and between networks in respect of access to resources and information, and the potential to exclude unwanted participants. Power can be seen as asymmetric exchanges, and dependence as the outcome of the exertion of power. There is a continuum of inter-organizational dependence in learning relationships, based on the type of compensation between the partners (Contractor and Lorange, 1988). In the learning of firms, technological training (in return for a fee) seems to be at one end of the spectrum and joint ventures (in return for shares) at the other end.

Like other networks, learning networks are relatively closed. They may be almost entirely closed if the knowledge involved is strategic and property rights are at stake. There are two other important characteristics of learning networks, namely, their spatial range and their socio-economic stability over time. The spatial range is variable and has increased in recent decades through telecommunications. As we have previously indicated, simple learning based on tacit knowledge needs physical proximity. Similarly, stability over time is variable, but seems to be relatively strong for tacit learning.

The above discussion underlines a differentiation in learning networks, but the common concern of network actors is to increase knowledge more efficiently than in the absence of networks. Networks are therefore vehicles for efficient behaviour. Network externalities may be derived from a higher speed, a greater coverage of knowledge, or synergy with other knowledge and so on. An interesting example of externalities can be found in telecommunication networks. Here, positive externalities increase with the number of subscribers to the networks (Capello, 1997). This seems to be equally true of learning networks using telecommunications, such as in a discussion on a web-site, but the situation appears to differ for learning networks based on face-to-face contact. With these, the optimum may be reached very quickly as the number of participants increases, because of diseconomies of density and the limited capacity of human beings to interact intensively with a great many actors.

3.3   DIVERSITY IN PATTERNS OF LEARNING

Several authors point to differences in knowledge development according to the dominant culture and conventions (den Hertog and Huizenga, 1997). Storper (e.g., 1996), for example, highlighted the differences between product types, dependent upon the uncertainty in the markets and technologies involved. Examples of product types are dedicated products and generic products. The critical condition for dedicated products is the existence of a community of specialists working on the redesign of the product within tight time limits, using their tacit and customary knowledge of the product. Such an interpersonal community of knowledge developers is often based on traditionally acquired skills. Constant communication is necessary to carry out the specific technological development, with communication between producers and users being the most essential. This pattern applies not only to certain craft-based European industrial districts, but also to the most specialist parts of high-technology industries, such as non-merchant semiconductor production in Silicon Valley and the medical and scientific instruments industry in Orange County (near Los Angeles) (Storper, 1996).

By contrast, the production of generic products depending upon highly specialized inputs, is based on formal processes of communication and learning. Knowledge development here relies on forms of communication that can be extended over large distances, because the information is codified and the exchange is planned at regular intervals (business meetings, seminars, etc.). At the same time, however, the producers are often tied to the same type of interpersonal communities of knowledge workers for the development of their newest technology inputs as in the previous case. This pattern means that regions dominated by such industries – such as fine chemicals – may include formal learning and tacit learning, but may equally lack substantial knowledge development *in situ* (in a disconnected case). We may therefore conclude that the importance of knowledge development and tacit learning in regional production may differ according to the product composition of firms in the region.

The above discussion refers to different types of learning as relatively stable patterns, but there may be a variation in the type and intensity of learning over time. We may distinguish between high levels of learning for a new product (design) or a new application followed by lower levels of learning for process innovation in order to reduce costs. Such time patterns are associated with the product life cycle and various variations of this cycle (van Duijn, 1984; van Geenhuizen, 1993), or with what Nooteboom (1998) calls the cycle of learning and organization. Needless to say, regional economies may show different compositions in this respect.

A broad discussion is now in progress about learning, knowledge, knowledge infrastructure, learning regions and the role of universities in all this. A very interesting paper has been published by Michael Gibbons *et al.* with the title 'The new production of knowledge'. It calls attention to a new form of knowledge production, the context in which it is pursued, the way it is organized, the reward systems it utilizes and the mechanisms controlling the quality of what is produced. In the authors' view, the social characteristics of knowledge production have been well articulated in the disciplinary sciences, chemistry, biology and physics, for example, which is the main reason why these are taken as paradigmatic of sound knowledge production in the sciences. Where social sciences and the humanities have tried to imitate the physical sciences, similar social systems have been put in place to govern the production of knowledge in these areas, too. In fact, 'the new production of knowledge' places science policy and scientific knowledge in its broader context within contemporary societies. For this reason, this approach to knowledge production is necessary not only for all those concerned with the changing nature of knowledge, but also for those involved in relations between R&D and social, economic and technological development. It is precisely here that we will be confronted with all kinds of problems inherent in the learning capabilities of regions.

The diversity of the patterns of learning has been described in several publications, often with reference to a pilot study. Peter Maskell, for example, describes and analyses the role of localized learning and regional embedded knowledge for the development of the furniture industry in Denmark. The success of this development is closely related to locally and regionally developed learning, in which the historical and social dimensions play an important part. Many case studies have been put forward in publications by John Goddard, who has studied the role of knowledge and the knowledge infrastructure in general and of the universities and higher education institutions, in particular. The OECD has even launched a project in which the role of higher education institutions has been highlighted in relation to regional needs. We might conclude from all these examples and case studies that the patterns of regional and local learning are highly diverse, as are the results.

3.4 COMPLEXITY OF LEARNING NETWORKS IN RELATION TO POLICY MAKING

This section focuses on three characteristics of learning networks, in view of the potentials for steering. Three characteristics have been put forward in recent literature on policy making, i.e., diversity, closeness, and dependence (de Bruijn and ten Heuvelhof, 1995; Koppenjan *et al.*, 1993). The section also discusses uncertainty in framing policy for learning networks arising from erratic moves and unpredictable outcomes.

As indicated in the previous sections, learning networks show a high level of diversity. This diversity is sometimes reinforced by a multi-layered network structure, in which actors at higher spatial levels influence the local level, as where multinationals decide upon the closure or opening of a local laboratory, or national governments lay down university budgets. Diversity often implies a different perception of problems and policy options and – in serious cases – a controversy. This may be true of the policy for learning-based economic growth itself, where it appears to be a time-consuming endeavour without immediate gains in terms of new employment (Morgan, 1997). A policy for learning regions may therefore face opposition from the labour unions or organizations for the unemployed. A situation of limited consensus between the relevant actors may lead to faint support for policy programmes and only a partial implementation of measures, leading to unexpected outcomes.

We stated earlier that learning networks are to some extent closed. This means that they have their own frame of reference and are therefore susceptible only to selected steering signals. The dependence in learning networks may relate to finance, for example, research budgets, or to political support or protection, etc. In the context of steering, a situation of dependence means that a powerful actor or network forms a useful starting point for the implementation of change, because the other actors (networks) tend to follow.

The characteristics described above result in a continuous change in learning networks within certain limits, such as the entry or exit of new actors, the merging or dissolution of networks, and shifts in power. What also happens is that the content of policy problems changes over time. Actors may redefine their problem, for example, because of a discrepancy between the original definition and the emergence of new insights or coalitions with other actors. For purposes of steering this means that there is a need for monitoring and evaluation.

It is important to note that the setting of knowledge creation is becoming increasingly complex. There is a shift from a hierarchical, disciplinary division of labour-based knowledge production to a mode in which research problems overlap disciplinary boundaries and focus strongly on application.

In terms of organization, a larger number of actors is involved (apart from universities, research centres), with an increased emphasis on teams (consortia) working on a temporary basis.

There is little experience of policies for learning regions, but there is experience of policies for innovative milieux, and of policies that similarly involve a multi-actor, multi-level and multi-disciplinary field, i.e. transport. We may accordingly expect policies for learning networks to produce erratic moves and unpredictable outcomes, firstly because decision making is still based on insufficient knowledge of the capability for learning and of learning itself. There is a limited empirical understanding of the conditions under which the localized collaboration of firms facilitates learning, or of the conditions under which localized learning leads to innovation and improved profitability or employment growth (cf. Brouwer *et al.*, 1993; Eskelinen, 1997; Oinas and Virkkala, 1997). It is also difficult to obtain and model reliable data of learning processes and knowledge in the regional economy. There is no standard production function of knowledge, no input–output recipe for assessing the impact of a unit of knowledge on economic performance, etc. This means that problem diagnosis and, therefore, solutions are insufficiently supported by solid quantitative data.

Even less is known about networks, particularly in the context of a relatively long-term dimension. Network dynamics are dominated by non-linear relationships, including chaotic dynamics. With the latter, small changes in the initial conditions or parameters may lead to disproportionately large dynamics, which may cause particular networks or regions to follow a different development path from others, e.g., they may suddenly become highly active in learning, while others may collapse or stagnate (cf. Kamann, 1997; Nijkamp and Reggiani, 1998).

Unpredictability also stems from the nature of policy making itself. The degree of rational and neutral behaviour in policy making is always limited, so that procedures are imperfect. Non-rational behaviour and subjectivity cannot be eliminated from decision making, particularly if the problems are complex (cf. Hofstee, 1996). The potential imperfections include: ill-defined and ill-structured problem definition, problem analysis that is hampered by lack of knowledge in the field concerned and of decisions in related fields, a disregard of potentially relevant alternative solutions, and absence of evaluation of current measures and developments (van Geenhuizen and Nijkamp, 1998b; Hall, 1990; Rietveld, 1993).

While exploiting its creative potential to acquire, digest, and deploy strategic knowledge more efficiently than its competitors, a region needs to become aware of the above imperfections and uncertainties in policy making. As an alternative to reducing uncertainty, a useful strategy is to use uncertainty creatively in order to find new policy solutions.

3.5   POLICY APPROACHES

This section first discusses important policy approaches to match the network and interactive nature of regional learning, i.e., network management and participatory policy making (de Bruijn and ten Heuvelhof, 1995). We then discuss the research needed to underpin policy initiatives.

Network management means influencing the diversity, dependence, and closeness of networks in order to provide opportunities for change. This is therefore a form of meta-steering, leading to changes in the network structure to facilitate an effective use of instruments (the operational level). For example, an important characteristic of learning capability is the fragmentation of intermediary networks (cf. Bartels, 1996). In this context, network management means first letting these networks merge or co-operate in a single 'platform' and then implementing measures by targeting the 'platform' in order to improve performance.

Moreover, in an interactive approach, much attention is paid to participatory policy making. The latter generally aims to achieve consensus between different actors, in order to increase support for policy solutions, although there may be various specific aims (Ester *et al.*, 1997). The aim may be merely to advise and provide information about actors' interests and values, in which case, the method works through citizen consultation, workshops and conferences where actors can disclose their information, opinions and values. An important result of the process is that the actors cross the borders of their own frame (frame reflective learning) and establish new networks and communication, based on a change of attitude. There are also participatory approaches, in which actors actively contribute to the design or redesign of policy solutions. The latter seems to be essential in learning region policies, because learning as a common action cannot work without the full support of all the local actors. A specific form of participatory policy making is 'creative steering', which has been developed in order to find new solutions in traffic infrastructure policy making. Creative steering takes chaos as a starting point and accepts contributions from all the actors who are willing to participate. A major aim is originality, rather than proving an argument right or wrong. The results of creative steering may be elaborated in several rounds in order to create a policy document of sufficiently high quality.

Apart from the policy areas of housing and community development and transport infrastructure, there is little experience with the participatory approach. A preliminary analysis suggests that the following factors influence the success of this approach (van Geenhuizen and Nijkamp, 1998b):

- *Motivation*; a sufficient number of relevant actors need to be convinced of the problem and of co-operation as an appropriate way of finding solutions.

- *Transparency* of aims and procedures, and *trust*, meaning that stakeholders are convinced of a potentially genuine participation (as opposed to symbolic participation).
- *Removal of barriers* between stakeholders, such as those created by 'languages' and types of argumentation.
- An *adequate role* for the process manager as the facilitator of communication and interaction between stakeholders (dependent upon the aim of the participation).
- A *short lapse of time* between participation and the implementation of the results. It seems that changes in actors' attitudes completely disappear after two years.

The above conditions indicate that participatory policy making requires careful preparation in terms of a clarification of the procedures to be followed (including competence and authority). More importantly, the selection of the appropriate actors and networks and a preliminary definition of the problem, including the level of aggregation and spatial scale, require careful preparation. This observation leads to a consideration of the empirical research that needs to be done. Research is needed on the specificity of the regions, so that a policy can be designed that matches the local situation. Various research lines can be mapped out in a (self)diagnosis:

1. To establish a picture of the interrelatedness of the regional economy, using micro-level data on input, output, and origin, destination, etc., in a *filière* or chain-like approach (Kamann, 1997). This analysis also reveals ownership structures, capital flows, knowledge flows, etc., in such a way as to provide indications of the regional embeddedness of firms.
2. To beam in on the relevant learning networks to which regional firms are tied and the key characteristics of these networks, including spatial range.
3. To explore the links between inter-firm collaboration, learning processes and the innovative behaviour of firms, particularly the circumstances under which localized collaboration leads to innovation and better performance by firms. The composition of the regional economy in terms of types and level of learning (related to product types) is relevant here.
4. To identify bottlenecks in learning networks and in the preconditions for their functioning. For example, to uncover the socio-cultural coherence, or lack of it, in the region. Cognitive maps of actors covering both the territorial dimension and the industrial dimension may be used (Kamann, 1997).
5. To analyse recent 'shocks' in the regional economy (such as the closure

of a large firm) and to uncover the composition of responses of key actors, i.e., in terms of wishes to protect an old technology (based on routines) or to restructure the industry with the aim of introducing new key technologies. This type of analysis serves to find out whether the region is tending to a lock-in situation (Grabher, 1993).
6. To identify labour market dynamics which influence localized learning processes, e.g., the match between labour demand and supply, in and out-migration of knowledge-based firms, and the supply of training programmes. To identify housing market dynamics connected with localized learning processes, such as the match between demand and supply of housing for knowledge workers, and the in and out-migration of the latter (Knight, 1995).
7. To design forms of participatory policy making that fit the local problem situation, e.g., taking into account the distribution of power.

The above research can certainly not be done overnight. Given a situation in which various future processes and policy outcomes remain uncertain, significant flexibility is needed in the steering and monitoring of ongoing developments.

3.6   CONCLUDING REMARKS

Learning regions is an attractive concept, because it calls for attention to be paid to the institutional side of regions. The concept suffers from some vagueness, however, particularly in regard to competition between regions. In addition, various cause-and-effect chains have not been very well tested. This presents interesting opportunities for cross-comparative regional research using a common analytical framework.

Learning takes place at different levels, for example, in and between firms, and in local and regional authorities. There is learning for product innovation, the unlearning of old routines, and the acquiring of learning skills. The diversity in the networks involved causes a wide differentiation in the regional composition of learning. Diversity is partly associated with the product types of local firms. An empirical part of this study might demonstrate a differentiation in innovation based on the stage in the life cycle of the products involved. In addition, it could be shown that only selected learning networks contribute to innovation. Within a broad range of networks – covering different activities and different degrees of dependence – training networks appeared to be the most important.

In general, policies for learning regions have to deal with diversity, closeness and dependence in a dynamic setting. According to the nature of the network (interaction) and the need for consensus, policy approaches should preferably follow models of network management, including participatory approaches aimed at increasing support. In this way, policy making itself becomes a specific type of regional learning. One policy line appears to be undisputed, that is, a sufficient investment in human capital. Other policy lines are dependent on the diagnosis of the specific shortcomings of the learning capability of individual regions.

The mission of the region, that is, to improve its learning capability, will yield significant results, mainly in the medium term, although particular measures may accelerate the pace of change. It would meanwhile be sensible to carry out a number of pilot projects in order to produce some short-term results in particular areas, and to test, through a systematic monitoring of current developments, whether the long-term objectives are still valid.

APPENDIX 1:   LEARNING NETWORKS IN EUROPEAN CITY REGIONS

This section presents the empirical results of a study of the relevance of different learning networks and different industrial sub-sectors in the context of innovation. The results are based on a data set derived from the URBINNO study and compiled from extensive structured interviews with manufacturing firms in the United Kingdom (208 firms), the Netherlands (33) and Italy (32) (Nijkamp *et al.*, 1997). The firms were selected to be representative of sectors both in the early stages and in the later stages of the product life cycle. The former include firms in machinery and equipment (SIC 29), electrical machinery and apparatus (SIC 31), medical precision and optical instruments, clocks and watches (SIC 33), and motor vehicles and trailers (SIC 34). In order to have a sufficient number of firms covering the later stages of the product life cycle, the database includes textile, clothing and leather industries (SIC 17–19), and basic metal and metal industries (SIC 27 and 28). The results reported here focus on the type of learning networks involving these firms and the local or regional university and the contribution of these networks to innovation, against the background of the different stages in the product life cycle. In selecting the type of learning networks, attention was paid to activity (such as consultancy and participation in seminars) and to dependence (low in consultancy and short training courses, but high in joint ventures). Labour market links were also included, that is, recruitment networks involving the local university.

Among the networks based on a commercial agreement, those representing low dependence tend to dominate (Table A3.1). Over 30 per cent of the firms

Table A3.1 Learning networks of firms[a] with local or regional universities and colleges

Type of activity	Dependence[b]	Participation (Percentage share of all firms)
Consultancy		
Consultancy	-	32.9
Testing (analysis)	-	31.6
Subcontracting	+	13.9
Joint ventures	++	9.3
Training networks		
Short courses	-	46.0
Courses for technical qualification	-	51.0
Courses for management qualification	-	36.1
Seminars	-	30.9
Recruitment networks		
Technical staff	+	27.0
Management staff	+	14.0

Notes:
a.   N = 273 (non-response of around 8 per cent).
b.   - = low; + = high; ++ = very high.

make use of consultancy and testing (analysis) services at the university, whereas under 10 per cent have established a joint venture with a view to knowledge sharing. Much more important than commercial links are training links with the university. Around 50 per cent of all firms take advantage of short training courses and training for technical qualifications. This means that universities are an essential actor in the learning network in city regions in terms of enhancing the skills and learning abilities of local firms. Training networks result in low dependence, but the impacts may last a long time, because they are embodied in human capital.

The next step was an explanatory investigation of the innovative behaviour of firms by using logit analysis. The independent variables were participation in the three types of learning network distinguished in Table A3.1 and the different manufacturing sectors (Annexe 1). Another learning network was also taken into consideration, that is, training supplied by local or regional public sector institutes or agencies. Because of an incomplete data-set, the logit analysis had to exclude a few indicators which may be expected to affect the propensity to innovate, such as size of firm and its growth rate. The results in Table A3.2 suggest that industries representing earlier stages in the product life cycle contribute significantly to the propensity of a firm to innovate. In addition, training networks are positively related to innovation, but commercial learning networks and recruitment networks are not.

In addition, a rough set analysis was carried out using the same database. Rough set analysis is a fairly recent classification method of an if-then type. The analysis classifies objects into equivalence classes using available attributes which act as equivalence relationships for the objects considered. A class which contains only indispensable equivalence relationships is called a core. An attribute is indispensable if the classification of the objects becomes less precise when that attribute is omitted. In order to carry out the classification, the values of the attributes of all the objects are subdivided into condition (background) attributes and decision (response) attributes. Rough set data analysis basically evaluates the importance of attributes for a classification of objects, reduces all superfluous objects and attributes, discovers the most significant relationships between condition attributes and the assignment of objects to decision classes, and represents these relationships in the form of decision rules (see van den Bergh *et al.*, 1997).

In the present analysis, the decision attribute (dependent variable) is that of whether the firm has introduced an innovation. The condition attributes (explanatory variables) are the same as in the above logit analysis.

It appears that 71.4 per cent of all firms can be classified into either the

Table A3.2   Results of a logit analysis[a]

-2Log Likelihood: 367.30157 (restricted model)
-2Log Likelihood: 323.41300 (full model)

Variable	Estimated coefficient	Standard error
IND29DUM	1.0613	0.3427
IND31DUM	1.2892	0.4229
IND33DUM	1.2720	0.5115
IND34DUM	2.0964	0.5507
LINKTRAI	0.9321	0.2799
Constant	−1.6011	0.2635

Note: a. Based on Theil's sequential elimination procedure

Table A3.3   Results of rough set analysis[a]

	Innovation	No innovation	Quality of classification
Classification with core attributes	69	126	0.714
Classification with a temporarily reduced condition attribute			
Industry	26	57	0.304
Training links	60	104	0.601
Assistance	56	110	0.608
Commercial links	56	112	0.615
Recruitment links	61	118	0.656

Note: a. Lower approximations for rough set classes.

innovation category or the no innovation category (Table A3.3). All condition attributes belong to the core, meaning that an exclusion of one of them would reduce the accuracy of the classification. In addition, the relative importance of the condition attributes can be investigated by dropping each of them successively from the core (the lower rows in Table A3.3). The results indicate that the quality of the classification is lowest when Industry is excluded (only 30.4 per cent can be classified). Further, of all the learning networks, those concerned with Training make the strongest contribution to the classification. These results confirm the pattern found using logit analysis.

The previous empirical study has demonstrated a specific participation of firms in learning networks with local universities. There is a clear preference for low dependence relationships leading to long-term impacts, that is, training or retraining of employees. The analysis has shown that training networks tend to promote more innovation than commercial learning networks and recruitment links. However, the basic determinant of innovation appeared to be the manufacturing sector, that is, relatively young sectors. The latter result confirms the need to take into account the sectoral composition of the regional economy in relation to the level and type of learning. The empirical research has also shown that rough set analysis is a helpful method for explanatory research into learning networks, because it matches a situation of qualitative research based on interviews using categorical (binary) data and often producing a relatively small number of observations.

Annexe 3.1

Independent variables in the logit analysis (Table A3.2):

Sector

IND29
IND31
IND33
IND34
IND17
IND18
IND19
IND27
IND28

Learning Networks
LINKCOMM
LINKTRAI
LINKRECR
ASSTRAIN

ACKNOWLEDGEMENTS

The authors wish to thank Aki Kangasharju, who undertook the data analysis as a part of a project funded by the Academy of Finland.

REFERENCES

Amin, A. and N. Thrift (eds) (1994), *Globalization, Institutions, and Regional Development in Europe*, Oxford: Oxford University Press.

Arthur, W.B. (1994), *Increasing Returns and Path Dependence in the Economy*, Ann Arbor: University of Michigan Press.

Bartels (Bureau Bartels) (1996), *Establishing Trust. A Knowledge and Innovation Strategy for the Region of Rotterdam*, Utrecht: Bureau Bartels.

Bergh, J.C.J.M van den, K. Button, P. Nijkamp and G. Pepping (1997), *Meta-Analysis for Meso Environmental Policy*, Dordrecht: Kluwer.

Bertuglia, C.S., S. Lombardo and P. Nijkamp (eds) (1997), *Innovative Behaviour in Time and Space*, Berlin: Springer.

Boschma, R. and J. Lambooy (1998), 'Economic evolution and the adjustment of the spatial matrix of regions', in J. van Dijk and F. Boekema (eds), *Innovation in Firms and Regions*, Assen: Van Gorcum, pp. 121–37.

Bramanti, A. and L. Senn (1997), 'Understanding structural changes and laws of motion of milieux: A study on NorthWestern Lombardy', in R. Ratti, A. Bramanti and R. Gordon (eds), *The Dynamics of Innovative Regions: The GREMI Approach*, Aldershot: Ashgate, pp. 47–73.

Brouwer, E., A. Kleinknecht and J.O. Reijnen (1993), 'Employment growth and innovation at the firm level. An empirical study', *Evolutionary Economics* 1993 (3), pp. 153–9.

Bruijn, J.A. de and E.F. ten Heuvelhof (1995), *Network Management. Strategies, Instruments and Norms* (in Dutch), Utrecht: Lemma.

Camagni, R. (ed.) (1991), *Innovation Networks: Spatial Perspectives*, London: Belhaven.

Capello, R. (1997), 'Telecommunication network externalities and regional development: policy implications', in P. Rietveld and C. Capineri (eds), *Networks in Transport and Communications: A Policy Approach*, Aldershot: Ashgate, pp. 13–36.

Contractor, F. and P. Lorange (1988), *Cooperative strategies in international business*, Lexington, MA: Lexington Press.

Cook, K. (1982), 'Network structures from exchange perspective', in P. Marsden and N. Lin (eds), *Social Structure and Network Analysis*, New York: Free Press, pp. 177–99.

Duijn, J.J. van (1984), 'Fluctuations in innovations over time', in C. Freeman (ed.), *Long Waves in the World Economy*, London: Frances Pinter, pp. 19–30.

Eskelinen, H. (1997), *Regional Specialisation and Local Environment. Learning and Competitiveness*, Stockholm: NordREFO.

Ester, P., J. Geurts and M. Vermeulen (eds) (1997), *Designers of the Future* (in Dutch), Tilburg: Tilburg University Press.

Geenhuizen, M. van (1993), '*A Longitudinal Analysis of the Growth of Firms. The Case of the Netherlands*', Rotterdam: Erasmus University (Ph.D. thesis).

Geenhuizen, M. van (1998), 'An evolutionary approach to firm dynamics: adaptation and path dependence', in G. Lipshitz, P. Rietveld, P. and D. Shefer (eds), *Regional Development in an Age of Structural Economic Change* (forthcoming).

Geenhuizen, M. van and P. Nijkamp (1998a), 'Improving the knowledge capability of cities: the case of mainport Rotterdam', *International Journal of Technology Management*, **15** (6/7), pp. 691–709.

Geenhuizen, M. van and P. Nijkamp (1998b), *Regional and Urban Policy Beyond 2000: New Approaches with Learning as Device*, Research Memoranda, Amsterdam: Free University.

Grabher, G. (ed.) (1993), *The Embedded Firm. On the Socioeconomics of Industrial Networks*, London: Routledge.

Håkansson, H. (1989), *Corporate Technological Behaviour: Co-operation and Networks*, London: Routledge.

Hall, P. (1990), *Great Planning Disasters Revisited*, London: UCL Department of Geography.

Hertog, F. den and E. Huizenga (1997), *The Knowledge Factor. Competition as a Knowledge-Based Firm* (in Dutch), Deventer: Kluwer.

Hofstee, W.K.B. (1996), 'Psychological factors in decision making' (in Dutch), in P. Nijkamp, W. Begeer and J. Berting (eds), *Considering Complexity in Decision Making: A Panoramic View*, The Hague: SDU Uitgevers, pp. 49–58.

Kamann, D.J.F. (1994), 'Spatial barriers and differentiation of culture in Europe', in P. Nijkamp (ed.), *New Borders and Old Barriers in Spatial Development*, Aldershot: Avebury, pp. 35–63.

Kamann, D.J.F. (1997), 'Policies for dynamic innovative networks in innovative milieux', in R. Ratti, A. Bramanti and R. Gordon (eds), *The Dynamics of Innovative Regions: The GREMI Approach*, Aldershot: Ashgate, pp. 367–91.

Knight, R.V. (1995), 'Knowledge-based development: policy and planning implications for cities', *Urban Studies,* (2), pp. 225–60.

Koppenjan, J.F.M., J.A. de Bruijn and W.J.M. Kickert (1993), *Network Management in Public Administration. Potentials for public steering in policy networks* (in Dutch), The Hague.

Kuklinski, A. (ed.) (1996), *Production of Knowledge and the Dignity of Science*, Warsaw: EUROREG.

Lambooy, I. (1997), 'Knowledge production, organisation and agglomeration economies', *Geojournal,* **41** (4), pp. 293–300.

Maillat, D., G. Lechot, B. Lelocq and M. Pfister (1997), 'Comparative analysis of the structural development of milieux: the watch industry in the Swiss and French Jura arc', in R. Ratti, A. Bramanti and R. Gordon (eds), *The Dynamics of Innovative Regions*, Aldershot: Ashgate, pp. 109–37.

Morgan, K. (1997), 'The Learning Region: Institutions, Innovation and Regional Renewal', *Regional Studies, 31* (5), pp. 491–503.

Nijkamp, P. (1996), 'Policy and policy analysis: narrow margins versus broad missions' (in Dutch), in P. Nijkamp, W. Begeer and J. Berting (eds), *Considering Complexity in Decision Making: A Panoramic View*, The Hague: SDU Uitgevers, pp. 129–46.

Nijkamp, P. and A. Reggiani (1995), *Interaction, Evolution and Chaos in Space*, Amsterdam: Elsevier.

Nijkamp, P. and A. Reggiani (1998), *The Economics of Complex Systems*, Amsterdam: Elsevier.

Nijkamp, P., A. Kangasharju and M. van Geenhuizen (1997), 'Local and innovative behaviour: A meta-analytic study on European cities', in G. Lipshitz, P. Rietveld and D. Shefer (eds), *Regional Development in an Age of Structural Economic Change* (forthcoming).

Nonaka, I. and H. Takeuchi (1995), *The Knowledge-Creating Company. How Japanese Companies Create the Dynamics of Innovation*, Oxford: Oxford University Press.

Nooteboom, B. (1996), 'Trust, opportunism and governance: a process and control model', *Organizational Studies,* (17), pp. 985–1010.

Nooteboom (1998), 'Innovation, location and firm size', in J. van Dijk and F. Boekema (eds), *Innovation in Firms and Regions*, Assen: Van Gorcum, pp. 75–9.

Oinas, P. and S. Virkkala (1997), 'Learning, competitiveness and development', in H. Eskelinen (ed.), *Regional Specialisation and Local Environment. Learning and Competitiveness*, Stockholm: NordREFO, pp. 263–77.

Ratti, R., A. Bramanti and R. Gordon (eds) (1997), *The Dynamics of Innovative Regions. The GREMI Approach*, Aldershot: Ashgate.

Rietveld, P. (1993), 'Policy analysis in traffic, transport and spatial planning; improving the quality of decision making?' (in Dutch), in P. Rietveld and H. Boerenbach (eds), *Policy analysis and decision making in traffic and spatial planning*, The Hague: Platform Beleidsanalyse.

Simmie, J. (ed.) (1997), *Innovation, Networks and Learning Regions?*, London: Jessica Kingsley.

Storper, M. (1996), 'Innovation as collective action: conventions, products and technologies', *Industrial and Corporate Change, 5* (3), pp. 761–90.

Williams, F. and D.V. Gibson (eds) (1990), *Technology Transfer. A Communication Perspective*, Newbury Park, London: Sage.

4. Distance and Learning: Does Proximity Matter?

Päivi Oinas

4.1 INTRODUCTION

To draw a caricature of how geographers have dealt with what are called the 'global' and 'local' scales during the past twenty years or so, one might visualize a seesaw with 'globalization' at one end and 'localization' at the other. It has been an up and down movement with different issues making the seesaw riders dizzy each time at each end. Examples of such issues are NIDL at the globalization end in the 1970s; industrial districts or new industrial estates at the localization end in the 1980s; the global dominance of multi- and transnational corporations at the globalization end at the end of the decade; and, most recently, learning at the localization end during much of the 1990s. As they witnessed this stage, economic geographers seem to have become convinced that success springs best out of proximate relations in specific kinds of local or regional surroundings which they dignify with the title 'learning region'.

Localized learning does not happen in a vacuum, however. The discussion in this chapter therefore concentrates on 'the question that is being asked more and more insistently today: what is the role of proximity in economic development?' (Crevoisier, 1996, p. 1684). Burmeister and Colletis-Wahl (1997, p. 235) note that 'propinquity in space only creates a potential for interactions, without necessarily creating them'. Conversely, distance may hinder interactions or make them difficult, but it does not eliminate them. The task remains to discover whether there is any systematization in the role that proximity and distance play in interactions between economic actors, in this case, the learning process.

It is therefore the aim of this chapter to outline grounds for questioning what is here called 'the received wisdom' about proximity and learning in economic geography. It will be claimed that while local relationships are important, it needs to be increasingly emphasized that the creation and maintenance of non-local connections also play a significant role in sustaining competitiveness. Such relationships allow centrally for the incorporation of new ideas into place-specific processes of technological learning. In certain sectors, international intra- or inter-firm networks are required to provide specialized knowledge that is still tacit and not widespread (cf. Cantwell, 1995; Patchell *et al.*, 1999). This question of the relative importance of local versus non-local relations in learning remains unsettled in recent research (Oinas and Malecki, 1999).

This chapter first provides an interpretation of the general line of reasoning in recent economic geographical literature on regional development. In the 1990s, the idea of 'localized learning' and the importance of local relationships has figured centrally in that literature. This general line will be brief, since earlier chapters also examine general theoretical issues and literature. Secondly, this chapter identifies reasons for questioning the strong focus on localized relationships and, thirdly, it outlines elements for an approach that accounts for different types of learning where proximity and distance play distinct roles. The chapter concludes by pointing out directions for future research on learning in a spatial perspective.

With regard to terminology, instead of the expression 'learning region', which is used frequently in the literature and elsewhere in this book (see, for example, Florida, 1995; Morgan, 1997; Simmie, 1997) this chapter will use the expression 'regional learning'. Regional learning is understood as '*inter-organisational learning* that is tied to the location where it takes place because it would be difficult or impossible to create the same circumstances for learning elsewhere' (Oinas and Virkkala, 1997, p. 270).

4.2   THE 'RECEIVED WISDOM' ABOUT PROXIMITY AND LEARNING IN ECONOMIC GEOGRAPHY

The interest in learning in the literature of economic geography dates back only a few years, but it has shown signs of being 'the discourse' of the 1990s (cf. Oinas and Virkkala, 1997, p. 263). A consensus seems to be emerging on the idea that learning requires proximity. Localized learning, in the current parlance,

> demands firms to be closely linked with, and deeply embedded in, their local economic and social environment where relevant business-specific knowledge is readily available. Local relations provide key resources that are not likely to be obtainable elsewhere. The local environment also endows a firm with the benefit of institutional support, based on social, economic and political institutions that grow up and evolve suited to the communities – including their firms and industries – in each place. Such an environment provides skills and experience that cannot be easily or quickly duplicated in other places. (Malecki and Oinas, 1999, p. 1)

This apparent consensus on these views seems to be a consequence of the line of thinking that has been developing in the field in the past ten years or so, asserting the importance of proximate local relations. These developments of recent 'fashions' in economic geography literature on regional development can be summarized roughly as follows:

- under the condition of globalization (Maskell, 1999)
- flexibly specialized networked actors (since Piore and Sabel, 1984)
- involved in collaborative and competitive relations (e.g. Harrison, 1992)
- are embedded in local social relations (Granovetter, 1985; Oinas, 1997)
- characterized by institutional thickness (Amin and Thrift, 1993)
- where interaction is governed by conventions (Storper, 1993, 1997; Storper and Salais, 1997)
- and results in learning (e.g. Lundvall, 1992)
- within localized relations due to its tacit elements (Asheim and Cooke, 1999)
- and enables the creation of unique assets for competitiveness (Maskell, 1999, Maskell *et al.*, 1998, Maskell and Malmberg, 1999b)
- of both firms and their regional environments.

Learning is regarded as a collective interactive and iterative process between actors which builds on organization-specific and region-specific resources. Processes of learning lead to growth of stocks of knowledge of the actors involved. The suggestion that tends to be drawn from the above thinking is that only proximate relations between actors enable the kind of interaction that is required between participants in innovation networks (see, for example, Kirat and Lung, 1999).

Maskell (1999), for example, acknowledges the fact that firms do connect to others at the local, national and even global level, while aiming to create new knowledge. He insists on the relatively greater importance of localized learning, however:

> It has been argued that firms in high cost areas of the world must be able to create or recreate valuable competencies at least as fast as they are destroyed by the U(biquitification) process. Firms do this by making connections at all levels from the local to the global. However, inter-organizational co-operation is frequently cheaper and faster when it takes place at the local level than at great distance and when their tacitness make the results less prone to be imitated. (Maskell, 1999, p. 50).

Tacitness and trustful relations, supported by a favourable local institutional environment, are the key points in arguments stressing the importance of proximate relations in the accumulation of organizational knowledge (Asheim and Cooke, 1999; Kirat and Lung, 1999; Maskell *et al.*, 1998).

Convincing as this line of thinking is, the following section provides a set of arguments suggesting that the 'received wisdom' might be questioned – or at least qualified – on several grounds.

4.3   GROUNDS FOR QUESTIONING THE 'RECEIVED WISDOM'

It is not the aim of this chapter to deny the importance of local relations and 'localized learning' as such. Instead, as the bulk of the literature of economic geography still seems to be predominantly interested in local relations and their significance for the success of regions and their firms alike, it seems warranted to highlight the relative importance of non-proximate relations as well (cf. Amin, 1999; Oinas and Malecki, 1999). Amidst all the talk about the contemporary tendency towards globalization, mere intuition makes one wonder why it is assumed that learning takes place among local actors only. The following – analytical as well as empirical – observations will help develop that intuition, and relativize what was called the 'received wisdom' above.

First, it should be remembered that all regions where learning takes place are not replicas of Silicon Valley. In other words, the regional contexts for learning in most cases are not the kinds of idealized – even mystified – self-contained entities with all the relevant leading-edge knowledge needed in a specific industry or business. Only in some very extreme cases could we say that all the relevant knowledge for the incubation or implementation of new ideas in a specific area of expertise is located in the same place. Most areas in the world are nothing close to such idealizations. Yet, learning takes place in them.

The above relates to the third point concerning collaboration and competition. The literature states that, in spatial industrial concentrations, even competing firms may be involved in collaborative relations. It seems, however, that this general statement needs to be qualified and particularly so in relation to learning, that is, mutually competing firms may find it advantageous to collaborate by exchanging goods and services, sharing information, improving local conditions, and so on. Yet, competition – when it is not price competition between identical products – requires producers to come up with products that provide higher customer satisfaction than those of their rivals (e.g., Conner, 1991, p. 132). This means that they are not likely to give competitors the knowledge that is most strategic for the creation of their competitiveness.

A firm may develop those resources itself, buy them, or collaborate with another firm in creating them (Oinas and van Gils, 1998). It is not evident that the novelty that is required to upgrade a firm's competitive edge derives from local relations. Rather, it might stem from creating something new with possibly rather distantly located partners.

What is in question here is Grabher's (1994; ref. Grabher and Stark, 1997) suggestion about the need to create diversity in order for new and potentially successful combinations to emerge in localities and regions. This is related to Harrison *et al.*'s (1996) findings to the effect that urbanization effects might be more relevant than location effects for fostering learning (see also Kelley and Helper, forthcoming). It is highly unlikely, however, that new combinations would be based solely on local resources and localized relations. This is why it seems warranted to emphasize the role of external connections in bringing new elements into local resource pools.

In addition to the above points, a few notes can be added on empirical evidence of localized learning. First, the problem with recent writing on localized learning is that empirical evidence of actual learning processes is scarce, if not non-existent (Malmberg, 1997, p. 578). One can cite research results that provide at least tentative evidence of the association between learning and proximity (e.g., Battista and Swann, 1998; Harrison *et al.*, 1996). While highly valuable in their own right, the problem in these quantitative studies from the point of view of the theoretical–hypothetical argumentation about proximity and learning is the lack of evidence of actual processes of learning. Learning is assumed rather than documented. Similarly, for example, in Maskell's (1997, 1998) well-known – and, in all fairness, quite plausible – case study of the Danish furniture industry, there is no evidence of actual learning. The point is that an observed positive correlation between agglomeration and learning – in quantitative or qualitative studies – does not yet prove the hypothesis on proximity and learning. Neither does it help to understand the processes behind that learning.

Secondly, a slowly increasing number of studies show that 'local' relationships are actually 'missing' where theoretically grounded hypotheses would suggest that they should exist, or are not as clearly related to performance as expected (see Alderman, 1999; Coe and Townsend, 1998; Grotz and Braun, 1997; Harrison et al., 1996; Sternberg, 1997; Suarez-Villa and Walrod, 1997). However, the literature makes few suggestions about how these puzzling results should be interpreted.

Thirdly, yet another line of research reports on innovation and learning taking place over space within or between firms (e.g., Cantwell, 1995; Lam, 1997) – regardless of obvious difficulties related to them (Lam, 1997). Observing one single firm, Herrigel (1993, p. 28) describes the Robert Bosch Corporation poignantly in this regard:

... because the technology in the businesses in which Bosch competes (specialised auto parts, microelectronics, consumer electronics, specialised machinery) is continuously changing, it is not possible for Bosch to define precisely which specific technologies it will need to produce in the future. It seeks, therefore, to remain abreast of developments in as many areas as possible. It does so by cultivating a broad array of intimate relations with subcontractors, and, logically enough, not exclusively in Baden Wurttemberg, but throughout Germany, Europe, and the world. ... The benefits for Bosch are clear, but the benefits to the region of its linkage through Bosch to a worldwide network of technological information is often underappreciated.

Cantwell (1995) provides detailed evidence based on abundant historical patent records. He suggests/concludes that 'technology leaders are now ahead ... in the globalisation of technology – that is, in the development of international intra-firm networks to exploit the locationally differentiated potential of foreign centres of excellence' (Cantwell, 1995, p. 157). Firms, in his view, are able to build upon or extend their core technological competence through internally coordinated learning processes. They thus complement external inter-firm networks in which knowledge is exchanged or in which learning occasionally takes place.

In an intriguing study, Sölvell and Bresman (1997) specify Cantwell's view by pointing out the need to look more closely at various stages in innovation in multinational enterprises. Their evidence of the relatively greater importance of non-proximate relations in the search and commercialization stages and the relatively greater importance of proximate relations in the actual development stage seems cogent. What also needs to be established is what is being learned at the various stages, that is, what kinds of learning processes firms go through (see the following section).

Besides MNEs, other types of actors also use non-local resources in various centres of excellence to receive support for the development of their assets, via units of their own or via network partners. Patchell *et al.* (1999), for example, suggest that 'large firms' (the firm segment between TNCs/MNCs and SMEs) are especially capable in this regard. SMEs may be more likely to learn in networks, surprisingly often non-local ones (Sternberg, 1997).

To sum up, despite all the talk about learning in economic geography, the case for the association of proximity and learning does not yet seem to have been made very convincingly. It seems possible to claim that this might be related to insufficient awareness of the nature of learning itself (cf. Hudson, 1999, p. 65; Odgaard and Hudson, 1998). The subject is vast and no comprehensive coverage is attempted in this paper. The next section, however, aims to point at some directions in developing a deeper insight into various types of learning and their possible manifestations in local versus non-local relationships.

4.4   VARIETY IN LEARNING

This section proposes making a few distinctions relating to learning as a basis for a tentative typology and for speculating on how distance affects the respective learning processes.

Much recent geographical writing on learning has been concerned with 'catching up' – that is, imitation or adoption of existing innovations from those in possession of 'best practice'; the creation of entirely new knowledge has been a rather neglected issue (Hudson, 1999, p. 65; Lagendijk, 1998). This observation provides us with the first distinction, that is, that between learning as the imitation of existing knowledge and learning as the creation of entirely new (leading edge, best practice) knowledge. At the level of a learning agent, imitation is also a learning process, even if it does not add anything new to knowledge already acquired elsewhere.

Secondly, a distinction can be made between what may be called incremental innovation (or single-loop or evolutionary learning) and radical innovation (or double-loop or revolutionary learning) (cf. Argyris and Schön, 1978; McKee, 1992). The former refers to slow progress building on repetition and routine; the latter to radical change in technologies and the associated practices and norms.

These basic distinctions give us three types of learning:

1.   imitation;
2.   incremental innovation;
3.   radical innovation.

Thirdly, the obvious distinction that arises from the discussions in the previous sections is that between learning in proximate relationships versus learning over space. These categories are the basis of Table 4.1, which provides a tentative typology of learning situations in a spatial perspective.

Two further distinctions can be made which are not obvious in the table, but which would provide subcategories of the types of learning identified in it. Namely, a fourth distinction is one that can be made based on the content of learning. While this can be done in many ways, I would like to suggest that a useful distinction might be related to the kind of knowledge or competence that is accumulated in the learning processes. Teece *et al.* (1994) make a useful distinction in this regard. They divide organizational resources into 'technical and organizational competences'. For Teece *et al.* (1994, p. 19), organizational competence refers to allocative competence ('deciding what to produce and how to price it'); transactional competence ('deciding whether to make or buy, and whether to do so alone or in partnership'); and administrative competence ('how to design organizational structures and policies to

Table 4.1　Distinguishing between types of learning in proximate and distant relationships

	Proximate relations	Distant relations
A. Learning as imitation	I　imitating local leaders	II　imitating global leaders
B. Learning as creating new knowledge		
Incremental innovation	III　learning in close interactive relationships	IV　learning in long-term relationships over space
Radical innovation	V　the emergence of novel combinations in variety-rich local environments	VI　projects designed for knowledge accumulation

enable efficient performance'). Technical competence refers to the ability to develop and design new products and processes, and to operate facilities effectively. Both basic types of competence do not, of course, remain static within organizations, but are subject to dynamic improvements: they are upgraded through incremental or radical learning.

A fifth distinction is concerned with whether learning takes place within organizations or in various types of network. Obviously, learning takes place in organizations within one location or as part of an interaction between units located in various places. With reference to intra-firm learning, Tushman *et al.*'s (1997) notion of 'ambidextrous organizations' (organizations that can combine processes characterized by continuous/incremental improvements and processes characterized by discontinuous innovations within the same organization) gives us a tool for thinking about the flexibility that firms may have in choosing locations suited to different types of innovation-related functions. The units performing different functions in innovation may be, but are not necessarily, located in the same place (cf. Cantwell, 1995). Units in multilocational 'ambidextrous organizations' communicate with each other. The information deriving from the incrementally innovating units is highly relevant for the units producing discontinuous innovations and vice versa. Similarly, the spatial extension of networks designed for learning purposes may be local or non-local; on closer inspection, various forms of both types are likely to be found.

4.5   CHALLENGES FOR FUTURE RESEARCH

Initially, there may seem to be a tension between the argument outlined in this chapter and the 'localized learning' argument. On closer reading, however, these arguments should be seen as complementing each other, i.e., an analogy can be drawn from the resource-based view of the firm which, in a basic formulation (Penrose, 1959; Wernerfelt, 1984), focuses on capabilities within the firm to upgrade resources for creating competitiveness. The existence of extensive network formations among contemporary business organizations points to the evident need to complement the resource-based view of the firm by analyses where networks are seen as means of upgrading resources within the firm (Oinas and van Gils, 1998). Similarly, the literature on localized learning should be complemented with analyses highlighting the importance of external (non-local or extra-regional) relations in adding new elements to local resource endowments, in addition to the role of proximate relations in upgrading regional resources. This may be done by digging deeper into types of learning in different contexts. For this purpose both conceptual and empirical analyses need to be carried out enabling distinctions to be made between types of learning in various contexts. Based on the discussion above, the following seem to be some of the areas in need of further investigation.

First, the distinction between technical and organizational competences (Teece *et al.*, 1994) mentioned above should be elaborated in order to identify the different types of resources that are upgraded in intra- or inter-organizational and local or non-local learning processes (Oinas and van Gils, 1998).

Secondly, the relevance of the different resources to the various firm-specific functions needs to be understood. This refers to the need to step down from abstract analyses of 'learning' in general and to pay detailed attention to various corporate activities such as strategy formulation, search and procurement of inputs, production, logistics, accounting, finance, leadership, organizational structures, PR, advertising, distribution and, of course, R&D – but not only R&D.

Thirdly, there are, of course, industry-specific differences in what kind of learning is needed, how much learning is needed, how learning is conceived of, how learning is organized, how learning is achieved, who participates in learning, and so on. All these can be only unravelled through detailed empirical research.

Fourthly, however, empirical research does not deliver good results if we do not have penetrating conceptual frameworks for organizing real world data. The next step for economic geographers, therefore, appears to be home-work in terms of building a theoretical framework that acknowledges the variety of learning in local and non-local relationships – and establishes more clearly the role of non-local relationships, even in 'localized learning'. This chapter hopes to have provided a few suggestions in that direction.

REFERENCES

Alderman, N. (1999), 'Local product development trajectories: A comparison of engineering establishments in three contrasting regions, in Edward J. Malecki and Päivi Oinas (eds), *Making Connections: Technological Learning and Regional Economic Change*, Aldershot: Ashgate, pp. 79–107.

Amin, A. (1999), 'An institutionalist perspective on regional economic development', *International Journal of Urban and Regional Research* (forthcoming).

Amin, A. and N. Thrift (1993), 'Globalization, institutional thickness and local prospects', *Revue d'Economie Regionale et Urbaine*, (3), pp. 405–27.

Argyris, C. and D.A. Schön (1978), *Organizational Learning: A Theory of Action Perspective*, Reading, MA: Addison-Wesley.

Asheim, B.T. and P. Cooke (1999), 'Local learning and interactive innovation networks in a global economy', in Edward J. Malecki and Päivi Oinas (eds), *Making Connections: Technological Learning and Regional Economic Change*, Aldershot: Ashgate, pp. 145–78.

Battista, R. and P. Swann (1998), 'Do firms in clusters innovate more?', *Research Policy*, **27**, pp. 525–40.

Burmeister, A. and K. Colletis-Wahl (1997), 'Proximity in production networks: The circulatory dimension, *European urban and regional studies*, **4** (3), pp. 231–41.

Cantwell, J. (1995), 'The globalisation of technology: What remains of the product cycle model?', *Cambridge Journal of Economics*, **19**, pp. 155–74.

Coe, N.M. and A.R. Townsend (1998), 'Debunking the myth of localised agglomeration: The development of a regionalized service economy in South-East England', *Transactions, Institute of British Geographers*, **23** (3), pp. 385–404.

Conner, K.R. (1991), 'A historical comparison of resource-based theory and five schools of thought within industrial organization economics: Do we have a new theory of the firm?', *Journal of Management*, **17** (1), pp. 121–54.

Crevoisier, O. (1996), 'Proximity and territory versus space in regional science', *Environment and Planning A*, **28**, pp. 1683–97.

Feldman, M.P. and R. Florida (1995), 'The geographic sources of innovation: Technological infrastructure and product innovation in the United States', *Annals, Association of American Geographers*, **84** (2), pp. 210–29.

Florida, R. (1995), 'Toward the learning region', *Futures*, **27** (5), pp. 527–36.

Grabher, G. (1994), *Lob der Verschwendung. Redundanz in der Regionalentwicklung*, Berlin: Edition Sigma.

Grabher, G. and D. Stark (1997), 'Organizing diversity: Evolutionary theory, network analysis, and post-socialism', in Gernot Grabher and David Stark (eds) *Restructuring networks in post-socialism. Legacies, linkages, and localities*, Oxford: Oxford University Press, pp. 1–32.

Granovetter, M. (1985), 'Economic action and social structure: The problem of embeddedness', *American Journal of Sociology*, **91** (3), pp. 481–510.

Grotz, R. and B. Braun (1997), 'Territorial or trans-territorial networking: Spatial aspects of technology-oriented co-operation within the German mechanical engineering industry', *Regional Studies*, **31** (6), pp. 545–58.

Harrison, B. (1992), 'Industrial districts: Old wine in new bottles?' *Regional Studies*, **26** (5), pp. 469–83.

Harrison, B., M. Kelley and J. Gant (1996), 'Innovative firm behavior and local milieu: Exploring the intersection of agglomeration, firm effects, and technological change', *Economic Geography*, **72** (3), pp. 233–58.

Herrigel, G. (1993), 'Large firms, small firms, and the governance of flexible specialization: The case of Baden Württemberg and socialized risk', in Bruce Kogut (ed.), *Country Competitiveness. Technology and the Organizing of Work*, New York: Oxford University Press, pp. 15–35.

Hudson, R. (1999), ' "The learning economy, the learning firm and the learning region": A sympathetic critique of the limits to learning', *European Urban and Regional Studies*, **6** (1), pp. 59–72.

Kelley, M.R. and S. Helper, 'Firm size and capabilities, regional agglomeration, and the adoption of new technology', *Economics of Innovation and New Technology*, (forthcoming).

Kirat, T. and Y. Lung (1999), 'Innovation and proximity. Territories as loci of collective learning processes', *European Urban and Regional Studies*, **6** (1), pp. 27–38.

Lagendijk, A. (1998), 'Regional anchoring strategies: Theoretical deliberations and evidence from the UK and Germany', *Mimeo*.

Lam, A. (1997), 'Embedded firms, embedded knowledge: Problems of collaboration and knowledge transfer in global cooperative ventures', *Organization Studies*, **18** (6), pp. 973–96.

Lundvall, B.-Å. (ed.) (1992), *National Systems of Innovation: Towards a Theory of Innovation and Interactive Learning*, London: Pinter.

Malecki, E.J. and P. Oinas (1999), 'Making connections: Introduction', in Edward J. Malecki and Päivi Oinas (eds), *Making Connections: Technological Learning and Regional Economic Change*, Aldershot: Ashgate, pp. 1–4.

Malmberg, A. (1997), 'Industrial geography: Location and learning', *Progress in Human Geography*, **21** (4), pp. 573–82.

Maskell, P. (1997), 'Localised low-tech learning in the furniture industry', in Heikki Eskelinen (ed.), *Regional Specialisation and Local Environment – Learning and Competitiveness*, NordREFO 1997 (1), pp. 145–70.

Maskell, P. (1998), 'Low-tech competitive advantages and the role of proximity: The Danish wooden furniture industry', *European Urban and Regional Studies*, **5** (2), pp. 99–118.

Maskell, P. (1999), 'Globalisation and industrial competitiveness: The process and consequences of ubiquitification', in Edward J. Malecki and Päivi Oinas (eds), *Making Connections: Technological Learning and Regional Economic Change*, Aldershot: Ashgate, pp. 35–59.

Maskell, P. and A. Malmberg (1999a), 'The competitiveness of firms and regions. "Ubiquitification" and the importance of localised learning', *European Urban and Regional Studies*, **6** (1), pp. 9–25.

Maskell, P. and A. Malmberg (1999b), 'Localised learning and industrial competitiveness', *Cambridge Journal of Economics* (forthcoming).

Maskell, P., H. Eskelinen, I. Hannibalsson, A. Malmberg and E. Vatne (1998), *Competitiveness, Localised Learning and Regional Development. Possibilities for Prosperity in Open Economies*, London: Routledge.

McKee, D. (1992), 'An organizational learning approach to product innovation',

Journal of Production and Innovation Management, **9**, pp. 232–45.

Morgan, K. (1997), 'The learning region: Institutions, innovation and regional renewal', *Regional Studies*, **31** (5), 491–503.

Odgaard, M. and R. Hudson (1998), 'The "misplacement" of learning into economic geography? A prelude to a theory of the "spatial" firm', *Mimeo*.

Oinas, P. (1997), 'On the socio-spatial embeddedness of business firms', *Erdkunde*, **51** (1), pp. 23–32.

Oinas, P. and E.J. Malecki (1999), 'Spatial innovation systems', in Edward J. Malecki and Päivi Oinas (eds), *Making Connections: Technological Learning and Regional Economic Change*, Aldershot: Ashgate, pp. 7–33.

Oinas, P. and H. van Gils (1998), 'Regional learning and firms – where is the learning?, *Mimeo*.

Oinas, P. and S. Virkkala (1997), 'Learning, competitiveness and development. Reflections on the contemporary discourse on "learning regions"', in Heikki Eskelinen (ed.), *Regional Specialisation and Local Environment – Learning and Competitiveness*, NordREFO 1997 (1), pp. 263–77.

Patchell, J., R. Hayter and K. Rees (1999), 'Innovation and local development: The neglected role of large firms', in Edward J. Malecki and Päivi Oinas, *Making Connections: Technological Learning and Regional Economic Change*, Aldershot: Ashgate, pp. 109–42.

Penrose, E. (1959/1995), *The Theory of the Growth of the Firm*, 3rd edition, Oxford: Oxford University Press.

Piore, M. and C. Sabel (1984), *The Second Industrial Divide*, New York: Basic Books.

Simmie, J. (ed.) (1997), *Innovation, Networks and Learning Regions*, London: Jessica Kingsley.

Sölvell, Ö. and H. Bresman (1997), 'Local and global forces in the innovation process of the multinational enterprise – an hour-glass model', in Heikki Eskelinen (ed.), *Regional Specialisation and Local Environment – Learning and Competitiveness*, NordREFO 1997 (1), pp. 43–64.

Sternberg, R. (1997), 'Innovative linkages and the role of the region – theoretical assumptions vs. empirical evidence', paper presented at the IGU Commission on the Organisation of Industrial Space Residential Conference, 3–9 August, Göteborg, Sweden.

Storper, M. (1993), 'Regional "worlds" of production: Learning and innovation in the technology districts of France, Italy and the USA', *Regional Studies*, **27** (5), pp. 433–55.

Storper, M. (1997), *The Regional World: Territorial Development in a Global Economy*, New York: Guilford Press.

Storper, M. and Robert S. (1997), *Worlds of Production: The Action Frameworks of the Economy*, Cambridge, MA: Harvard University Press.

Suarez-Villa, L. and W. Walrod (1997), 'Operational strategy, R&D and intra-metropolitan clustering in a polycentric structure: The advanced electronics industries of the Los Angeles Basin', *Urban Studies*, **34** (9), pp. 1343–80.

Teece, D.J., R. Rumelt, G. Dosi, and S. Winter (1994), 'Understanding corporate coherence. Theory and evidence', *Journal of Economic Behavior and Organization*, **23**, pp. 1–30.

Tushman, M.L., P.C. Anderson and C. O'Reilly (1997), 'Technology cycles, innovation streams, and ambidextrous organizations: Organization renewal through innovation streams and strategic change', in Michael L. Tushman and Philip C.

Anderson (eds), *Managing Strategic Innovation and Change*, New York: Oxford University Press, pp. 3–23.

Wernerfelt, B. (1984), 'A resource-based view of the firm', *Strategic Management Journal*, **5** (2), pp. 171–80.

PART TWO

Institutions and Policy

5. Innovation and Regional Development Policy

Mikel Landabaso[1]

5.1 INTRODUCTION: REGIONAL POLICIES AND THE CONDITIONS FOR ECONOMIC DEVELOPMENT

The basic question to which regional policy has to find an answer is that of how it can help a territory to consolidate and develop its economic activities in order to retain and expand sustainable employment and create wealth. This also applies to European regional policy. In this sense, regional economic development is the end-product of socio-economic and institutional conditions conducive to sustained and sustainable development as a means of generating jobs. One of these conditions is creating a learning environment. This chapter will focus on how such a learning environment can be stimulated through European channels.

Setting the less developed regions on an upward path therefore depends primarily on two types of micro-economic conditions, regardless of macro-economic conditions (inflation, debt, deficit, etc.), most of which will be largely outside the control of national and regional public administrations once the euro has been introduced. This also implies that traditional policy instruments of macro-economic regulation, such as national monetary policies, including exchange rate and interest rate manipulation, will no longer be available. This reinforces the need for efficient 'supply-side' industrial and regional policies as almost the only remaining policy options available to governments for economic regulation.

The first requirement is basic physical infrastructure (communications by road, air, sea and rail, telecommunications, energy, the environment, etc.) and human resources with a minimum level of training. If these are lacking or do not reach a certain level, efforts to promote regional development cannot prosper. We will refer to these requirements as 'necessary conditions'.

The second target is the improvement of intangibles, which assumes the existence of regional strengths such as the capacity of regional firms to innovate; the quality of management; a business culture which promotes entrepreneurship; an institutional framework which encourages inter-firm and public-private cooperation; a dynamic tertiary sector providing business services and the transfer of technology; a minimum level of R&D capabilities; the availability of appropriate interfaces between the demand for innovation, particularly from small firms, and supply; the existence of adequate financial instruments conducive to innovation and new economic activity, and so on. We will refer to these as 'sufficient conditions'. We assume that these conditions are also subject to improvement through public policy.

These are the conditions most closely linked with the competitiveness of the regional economic fabric and the interrelations between firms (particularly small ones) and their surroundings (which we will refer to as the 'productive environment'). Both economic (relations with other firms, subcontractors, suppliers and customers) and institutional (industrial and regional policies, cooperation with universities, consultants, centres of expertise, etc.) conditions are included.

The improvement of the 'sufficient conditions' is critically dependent on the assumption that the competitiveness of firms relies not only on its own forces but, to no less an extent, on the quality of its environment, sometimes referred to as 'structural competitiveness' (Chabbal, 1994). This assumption might particularly apply to small and medium sized firms, whose key economic difficulties are related not so much to size as to isolation. This is increasingly true of SMEs located in less favoured regions, which are often family owned, working in traditional sectors for local markets and ill prepared for new competitive pressures generated by globalization, to which they are increasingly exposed.

These sufficient conditions are closely related to 'intangibles' and 'real business services' concepts, as opposed to traditional horizontal aid schemes and 'automatic' business subsidies, the idea being not simply to alleviate costs

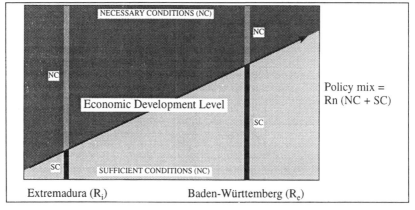

Figure 5.1   The conditions for economic development

to an individual entrepreneur, but to change corporate strategies and business culture (Bellini, 1998). The assumption here is that businesses and SMEs in less favoured regions, in particular, because they are working in imperfect markets with limited information access (including access to know-how[2]), may need assistance in tapping the necessary resources (mainly related to knowledge) in the form of technology or qualified human capital, in particular, in order to face up to the new forms of competition developing in the global economy. Thus, they may need more than simply fewer taxes and lower interest rates (because 'they know better') in order to exploit fully their competitive position and so maximize their contribution to the regional economy in the form of more jobs and higher wealth, thus ultimately justifying public financial support for a policy aimed at improving 'sufficient conditions'. This approach can be exemplified in Bellini's words: 'the provision of real services transfers to user firms new knowledge and triggers processes within them, thereby modifying in a structural, non transitory way their organisation of production and their relation with the market'. In short, the creation of sufficient conditions implies the triggering of learning processes in the regional economy to allow regional firms to become more innovative, anticipative and adaptable to rapidly evolving markets and economic conditions.

An effective regional policy must help to create both types of conditions, the 'necessary' as well as 'sufficient' ones; if either is missing, development will be adversely affected. The policy mix of these conditions will be different for each region, depending on its level of development, since the higher the region's level of development, the more important intangible factors become. This also implies that a regional policy that supports and stimulates development efforts will have to change constantly over time in order to become more effective.

That is now the position with Europe's regional policy as it approaches the year 2000 and has to cope with fresh challenges such as the accession of new member states, monetary union and budgetary constraints. Regional policy will have to advance in terms of both its content and policy delivery systems.

Hitherto, in the regions whose development is lagging behind, the Structural Funds have concentrated their efforts primarily on infrastructure[3]. However, intangibles are becoming an increasingly important priority for structural policy as the regions develop and infrastructure provision reaches a satisfactory level. The focus is therefore shifting to conditions more directly linked with the competitiveness of the fabric of production in the region, since it is these conditions which will permit the firms in these regions, particularly small firms, to become more competitive and so develop new job-creating economic activities.

What we are looking at now are structural operations for regional policy in the next century, starting from an exploration of new paths by bolstering intangibles and regional 'learning' capacities. This process will give priority to innovation in order to make the Community's regional policy more effective in creating appropriate conditions for development in the disadvantaged regions.

5.2   WHY IS INNOVATION IMPORTANT FROM THE EU REGIONAL POLICY PERSPECTIVE?

5.2.1   Innovation and Regional Policy

As has also been stated in the earlier chapters, there is growing empirical evidence that the innovative capacity of a regional economy correlates with the capacity of that economy to adapt to accelerated technological change and withstand competition in a progressively global economy. Many of the causes of disparities among regions can be traced to disparities in productivity and competitiveness. Research, technological development and innovation are vital components of regional competitiveness. Unfortunately, as Townroe has recognized, it has not been until relatively recently that innovation has been fully incorporated into the core of regional policy making: 'Until the 1980s, technology and innovation were under-recognised influences in the explanation of differences in the rates of economic growth between regions in advanced industrial nations ...' Townroe (1990).

The small and medium sized firms constitute the basis of the productive fabric of those regions whose development is lagging behind. For these firms, as explained before, competitiveness depends partly on their internal efficiency and partly on the type of interaction and quality of their environment. The latter is what makes available to them such assets as a skilled labour force, quality service centres in areas where internal provision would not be efficient and, where necessary, facilitates cooperation links with other firms and technology transfer centres and universities etc.

The high road to competitiveness for these firms that are exposed to international competition runs through innovation, which enables them to adapt at the right time to the competition posed by globalization and the fast pace of technological change. Innovation must apply to all aspects of a small firm's activities (new markets, new, different or better products, processes and services). In this sense, the concept of innovation embraces research and development, technology, training, marketing and commercial activity, design and quality policy, finance, logistics and the business management required for these various functions to mesh together efficiently.

Since small and medium sized firms do not usually have either the necessary strategic information or the staff specializing in all of these functions, some of the latter will have to be carried out by outside contractors. This means that the competitiveness of a small firm depends in part on the quality of the links with and the efficiency of its geographical neighbours (research and transfer centres, training centres, business services companies etc.). The firm is also very largely dependent on the quality of the institutional system providing support for innovation (regional authorities responsible for industrial/regional policy, in particular).

In this sense, innovation is more accessible to small and medium sized firms when they are working within rich and dynamic regional innovation systems, which is not usually the case in the disadvantaged regions. Regional innovation systems have been defined (Autio, 1998), as a distinct concept from national innovation systems (Lundvall, 1992), as 'essentially social systems, composed of interacting subsystems; the knowledge application and exploitation subsystem and the knowledge generation and diffusion subsystem. The interactions within and between organisations and subsystems generate the knowledge flows that drive the evolution of the regional innovation systems.'

From a regional development perspective, R&D and innovation policies are important insofar as they increase the capacity of producers to consolidate and develop production activities through modernization and diversification, thereby helping them to maintain or increase their competitiveness in a continually changing international market. Specialization in segments of production offering greater added value, particularly those outside the reach of competition from newly industrialized countries with their lower wage and other costs, is a way in which small and medium sized firms in less favoured regions can respond competitively with the help of public policies for the promotion of innovation.

This is dependent, *inter alia*, on non-cost factors of competitiveness related to innovation, which could be subject to indirect policy support. Examples might be (i) reduction in the time required to respond to changes in demand, (ii) reduction in the life cycle of products, (iii) quality, design, customization, product differentiation and adaptation to niche markets, (iv) new methods of management and business organization, (v) quality of networks for co-operation between businesses and between businesses and service providers (notably the R&D and innovation infrastructure), (vi) quality of the business and institutional environment, etc.

To conclude, a regional strategy for the less favoured regions, which will be viable in the medium and long-term, is one that seeks to modernize the regional economies and diversify them towards activities offering greater added value and new markets. The Community's regional policy must be there to help the less developed regions achieve this. A large part of the response to the question of how to develop competitive advantages for the regions in order to achieve the key European regional policy objective of reducing the disparities between them lies in innovation. In this sense, promoting innovation must form an integral part of the new regional policy. This probably explains why the European Commission has made several institutional statements on this issue over the past two years.

5.2.2   The Sources of Regional Innovation

The innovative potential of a region can be considered to be dependent not only on the RTDI resources or competitive pressures to adapt, but also on the density and quality of networks of co-operation between regional actors (and indeed extra-regional linkages with stimuli or sources of innovation). This means that these collective learning and diffusion mechanisms based on socio-cultural factors can be developed,[4] unless we accept a fatalistic 'historical determinacy' view of the world.

SME innovation capacity, particularly in less favoured regions, is directly linked to co-operation with other firms (firms learn best from other firms, their clients, other manufacturers or suppliers) and co-operation with the public sector and the RTDI intermediaries and infrastructures: technology centres, universities, polytechnics, business services, etc.).

This has been confirmed by recent empirical evidence (Sanz and García, 1998): 'most firms which have developed, within the last three years, new products have been engaged in collaborative arrangements (82.5 per cent of the total)'. Similar results were found in a recent survey of regional firms carried out in the region of Niederösterreich and in several other regions undergoing a Regional Innovation Strategy (RIS) exercise (see the next section). In those regions it was found that co-operation at the regional level is the key to innovation for SMEs and that the most important partners in the innovation process for regional firms were, in order of priority: (i) clients, (ii) suppliers, (iii) competitors and (iv) support organizations.

This has also been substantiated by previous studies, which see innovation in terms of a functional relationship between users, manufacturers and suppliers, through which they derive benefit from a given product, process or service innovation (Von Hippel, 1988). This innovative capacity of the regional firm is directly related to the 'learning' ability of a region. That is, innovative capacity and the regional 'learning' ability associated with it are directly related to the density and quality of networking within the regional productive environment.

Inter-firm and public–private co-operation and the institutional framework within which these relationships take place are the key sources of regional innovation, where innovation is the end product and the regional 'learning' dependent on the quality and density of the above relationships is the process.[5]

This co-operation and networking among key regional players conducive to innovation may take a conscious collective learning form or an unconscious one (Keeble *et al.*, 1998). The latter is 'arguably more important (than the former), operating through the transfer and diffusion within the region of technological know-how and "embodied expertise" in the form of entrepreneurs (via start-ups and spin-offs) and professional, managerial and scientific staff (via the regional labour market)'.

In this sense, Spielkamp in recent work based on a survey, concludes that for small firms (up to 49 employees) in the manufacturing sector:

- Cooperative projects are the most effective form of technology transfer; they presuppose in-house capabilities and the foundation is personal experience and mutual trust;
- Interchange of know-how is the widest technological transfer channel among SMEs. Informal outside contacts are utilised by most companies for acquiring new technical knowledge ... (Spielkamp, 1997).

Finally, it is important to note that regional 'collective learning' takes place in a context of co-opetition (co-operation and competition happening at the same time among the same actors). This is important from the policy-making point of view, since it adds a novel role to public action; that of a broker/mediator and facilitator among economic agents in order to create the right conditions for collective learning. In the right context, entrepreneurs could then, through 'enlightened self-interest', maximize their contribution to this collective learning task, thus providing further impetus to the broader regional development goals. This has happened with a number of RIS pilot actions, as explained in a later section.

5.2.3 The Regional Innovation Paradox

The 'European innovation paradox' is a well-known phenomenon: Europe is at the leading edge of R&D activities internationally, but it is nevertheless unable to maximize this potential successfully through increased innovation (for example, in the form of new firms and increased high quality jobs), particularly in comparison with other global competitors such as the US,[6] as the EU has recently recognized.

This is why the EU Commission has been insisting on the development of a European policy aimed at solving this problem, notably the recently published Innovation Action Plan, which follows from the analysis made in the Delors' 'White Paper':

... Steps must be taken to allow better application of the results of the research carried out in the Community, i.e. the establishment of operational mechanisms at national and European level for the transfer of technologies from university laboratories to companies, from one company to another ... One key aspect must be substantially to step up measures to improve the business environment, in the form of scientific and technical information, financial services, aid to protect innovations, training in new technologies.

The regional innovation paradox is a less well-known phenomenon. Basically, it refers to the apparent contradiction between the comparatively greater need to spend on innovation in less favoured regions and their relatively lower capacity to absorb public funds earmarked for the promotion of innovation, in comparison with more advanced regions. In other words, the more innovation is needed in less favoured regions to maintain and increase the competitive position of their firms in a progressively global economy, the more difficult it is to invest effectively and therefore 'absorb' public funds for the promotion of innovation in these regions. Such is the nature of the regional innovation paradox. Today, in Europe, advanced regions spend more public money (and in a more strategic way) for the promotion of innovation for their firms than less favoured regions do, thus increasing the innovation gap across Europe.

That is, regions that suffer more from underdevelopment have a greater need to modernize and diversify their productive capacity through innovation. In that way they can minimize threats from new competitors (for example, newly industrialized countries with lower wage and production costs). At the same time, it is very difficult for these regions to spend public money (aid) on promoting innovation. In other words, one might have expected that once the need has been identified (the innovation gap) and the possibility exists of responding to it through public means, these regions would have a greater capability of absorbing the resources destined to meet this need, since they are starting from a very low level ('everything is still to be done').

The main cause of this apparent paradox is not primarily the availability of public money in the less favoured regions. Its explanation lies elsewhere: in the nature of the regional innovation system and institutional settings to be found in these regions. The regional innovation system in less favoured regions is characterized by underdevelopment and fragmentation (lack of integration and coherence). The institutional setting in less favoured regions is characterized by the absence of the right institutional framework and policy delivery systems, public sector inefficiency and lack of understanding by policy makers of the regional innovation process. These two factors combined explain the regional innovation paradox.

The underdevelopment of the regional innovation system in less favoured regions and the incoherence of its different subsystems and innovation players is illustrated by some of the following characteristics of less favoured regions.

Money earmarked for innovation is sometimes used exclusively for the creation of R&D physical infrastructures and equipment for which no real demand has been expressed by the regional firms. Funding falls into the hands of those responsible for research/science or technology policies which do not have an economic development perspective, innovation being primarily about economic competitiveness and the exploitation of new markets, products and services. In other words, there is often no multidisciplinary approach in the planning of funding, which is critically important for a successful innovation policy. University departments from relatively new universities, for example, which do not have a long tradition of university–industry collaboration, use new funding to strengthen research activities which do not always reflect the needs of the regional firms, but rather the university's academic expertise.

On top of that, regional innovation systems in less favoured regions are isolated from the international R&D networks of 'excellence', so that they find it hard to access the technology sources and partners, including informal personal contacts, which are necessary for the continuous feeding of the innovation system in order to keep abreast of technological change in the global economy.

The regional firms, often small, family-owned and competing among themselves in relatively closed markets, do not have a tradition of co-operation and trust, either among themselves or with the regional R&D infrastructures, particularly the universities. This can be illustrated, for example, with reference to Spain, where '... 80 per cent of firms in Spain with fewer than 200 workers undertook no R&D in 1994, whether internally or through outside contractors ...' (Fundacion COTEC, 1997). Co-operation for innovation is particularly critical in their case, because of their limited internal human resources and lack of 'know-how'. Firms do not express an innovation demand and the regional R&D infrastructures are not embedded in the regional economy and so are unable to identify the innovation needs and capabilities existing in the regional economy, thus reflecting a lack of integration between regional supply and demand for innovation.

In short, the regional innovation system in these regions has neither the necessary interfaces and co-operation mechanisms for matching supply and demand, nor the appropriate conditions for the exploitation of synergies and co-operation among the scarce regional R&D actors which might eventually eliminate gaps and duplications and so increase the economic development impact of the RTDI funds. In this situation, investing more money in the creation of new technology centres, for example, without first co-ordinating and adapting the work of the existing ones, risks further distorting the system. It also risks imposing a new budgetary burden on public budgets through the running costs of these institutions, which are unlikely to reach a satisfactory level of self-financing in a reasonable time period because of the mismatch referred to above. The same applies to a number of technology park initiatives in Objective 1 regions, which end up becoming property development operations dependent on external capital attraction, poorly linked to the regional industry and playing a very limited role in the economically strategic function of regional technology transfer.

Moreover, advanced business services and networking agents/interfaces, such as those existing in advanced regions, are few and not necessarily specialized in innovation. This limits the innovation opportunities of firms through proper technology auditing and accessing strategically important services such as innovation management, technology forecasting and training. These initiatives, particularly private ones, become trapped in the vicious circle of low demand and poor supply, which is rarely spontaneously broken from within the system. When they do break the circle, as a result of adaptive reactions (rather than proactive ones) to market pressures, it is often as late technology followers, and innovation opportunities are lost to local industry. Something similar can be said about financial instruments and institutions in less favoured regions which, in addition to imposing above average (community) interest rates, pay little attention to the long-term, higher risk and intangible investments which are characteristic of innovation projects.

Finally, the quality of the institutional setting in these regions is often the main obstacle to the creation of an efficient regional innovation system. Over and above the different degree of regional autonomy in the conduct of regional/industrial policy, some regional government structures in less favoured regions suffer heavily from lack of credibility, political instability and absence of professional competence (and awareness) in the field of innovation. These are three critical illnesses of underdevelopment.

The lack of credibility of these governmental structures, notably *vis à vis* the private sector, is reflected in their incapacity for consensus building and partnership arrangements with private firms and other institutional actors, be it universities or national R&D correspondents. Political stability undermines any serious effort in the implementation of an innovation policy which, by its very nature, is medium to long term. Moreover, it makes the necessary regional leadership for the development of a regional innovation system even weaker and more prone to fall into the hands of consolidated lobbies and parochial interests which hinder innovation. Lack of professional competence is reflected in the fact that these administrations tend to favour 'traditional' and 'easy to manage' regional instruments rather than more sophisticated and complex policies such as innovation policy. In some instances, even where the political commitment has been clearly expressed in such a policy, these governmental structures have been unable to find the management resources to carry it out efficiently.

All this helps to explain why the experience of some of the Structural Funds in this field, as illustrated by the experience of STRIDE[7] in Objective 1 regions, has been relatively frustrating. Firstly, the funds were difficult to absorb and, secondly, their use lacked a strategic approach more strongly linked to general regional economic development objectives. Finally, the regional development impact of the aid was relatively weaker than in other more advanced regions, for example, Objective 2 regions (regional industrial decline).

5.2.4 The Learning Region

Learning as an economic process can be subject to vicious circles and increasing complexity. The more a region or a company is in a position to learn (identify, understand and exploit knowledge, for example in the form of technological expertise, to their own economic benefit) the more capable, and possibly willing, they become to build on it and increase their demand and capacity to use further new knowledge. But learning depends critically on two key factors: a certain degree of business–economic intelligence, to trigger the demand for new knowledge, and access to and availability of knowledge.[8]

At micro-economic level, for example, it could mean that a small family-owned company working in a traditional sector and exploiting local markets may require a new 'intelligent cell' in the form of university graduates, for example, in order to trigger a learning process as a stage towards adopting a more competitive business strategy.[9] The graduates (perhaps recruited through a regional policy scheme) may open access to new sources of knowledge which contribute to an evolution in its business culture, making it more adaptable to economic change and willing to consider further innovations, thanks to the initial successful experience. These graduates may themselves bring useful new knowledge to the firm or they may act as 'bridges' or 'open gates' to existing, but so far unexploited, sources of knowledge, e.g., in the form of university departments or technology centres operating in the region. A positive first experience in this new relationship between the firm and a regional 'knowledge centre' may build trust and understanding between the two and engender a longer-lasting relationship through new projects, thus generating more 'knowledge' demand on the side of the firm and, at the same time, new and better adapted knowledge supply on the side of the local university or technology centres. The triggering of this vicious circle of learning, as an economic relationship between firms and regional knowledge centres which may help the clustering of local firms around these institutions, depends critically on the formulation of an initial 'knowledge' demand on the side of the firm, which can be sparked only by a certain degree of business intelligence, which we could refer to as innovative capacity. There is no learning in the absence of intelligence.

We also need an 'intelligent cell' at meso-economic level to trigger a learning process in a regional economy. The regional government (and its development-related agencies) can play a major role in articulating and dynamizing a regional innovation system, understood as the process of generating, diffusing and exploiting knowledge in a given territory with the objective of fostering regional development. In this dynamic and systemic sense, the regional innovation system is in itself the process of learning which 'learning regions' are aiming for. The regional innovation system is what determines the effectiveness and efficiency of regional knowledge building and transfer among the different integrating parts of the system, including individual firms, sectoral/value-chain clusters, business consultants, technology centres, R&D centres, university departments, laboratories, technology transfer and valorization of R&D centres, development agencies, etc. The regional innovation system is what makes the whole bigger than the sum of the individual parts.

Thus, the regional government can play the role of the 'collective intelligence' necessary for a region to spark the process of becoming a 'learning region'. In terms of political legitimacy and economic powers, including its ability, if necessary, to use the carrot (e.g. with financial backing, not least as a key decision maker in allocating Structural Funds) and the stick (e.g. through its regulatory powers and public procurement policies), it is best placed to facilitate the articulation of the regional innovation system. Articulating means linking (regional actors: firms, technology centres, universities, business service providers, etc.) and matching (innovation needs with knowledge supply) in search of synergies and complementarities among the different actors, policies and subsystems which integrate a regional innovation system. Links, synergies and complementarities are precisely the 'learning vehicles' which may allow a region to learn effectively and increase its innovative potential, thanks to the nature of innovation at the regional level.[10]

The first form of articulation is the matching of innovation (the capacity to use knowledge) demand from firms with existing RDTI regional supply (the availability of knowledge centres) and possibly finding open gates to external innovation sources and partners capable of addressing the innovation needs of the regional economy. This includes the initial important task of identifying and assisting the expression of innovation demand and needs, latent or otherwise, from regional organizations, particularly SMEs.

The second form is the facilitating of co-operation and coherence between the different agents and policies (science policy, research policy, industrial policy, regional policy, human resources policy, competition policy, ...) which are integral parts of the regional innovation system.

In this sense, the regional government, as evidenced by the RIS experience explained in the next section, can and should play an important role as a catalyst, a facilitator and a broker in the articulation of the regional innovation system. This is particularly important for less favoured regions where the regional innovation system is more fragmented and its subsystems and integral parts are less developed or, at times, simply absent. It is, above all, a necessary 'agent for change' which stimulates and develops networking among the different actors of the regional innovation system. In this 'enabling' capacity it can energize the regional endogenous potential of the entrepreneurship, technical expertise and know-how within the existing business culture and distinctive economic characteristics of the region, notably by building its own distinctive path to an efficient regional innovation system, since there is not and cannot be a unique model of a regional innovation system exportable to all regions (although some insist on trying to find it in Baden-Württemberg or Emilia Romagna). It is precisely regional diversity that is an asset for regional innovation to build upon.

For the regional government to be able to play this progressive role in the articulation of the regional innovation system, a major cultural and organizational change has to occur in the regional governmental structures (where they exist at all) in most regions, and the less favoured, in particular. This change should go along the lines of more flexible, less bureaucratic structures, capable of much tighter partnerships with the private sector (and with a higher degree of professional competence in strategic planning capabilities, in particular). It also means an increased disposition towards consensus-building and inclusiveness in the policy process, including the policy delivery system, away from stop-and-go policy decisions dictated by short-term political instability and parochial interests. It is only when the necessary 'social capital' and 'institutional thickness' has been reached that the public sector, and regional government in particular, will be able to lead the process of articulating and energizing the regional innovation system, i.e. the process of learning conducive to the practical realization of a 'learning region'.

5.3   EU REGIONAL POLICY AND INNOVATION PROMOTION: POLICY RESPONSES

5.3.1   Innovative Actions under Article 10 of the European Regional Development Fund

It has been recognized that the effectiveness of Structural Fund interventions aimed at technological innovation depends on the quality of the partnership between public authorities, the principal innovation support organizations and local firms. Indeed, technology cannot be expected to assist in resolving the problems of competitiveness unless it functions as part of a system which is institutionally and organizationally capable of adapting to changing demands on a continuous basis (Landabaso, 1993).

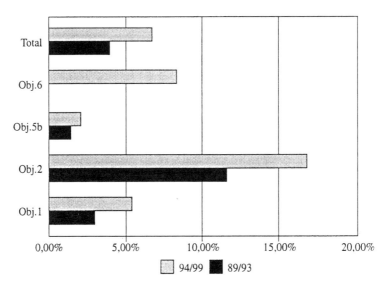

Figure 5.2   Change in the RTDI component of structural interventions

As the graph in Figure 5.2 shows, Structural Funds support for R&TD and innovation has been quite substantial in the last two programming periods up to 1999. Moreover, it has been growing from one period to the next, thus showing the increased interest that this type of investment has had for those responsible for regional policy planning at both the national and regional levels. In view of this fact, the European Commission has been trying to explore new, more efficient, ways of developing policy in this field of innovation promotion through some of the innovative actions financed under Article 10 of the European Regional Development Fund (ERDF), as described in Figure 5.3.

5.3.2   RIS: Towards Collective Learning in Less Favoured Regions

A short definition of RIS (Regional Innovation Strategies) might be that they are an instrument for translating 'knowledge' into regional GDP. RIS are an instrument for creating and/or strengthening Regional Innovation Systems (territorial systems that efficiently create, diffuse and exploit knowledge that enhances regional competitiveness) in less favoured regions.

			1994-1996[11]		1996-1998[12]
	Strategies	>	**IRISI**: 6 regions (Inter-Regional Information Society Initiative)	>	**RISI**: 22 regions (Regional Information Society Initiative: Strategy and Action Plan)
Information Society			2 MECUs		15 MECUs
	Regional Telematic Applications	>	**WOLF**: 7 regions (World Wide Web Opportunities in Less Favoured Regions)	>	**RISI2**: 7 projects involving 30 regions (Regional Information Society Initiative: Pluri-Regional Telematic Applications
	Strategies	>	**RTPS**: 8 region (Regional Technology Plans)	>	**RIS**: 19 regions (Regional Innovation Strategies)
Regional Innovation			5 MECUs		15 MECUs
	Regional Technology Transfers	>	**Technology Transfer**: 4 regions (Transtex, Reporting, Implace)	>	**RTTs**: 6 projects involving 30 regions (Regional Technology Transfer Projects)

Figure 5.3   Article 10 of the ERDF: pilot actions in the field of Information Society and Innovation 1994-1999

The RIS are a 'social engineering' action at the regional level whose main aim is to stimulate and manage co-operation links among firms and between firms and the regional RTDI actors, which may contribute to their competitive position through innovation, notably by facilitating access to 'knowledge' sources and partners. In this sense, RIS 'social engineering' means creating the right environmental conditions, particularly institutional ones, for increasing the innovative capacity of the regional economy.

The general objectives of RIS are:
- Setting the foundations of a regional innovation system as an actively learning regional economy;
- Aiming at promoting public/private and inter-firm co-operation and creating the institutional basis for a more efficient use of scarce public

and private resources for the promotion of innovation (bigger and better spending in this field through regional policy);
- New ways of introducing technological innovation in the regional economic development agenda of the less favoured regions.

The specific objectives of RIS are:

- Internal coherence of the regional innovation system through connecting its different key elements: RTDI supply with well-identified demand and business needs, from SMEs in particular;
- Creating and/or strengthening inter and intra-regional co-operation networks, between the public and the private sectors and among firms, in particular;
- Setting the promotion of innovation as a priority for regional policy;
- Increasing the amount and, more importantly, the quality of public spending on innovation through innovation projects;
- Rationalizing the regional innovation support system by raising awareness, eliminating duplications, filling gaps and promoting synergies.

The RIS provide the regions with a methodology which is flexible and respects regional diversities and financial aid (50 per cent of a total budget per project of ECU 500 000) to develop a strategy and an action plan to promote regional innovation over a two-year period.

This means that the RIS are essentially a process for imparting social and institutional dynamism to the policy of support for innovation in a way which takes account of the actual needs of the regional production fabric. The two RIS priority aims are based mainly on the lessons drawn from the previous experience of the European Regional Development Fund in the promotion of innovation. It is interesting to note here that both the methodological characteristics of the RIS process (bottom-up and demand-led, based on public–private partnership, integrated approach to innovation, and so on) and the 'good practices' identified in the management of these projects (clear regional leadership, built on existing delivery systems, based on a thorough understanding of the regional industry and R&D resources, and so on) are mirrored by other experiences, notably, the lessons learnt from experience in the US with 13 science and technology plans developed by the states between 1991 and 1995 (EDA, 1997).

The first lesson to be learned is that innovation should be made part of the regional development policy agenda and that this should be done in an appropriate way. This means not restricting the concept of innovation in the RIS simply to R&D, nor even to technology, in the narrow sense, even though

R&D and technology are often vital components of innovation. Innovation, in this economic sense of the term, means doing better[13] what we are doing already, or doing something new, or doing something different[14] in order to become more competitive. That is why innovation must affect not only research and technology, but also a variety of functions, both within firms, such as management, training and marketing, and outside them, such as finance, administrative restrictions, relations between firms and the regional R&TD and innovation infrastructure. The latter group form part of the quality of what we call 'the productive environment', the institutional climate and the density of networks of co-operation among firms and with R&D institutional agents.

The ultimate aim is to facilitate access to 'knowledge' and the economic use of knowledge for productive purposes. That is why the RIS have chosen a multidisciplinary and integrated approach to regional development.

In this sense, universities and technology centres are members of all the steering committees for the RIS on the same footing as the representatives of the private sector or regional development agencies. For example, the Strathclyde RIS includes some 40 partners associated with the project, who contribute financially to the regional part, including the four universities and colleges providing vocational training and the 'Local enterprise companies'. More than 100 organizations in the public network of support for innovation and over 400 firms helped to draw up the action plan.

The establishment of a RIS requires a strategic and bottom-up approach based on genuine demand from firms, particularly small ones. This entails identifying the most appropriate measures for linking demand for innovation, which may be hidden or sometimes badly expressed among small firms, with the 'knowledge' resources available (technology centres, universities) at regional level and, if necessary, at national and international level.

In Aragon, the RIS reviewed and carried out interviews in over 160 firms. In central Macedonia, over 200 businessmen, scientists and civil servants participated personally in the working parties which prepared the RIS action plan.

This, in turn, requires the development of co-operative links between the various components of the supply of RTDI and services: technology centres, universities, public laboratories and so on, in order to eliminate duplication, remedy deficiencies and improve mutual assistance. The final aim is to help to establish a reference policy framework for putting public expenditure on innovation to the best possible use.

The RIS have led to the emergence of new, better co-ordinated and more efficient regional networks for RTDI in regions such as Leipzig-Halle-Dessau, Lorraine and Castilla y Leon. In the latter region, nearly 800 companies were involved in the RIS process through a dozen sectoral strategic discussion meetings, and a total of 447 million ECU has been pledged for the first four years of implementation (1997–2000), with the objective of increasing the regional 'technological effort' (R&D expenditure over GDP at factor costs) to reach 1 per cent in the year 2000, from a current 0.8 per cent.

The regions are the most appropriate level for action on innovation. A policy of stimulating innovation in small firms is, in fact, regarded as primarily a proximity policy and so a prime concern of regional development policy. The ultimate goal is to foster effective regional innovation systems which will create, disseminate and use 'knowledge' for economic purposes and innovation in order to modernize and diversify the regional fabric of production. For example, the Limburg regional government and the Welsh Development Agency adjusted their regional economic development strategies in the light of the results of the RIS. In Dutch Limburg RIS for example, over 50 projects were started in 1996–1997 for a total sum of nearly 38 million ECU, involving some 375 companies, leading to the preservation and/or creation of approximately 2000 jobs.

In Wales, where 350 companies undertook an 'innovation' audit and over 600 organizations were involved in the RIS process, nearly 70 new projects were identified and the industrial South Wales Objective 2 Structural Fund programme for 1997–99 now includes up to £40 million for innovation-related projects. Moreover, the Wales Development Agency incorporated the RIS priorities in its Agency Business Development Programme and the universities' strategies for business. In both cases, specific structures were established to manage the RIS action plan.

Finally, the RIS depend on a broad public/private partnership for one very good reason: co-operation among firms (clusters) and between firms and the public sector is the main force for innovation in a region. The RIS approach considers that the competitiveness of small firms and their ability to innovate depend on their internal resources, but they also depend on the quality of their links with their environment and how they interact with it, which is an integral part of the regional innovation system.

It is interesting to note here that virtually all the RIS regions work to create clusters and networks in the broad sense. For example, in Yorkshire and Humberside, 11 Business Sector Networks have been set up. Each has what is called an 'Innovation Board' headed by a local businessman, who mobilizes hundreds of his colleagues to stimulate innovation through close business co-operation. The same goes for the RIS Basque Country which is one of the pioneering regions in Europe in developing a comprehensive cluster approach, which has significantly contributed to the revitalization of the regional industry through a very active regional innovation promotion policy.

The second aim of the RIS has been to secure better use of the financial resources allocated to the Structural Funds. RIS projects are pilot projects intended to feed into the mainstream operational programmes. Their purpose is to explore new ways of improving regional policy through our operational programmes and Single Programming Documents.

Even today, most RIS projects are having some impact on the Community Support Frameworks of the Structural Funds, and are increasing the number of projects concerned with innovation. For example, the Objective 2 operational programmes for the Basque Country, West Midlands and Weser Ems, will dedicate substantial budgets to projects in the RIS action plan.

The RIS has acknowledged past experience in the promotion of innovation in the mainstream operational programmes, including the Stride Community Initiative, which concentrated on the provision of physical infrastructure (buildings) and equipment for R&D, most frequently in universities and public technology centres. There was an absence of a strategic approach to link this expenditure more closely to regional development targets which could meet the needs of firms for innovation. This would have entailed a different policy, one that was more sophisticated and more difficult to implement than traditional regional policies. Non-material investment and the supply of 'real services' to businesses are more difficult to organize and finance than investment in infrastructure, even though they are just as important, if not more so.

The preliminary results of an evaluation being carried out for the Commission on the theme of research and innovation actions financed within the framework of Objective 2 (Regions in Industrial Decline) programmes over the decade since 1989 has underlined the impact that the RIS projects have had on the mainstream Structural Fund programmes. This is the case, for example, in Austria, where the evaluation concludes that RIS seem to have

> strong effects on partnership building, awareness raising, capabilities to design strategies, the development of new innovative measures and integration of international expertise ... RIS are an effective way to influence and improve the profile of technology and innovation actions in the Structural Fund programmes (White Paper, 1993).

Promoting innovation will be one of the Commission's main guidelines during the next programming period (2000–06). The RIS may help to prepare the ground so that those responsible for structural policies at the regional and national levels can respond to this guideline in the most effective way, more specifically through work on basic strategic planning involving those mainly concerned at regional level and resulting in new innovation projects which are consistent with regional policy objectives.

The RIS pilot projects are about opening new perspectives for regional development in the coming decade. During the last five years, almost 600 leading figures in the public and private sectors devoted time to and participated directly in the steering committees of the 27 RIS. More than 5,000 small firms were reviewed and several hundred RTDI organizations were consulted in the process of drawing up strategies and action plans based on the RIS.

The external evaluation results from the first seven RIS[15] clearly show that the pilot projects in each of the regions have made a significant contribution to creating a strategic planning culture and to increasing substantially the quantity and quality of public finance for innovation.

The RIS, as strategic planning measures based on an extended partnership and mindful of subsidiarity, are an example of the value which the Commission can add to regional policy making at the European level. A sound regional policy inevitably has three key components: ideas, political will and commitment, and money. All three, strictly in that order, are essential to success. The RIS operate mainly on the first two: ideas (what to do and how?) and political will (with whom? – convergence of resources and will based on a broad public–private partnership). With the first two components in place, the money will normally follow in less favoured regions through the Structural Funds. In conclusion, RIS is becoming a useful strategic planning tool, as well as a channel for discussions with the appropriate institutional bodies on defining measures to support innovation in regional policy.

The Commission's privileged position as an observer of virtually all the regions of Europe means that it is well placed to organize exchanges of experience and good practice and to promote interregional co-operation in order to avoid constantly reinventing the wheel, while at the same time turning the European dimension to good account. In other words, EU regional policy can act as a catalyst for 'collective learning' on the path towards the learning regional economy.

NOTES

1. The opinions expressed in this paper are the author's alone and not necessarily those of the European Commission.
2. We will use Von Hippel's definition of know-how as 'the accumulated practical skill or expertise that allows one to do something smoothly and efficiently' (e.g. the know-how of engineers who develop a firm's products and develop and operate its processes. Firms often consider a large part of this know-how proprietary and protect it as a trade secret).
3. Motorway provision in Spain, for example, is already at the EU average, even though the density of its road network is only half the EU average, and the percentage of the population of working age educated at university is above the EU average (23 per cent in Spain as compared with 22 per cent in the Union as a whole) ... although unemployment in Spain is over twice the EU average (24 per cent in 1994 as compared with 10 per cent in the Union) and productivity (output per worker) is still below the EU average. Labour productivity in

Greece and Portugal is even lower (70 per cent and 60 per cent respectively of the EU average). It is interesting to note that the Spanish example, with an intensive investment in the creation of the 'necessary conditions' contrasts strongly with the situation and strategy followed in Ireland, which has concentrated more on the 'sufficient conditions' through constant investment in skills/education upgrading, strong emphasis on an integrated approach to RTDI, based on innovation rather than simply R&D, focus on indigenous firms and first time R&D and innovation performers, priority to product rather than process innovation etc., while motorways in Ireland are still at 12 per cent of the EU average.

4. A more detailed explanation of this section can be found in the chapter called 'Developing Regional Innovation Strategies: the European Commission as an Animato' (M. Landabaso & A. Reid) in the book *Regional Innovation Strategies: key challenge for Europe's less favoured regions* (K. Morgan and C. Nauwelaers (eds)), Jessica Kingsley Publishers, London, 1998.

5. An excellent account of this 'learning' ability can be found in B.A. Lundvall and S. Borras. 'The globalising learning economy: implications for technology policy'. Final Report under the TSER Programme, EU Commission, December 1997. Chapter 7 in particular, on the creation of networks and stimulation of interactive learning is most enlightening.

6. Two-thirds of the 10 million jobs created in the United States in the last four years were in the high-technology sector and half were in small firms.

7. Science and Technology for Regional Development in Europe. A Community initiative with a budget of 400 million ECU of grant aid for the period 1990–94, two thirds of which was earmarked for Objective 1 regions in Europe (regions with an income per capita which is less than 75 per cent of the EU average).

8. Similarly, once someone who starts reading for the first time enjoys a book, they will look for more, while increasing their capacity to understand books better, to read faster and combine the new knowledge with previously recorded knowledge from other books, thus extending their learning capabilities in a sort of virtuous circle.

9. These graduates may, for example, help the firm to break the 'cultural' barriers and establish a common 'language' between the business owner and the university researcher, who belong to two very different worlds and working cultures in many regions. This may be particularly relevant in less favoured regions where, as in the Spanish case, three quarters of the businessmen running firms with under 200 employees do not hold a university degree. If we go back to our reader's example, there might be nothing more frustrating for them than to want to read a book which is written in a language they do not understand. The knowledge might be there but they cannot access it.

10. For a further tentative explanation of the characteristics and nature of innovation at the regional level see M. Landabaso, 'The promotion of Innovation in regional policy: proposals for a regional innovation strategy', Entrepreneurship & Regional Development, 9 (1997), 1–24.

11. In collaboration with DG XIII (IRISI), DG III (WOLF and IMPLACE) and 'The Innovation Programme – DG XIII' (RTPs, Transtex and Reporting).

12. In collaboration with DG V (RISI and RISI2), DG XIII (RISI) and 'The Innovation Programme – DG XIII' (RIS and RTTs).

13. Doing something better may mean here: improving the quality of production, reducing production cycles, introducing new methods of management which reduce the time required to respond to market changes, etc.

14. Doing something new or something different may mean: incorporating design, using new methods of marketing, adapting products to new market opportunities, improving after-sales service, personalizing services, customization, and so on.

15. Technopolis Ltd. (Boeckhout & Arnold) & Athens University (Tsipouri), 1998, 'Regional Technology Plan Evaluation'. Evaluation Study for the EU Commission (DG XVI). An executive summary of this evaluation and a two-page summary of results to date of each of the 27 RIS in operation can be found in the brochure 'Innovative actions of Article 10 ERDF: regional innovation strategies', published by the EU Commission – DG XVI, January 1999.

REFERENCES

Autio, E. (1998), 'Evaluation of R&TD in regional systems of innovation', in *European Planning Studies*, **6**, (2).

Bellini, N. (1998), 'Services to industry in the framework of regional and local industrial policy', OECD draft paper Modena Conference (May 28-29) on 'Upgrading knowledge and diffusing technology to small firms: building competitive regional environments'.

Chabbal, R. (1994), *OECD Programme on Technology and Economy*.

EDA (1997), Report by the State Science & Technology Institute prepared under an award of the Economic Development Administration, US Department of Commerce, *Science and Technology Strategic planning: creating economic opportunity*, October.

European Commission, *European regional disparities and policy in the 1990s*, DG XVI internal document, July 1997.

European Commission, *Premier Plan d'Action pour l'Innovation en Europe: l'innovation au service de la croissance et de l'emploi*, Luxembourg, 1997.

European Commission, Préparation du rapport conjoint sur l'emploi et des orientations pour la création d'emplois en Europe: contribution de la DG XIII, 1997.

Fundacion COTEC, *Tecnologìa e Innovaciòn en España*, report 1997, Madrid 1997.

Keeble, D., C. Lawson, B. Moore and F. Wilkinson, F. (1998), *Networks, collective learning and R&TD in regionally-clustered high-technology small and medium-sized enterprises*, Cambridge regional report, June, prepared for the EU Commission project, *Networks and collective learning*, SOEI CT 95-1011.

Landabaso, M. (1993), 'The European Community's regional development and innovation: promoting "innovative milieux" in practice', *European Planning Studies*, **1** (3).

Lundvall, B.A. (ed.) (1992), *National Systems of Innovation: Towards a Theory of Innovation and Interactive Learning*, London: Pinter Publishers.

Sanz, L. and C.E. García (1998), *Inter-firm collaboration in Spain*, draft notes of the Spanish report for the 'Inter-firm Collaboration' Focus Group of the OECD project on National Innovation Systems (phase 2) based on the 1994 (First) Technological Innovation Survey in Spain.

Spielkamp, A. (1997), *Innovation as a Transfer Result of Cooperation between the business and Academic Communities* (ZEW – Centre for European Economic Research), paper presented at the International Conference on Industrial Policy for Europe, London, 26-27 June.

Townroe, P. (1990), 'Regional development potentials and innovation capacities', in H. Ewers and J. Allesch (eds), *Innovation and Regional Development: Strategies, Instruments and Policy Coordination*, Berlin: Walter de Gruyter Ed.

Von Hippel, E. (1998), *The Sources of Innovation*, Oxford: Oxford University Press.

White Paper on *Growth, Competitiveness and Employment: the challenges and ways forward into the 21st Century*, 1993, p. 103.

6. Planning the Learning Region: an Italian Approach

Nicola Bellini

6.1 INTRODUCTION[1]

This chapter discusses the role of regional governments in economic development and suggests possible ways of interpreting it in line with the emerging paradigm of the 'learning region' (Chapter 1 of this volume). The learning region paradigm offers a new way of shedding light on the role of regional governments in their attempt to further economic development. The objective of this chapter is to analyse the new role of regional governments as it has developed in Italy over the past few decades. Learning and building learning capacity play an increasingly important role in regional policy in Italy. The lessons learned in Italy may serve as an example for regions elsewhere which are trying to get a grip on the realities of today's global economy.

Regional governments are fundamental players in the construction and evolution of learning regions: they promote the experimentation with new disciplines of co-ordination and co-operation and strengthen the untraded interdependencies that form the supply architecture for learning and innovation (Storper, 1995; Sabel, 1996; Belussi, 1997). To some extent, their policy problem is not significantly new: 'how to design an enterprise support system which resonates with firms' immediate needs on the one hand and yet stimulates their long-term learning capacity on the other' (Morgan, 1996, p. 59). However, the requirements in terms of policy styles and capabilities are unmistakably different from the past and provide an exemplary case of the more general reshaping of industry–state relations in contemporary economies (Bellini, 1996b). This chapter suggests that reference to learning processes should lead to a reappraisal of regional economic policies, throwing light upon three distinct, but tightly interrelated, aspects:

1. the intraorganizational learning of regional governments and agencies, involving both political and bureaucratic élites, internal bodies and external agencies;

2. the learning relations of the regional governments, including both down-
    stream knowledge management (an essential condition of policy
    effectiveness) and upstream knowledge transfer (an essential condition of
    policy network building and management);
3. the engineering of the learning infrastructure of the regional economy as
    a fundamental object of regional policies.

This chapter further focuses on regional planning and plans,[2] rather than on
the analysis of actual and/or specific policies. While planning can be seen as
the collective 'exercise' that makes explicit the advance of both the
intraorganizational and interactive learning of the regional government, plans
include (more or less explicitly) the design of the learning region, at least in
the eyes of the regional government. This is done by selecting the participants
in the relevant networks, especially the policy networks.[3] This discussion
takes as its example two important documents that have been issued recently
in Emilia-Romagna and Tuscany:

*   the paper on 'The global region', a proposal for the updating of the
    'Regional Territorial Plan' of Emilia-Romagna (issued July 1997),[4]
    and;
*   the new 'Regional Development Plan 1998–2000' of Tuscany (issued
    October 1997; approved December 1997).[5]

The reference to these two cases must be partially attributed to the personal
opportunities of the author, yet it is worth recalling that, to scholars
worldwide, the significance of the events in these 'Third Italy' regions often
exceeds that of other case studies. Both regions have often been the
subject of international research. Both have reached a high level of
industrial development, starting from an economic structure dominated by
small companies and characterized by district patterns. Both have a
tradition of high-quality policy-making and planning. Furthermore, these two
regions have already experienced most of the networking policies, based
on inter-firm co-operation, that nowadays are indicated as constituent
parts of a learning economy. In both cases, the policies have been subject to
critical reappraisal.[6] In the following section the evolution of regional
planning is outlined, together with the different learning mechanisms that
were created. Section 6.3 defines the main requirements of effective regional
government for learning regions: the idea of 'intelligent government' is
articulated into a number of specific features. In Section 6.4 the main tasks of
the regional government within the 'learning region' perspective are
discussed.

6.2 REGIONAL PLANNING AND THE LEARNING GOVERNMENT

Planning in Italy has been a central element in the establishment of the new level of government as a result of the devolution process started in 1970 (Bianchi, 1982). Even when it turned out to be a rhetorical exercise and, in fact, a confession of impotence, planning was nevertheless a means of affirming the identity of the new institution and of educating the administrative and political élites to the full awareness of the limits and potential of this 'meso' level of government.

This has been especially true in Italy where, because of the very slow and uncertain pace of regional devolution, planning had (and still has) to deal with the structural asymmetry between ambitions and powers. Even when all the components of a real 'plan' are found in the resulting documents (analysis and scenarios; definition, ranking and quantification of priorities; verification of vertical and horizontal consistency; guidelines for evaluation and control), the possibility of translating ideas into facts was always limited. Not only were policies typically pertaining to the national level excluded, but the toolbox of regional policies lacked most of the instruments for industrial policy, including those for small and medium-sized enterprises. In fact, regional planning was born in Italy before the regions themselves. Planning activities were started during the 1950s and the 1960s, but this was done on the initiative of provincial administrations and chambers of commerce. It was a way of gaining a better understanding of territorial imbalances of a more limited nature than the one, overwhelmingly present in Italian political economy and history, between North and South. At that time – with the exception of the 'special statute' regions[7] – regions were little more than geographical, sometimes artificial entities: a list in the Constitutional Chart and an unaccomplished promise for institutional reform. Planning activities were, in a sense, 'simulating' regions, by defining 'development platforms' for the areas concerned.[8] This 'regional planning without regions' proved to be crucial in reconstructing, a century after unification, the forgotten identity of the Italian regions and in selecting the future leadership of the regional institutions.

These early experiences also mark the first step toward a differentiation of experiences that is still the most visible feature of the Italian case. On the one hand, not all regions engaged in planning activities: at the end of the 1960s the national government itself introduced a law establishing 'regional committees for economic planning' with the task of extending that practice to all areas of the country. On the other hand, it was precisely in the 'special statute' regions that planning did not take off. They were institutionally active, had financial resources and the legal means to operate; they even had statutory provisions for preparing plans. But very little occurred.[9] Plans were not drawn up by the local intelligentsia, but mostly by external consultants. In most cases, plans were the ritual advocacy of the local claims to the national governments to justify transfers of financial resources, rather than statements of possible and intended policies. No 'government culture' could grow on such grounds; no learning process was triggered. Instead, it resulted in a loss of sense of responsibility that has negatively characterized the history of several regional governments in Italy.

Regions were eventually established during the 1970s: the number of 'plans' increased dramatically; their quality, however, did not. A few of them stayed realistically within the boundaries of territorial planning (the final approval of the *Comuni*'s urban plans being the main power that regions had from the beginning). Other regions proceeded to define economic development plans, but their realization was clearly outside the scope of the new power. Plans then became 'dream books', where growth and modernization objectives could easily be listed without real verification and without taking responsibility for their realization. In retrospect, however, the 'dream books' did have some value. The new institution approached concrete problems by placing them in a more general framework. Also the political debate was stimulated. In fact, 'learning-by-dreaming' was to some extent a surrogate for 'learning-by-doing'. The DPR 616 of 1977, i.e. the bill that brought about the first massive transfer of jurisdiction from the centre to the regions, made planning compulsory: it was the first and last national regulation on this matter. Regional budgets were to be part of a three-year budget and the latter had to refer to a 'regional development plan' (*programma regionale di sviluppo*, PRS). However, nothing was said about the contents. As a consequence, the PRS has been primarily regarded as a legal precondition for the approval of the regional budget by the State authorities. Planning had, of course, become a mandatory step but, when not otherwise decided, it could easily be reduced to the bureaucratic need for an 'attachment' to the budget.

During the 1980s, regional planners embraced approaches that claimed to substitute dreams with reality. Scenarios and platforms were replaced by lists of projects: plans lost their theoretical content and acquired practical reference to actual policies. In fact, the regional toolbox grew incrementally, but rapidly during this period. The most significant additions concerned 'real service' policies, innovation policies for SMEs, networking and promotional actions within territorial productive systems (cf. Bianchi and Bellini, 1991) and – in some, more debatable, cases – even indirect shareholding (through development agencies and regional *finanziarie*) in companies. Regional governments started to learn by doing, although very often through a clearly delayed, *ex post* rationalization of what contingent problems and the perceived societal demand for policy action had 'forced' them to do. Once again, history was not the same everywhere: activism in some regions pushed forward their governments on the learning curve of regional economic and industrial policy; others just watched and tried little more than pale imitations of the most successful experiences. Sadly, the dividing line between these two kinds of regions was often the same as the borderline between the developed North and the depressed South. After decades of centrally-managed subsidization, the *Mezzogiorno*'s political economy did not wake up from its addiction to political irresponsibility (Trigilia, 1992).

Planning was once again reconsidered at the end of the 1980s. The regional development plans had proved to be increasingly weak tools in shaping strategies and policies. Technical sophistication and, especially, the massive adoption of cost-benefit analysis,[10] had only a superficial and instrumental compliance with supraregional procedures required for either State or European co-financing, often hidden behind a façade of stringency. In fact, constituent elements of plans, such as the quantification of targets, the setting of strategy-generating procedures, the formal evaluation of alternative policy options, the provision for monitoring procedures, were still missing. Innovation was decisively stimulated by the interaction with the European Community procedures. The experience of the Integrated Mediterranean Plans (*Programmi integrati mediterranei*, PIM) marked a real turning point in this respect (Bianchi, 1990). New concepts were introduced that had so far been mostly unknown to the planning practice of Italian regions. Integrated planning replaced sector planning; evaluation and monitoring eventually entered the political and administrative vocabulary.

It was much more than simple technical contamination. Planning abandoned its old 'authoritarian' style (stating policy intentions with no actual obligation to realize them, except for the political evaluation that would be given by elected assemblies and voters; plans turned into contracts. They began to include commitments, duties and sanctions for non-fulfilment: the escape hatch of being substituted by some higher-level authority was no longer available and funds could be withdrawn. Furthermore, PIM established the principle of partnership: participating actors were committed not only to generic consensus (of the kind that could easily be granted as ordinary political exchange), but to the co-financing of the initiatives as well. PIM (and later the EU Structural Funds) were not only an influential laboratory of a new planning and policy style. They also educated a new generation of politicians and managers. Since then, the European style has supplied new concepts and references to regional planning, even if this has happened in most cases without conscious investment in human resources and scarce and delayed organizational changes,[11] i.e. through an almost spontaneous learning-by-doing process.

In fact, the European Union abstained from taking a proactive approach to this problem, sheltering behind the non-interference principle. Not surprisingly, therefore, the adoption of the European practices has further increased the gaps between the Italian regions, both in the exploitation of funding opportunities and in the degree of consistency between local and European policies. Three patterns have emerged as a result of different attitudes to European policy-making and to actual administrative capabilities (Figure 6.1). Emilia-Romagna is often said to have performed as 'Euro-leader', combining an active presence in Brussels' lobbying and trans-regional network building circuits with its long tradition of efficient administrative implementation. Tuscany may now be seen as slowly moving from a 'follower' attitude towards a more active one, partly as a result of its newly-acquired awareness of the distortions caused by European policies. The PRS itself, for example, reflects a critical attitude towards the perverse effects of the 'zoning' method.

However, the most dramatic result of this Europeanization process of planning and policies can be seen in those cases where regions have been trapped into their inability to sustain European standards of policy-making because of their inadequate administrative structures and governing élites. But for short-lived attempts to 'Euro-bluff', these regions, which include most of the Italian *Mezzogiorno*, seem to be locked into the vicious circle of ineffective government and are progressively marginalized in a scenario of decreasing available resources and increasing competition from other low-income regions.

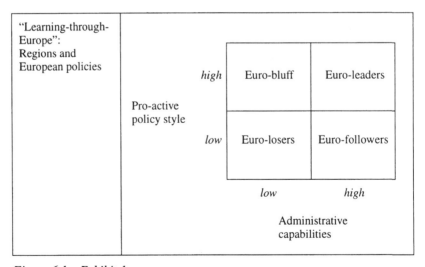

Figure 6.1   Exhibit 1

6.3   THE INTELLIGENT GOVERNMENT

The two documents issued in Emilia-Romagna and Tuscany are the result of the evolution described in the previous section. They are possibly the best expression of the state of the art in regional planning in Italy. None of them explicitly use the 'learning region' framework, but they can easily be interpreted along those lines and are extremely suggestive of more general points. Looking at the picture of regional government that emerges from these documents, 'intelligence' appears to be the most adequate definition summarizing the main requirements of regional government in the 'learning region'. Intelligence includes:

- a sophisticated and updated interpretation of relevant scenarios;
- continuous monitoring and evaluation of policies;
- substantial policy flexibility.

6.3.1   Updating Visions

The two documents clearly show the relevance of an updated vision of both past performance and prospective scenarios of the regional economies in global competition. The documents are dominated philosophically by the awareness of global competition as the driving force of economic development and by a sharpened sensitivity to the theme of competition between territorial systems. Both documents show the conviction that an updated interpretation of economic trends should be translated into a strategic reappraisal. In the Emilia-Romagna document the most interesting contribution in this direction comes from the critical reconsideration of the industrial district. The following is a central quote:

> The fact that the districts' internal efficiency and external success could be largely attributed to the district as a system left the strategic problems of individual companies in the background. It is now clear, however, that the economic evolution of territories and districts depends above all on the control of company-specific strategic resources. Districts and their associated territories are different not only because of historic processes of socio-economic accumulation or because of their industries and, consequently, the production and distribution technologies employed. They are also different (even when the social bases or the industry-specific competence are the same) for the potential of network strategies that individual companies can put into the field within the globalization scenarios. ... It is evident that evolution potentials increase as one moves from small company structures, without hierarchy and with local production links, towards mixed systems including companies of different size, where local networks integrate themselves with global networks and exploit accumulated knowledge partly through working out new entrepreneurial ideas.[12]

These trends imply serious threats to the regional economy: the reduction of the industrial base (when globalization implies delocalization of activities) and the migration of leading companies to other areas where external economies typical of large metropolitan areas are available, unlike in the medium-sized towns of Emilia-Romagna. The shift in vision emerging from the Tuscany document seems even more radical, as it outlines wider (and more widely instructive) implications in the method of policy making itself.

In Tuscany, indeed, a more pessimist view of economic prospects is diffused. There are conflicting views about the desirable future in the political debate. Rapid de-industrialization, which has been occurring since the 1970s, is interpreted accordingly. Some are even tempted by the idea of fostering the shift of wealth-creating activities from the manufacturing sector in order to speed up the movement towards the 'post-industrial' society in a region highly endowed with extraordinary tourist assets. To others, the decline in the regional gross product share of industry is just the local reflection of the more general trend in all developed economies and services and does not outline a real alternative to the central role of industry.[13] For those people taking a traditionally very strong 'industrialist' view (both within the entrepreneurial associations and within the trade unions and the dominating Left), Tuscany runs the risk of a future that may be neither post- nor neo-industrial, but of general decline.

The problems of industry return to the foreground.[14] Tuscan industry has lost the traditional advantages of flexibility that are no longer monopolized by small enterprises. At the same time, the traditional industries have shown a low propensity to invest, partly due to the lack of medium-sized and leader enterprises. Problems of competitiveness, however, are not automatically related to the sectorial composition of the economy (that is, the structural decline of traditional sectors that have traditionally driven the regional economy). A small hard core of dynamic and innovative companies, with high rates of growth, have indeed introduced significant innovations in organization. They have moved to more complex and strategically relevant relations with contractors and subcontractors and have strengthened their technical command of specialized areas. These firms have also established a new relationship with the market, while innovating their corporate finance. An 'excellent' Tuscany, where excellence is not hindered by structural factors, seems possible and practicable, but how can it be achieved? The PRS acknowledges that a winning model is lacking. Various paths lead to success, but none can be labelled as the 'recipe'.

In conclusion, we can generalize from the two examples that intelligent governments feel the pressing need to bring policy making back in line with the historical context of their region. This is, above all, an intellectual challenge. In different times, it was probably acceptable for the intellectual support to political decision-making to forget Hegel's warning 'about giving instruction as to what the world ought to be', which can also be applied to economic matters, 'it is only when actuality is mature ... that the ideal apprehends this same real world in its substance and builds it up for itself into the shape of an intellectual realm'. Economics may also come onto the scene too late. Nowadays, however, the 'owl of Minerva' syndrome[15] must be overcome by effectively providing the government with intellectual keys that are not mere projections of images from a (more or less successful) past.

6.3.2 Monitoring and Evaluation

As stated in Section 2, policy monitoring and evaluation has traditionally been the weakest point of policy-making. That made it essentially 'blind' and dependent on ambiguous indicators, such as the 'customer satisfaction' of companies applying for subsidies. In contrast, continuous and sophisticated monitoring and evaluation procedures are an integral part of 'intelligent government'. They are essential both to intra-organizational learning and to interactive learning, as they are instrumental to the transfer of information flows to and from government. Both documents show awareness of this. This topic cannot be developed to full length in this chapter and only a few fundamental aspects will be highlighted. First, it is important to note that technicalities appear to be a problem of diminishing importance. The old problem of fixing appropriate connections between budgets and plans is finding increasingly effective (although not definitive) solutions. Only benchmarking techniques (which are also a potentially powerful tool for learning in policy-making organizations) still seem to be unknown. The crucial issue, however, is organizational (rather than technical) in nature and provides evidence that basic power relations between sections of the regional government's structure are at stake in the internal learning process.

Secondly, through evaluation, risk finally enters the realm of policy making. Risk aversion is a distinctive feature of traditional policy making, especially in the legalistic culture that dominates Italian bureaucracy. Failures are inherently linked to guiltily mistaken behaviour. In a country like Italy, inefficiency, corruption and other pathologies are too well-grounded stereotypes, ready to use in order to interpret policy failures. Indeed, the two documents assume a departure from this attitude, but not to the point of stating it unambiguously. Intelligent governments, on the contrary, accept risk as an ordinary condition of policy making, to the extent that policies reinforce investment and the risk-taking propensity of the economy and do not limit themselves to subsidizing present behaviour and ventures. In other words, risk acceptance is tightly linked to policy additionality.[16] It puts value on the policy of sharing the 'excessive' risks of entrepreneurship in order to increase the level of 'confidence' in the economy, as was already limpidly clear to Alexander Hamilton.[17]

6.3.3 Policy Flexibility

The PRS of Tuscany goes beyond the recognition of a changed scenario. The discontinuity with the past leads to a more fundamental shift that can be assumed in our discussion to be a distinctive feature of 'intelligent government'. In what follows we try to read the indications of the PRS in a way that is consistent with our conceptual framework. In fact, the acknowledgement by the PRS that it is impossible to define *a priori* a desirable model for development has important consequences for policy. There is no clear reference to policy, and the learning process (both in its intra-organizational dimension and in relation to the interactions with actors in the economy) is also more difficult. Diversity itself becomes the policy objective: a wide portfolio of entrepreneurial responses to the challenges of global competition ensures economic success against the vagaries of future scenarios.

The policy (and learning) must therefore focus less on a precise strategy than on the ability to manage a sufficiently wide range of options, as each one of them may turn out to respond adequately and to provide opportunities to take advantage of unforeseeable future conditions. In fact, a 'lean' policy-making must place the greatest priority on the control and management of information flows. Analogies with lean manufacturing and flexible production systems may provide more than mere images to the understanding of policy flexibility. Learning functions lie at the core of flexible policy making.

6.4 THE REGIONAL GOVERNMENT AND THE LEARNING REGION

The role of the regional government within the learning region is characterized by two main tasks (and sets of problems):

1. the *animateur*/engineer role in relation to inter-firm networks and policy networks: in this respect, regional governments are crucial in defining the appropriate mix of diversity and proximity in networks, selecting local subjects and establishing extra-regional linkages;
2. the rule-maker for inter-institutional co-ordination: in this respect, regions must work out a balance between *ex ante* policy coordination and policy pluralism (competing policies and networks) with *ex post* co-ordination.

Both tasks reflect the 'meso' character of regional governments, that is, their intermediate position between localities and the traditional power structures of the state. Although inherently ambiguous, the 'meso' character may be interpreted as a source of great potential for innovative economic policy, integrating diversity in a territorial space that is larger, but not to the point of losing the proximity needed to support effective communication (cf. Humphries, 1996; Gregersen and Johnson, 1997; and Grassi and Cavalieri, 1997). At the same time, however, the 'meso' character may suffer from equally great problems: it may be the object of the converging pressures of centralist bureaucracies and of localities (Bellini, 1996a); it may be 'too large to respond to the malaise of many entrepreneurs under duress and too small to accompany the internationalization of leading companies'.[18]

6.4.1 Animateur and Engineer

The PRS of Tuscany (together with the related preparatory work) provides some interesting suggestions that are elaborated in the context of the conceptual framework of the learning region in this section. Change is identified as a logical sequence of three different levels of innovation (Figure 6.2). In turn, the shift from each level of innovation to the other identifies the areas for industrial policy action, as in Figure 6.3.

In supporting 'possible innovation', policies 'accompany' the diffusion of innovative behaviour patterns that have already been experimented with by companies. They therefore support an inward-looking kind of learning within the regional economy, which is based on imitation and results in incremental adjustments. To 'accompany' means to optimize all those actions that provide the supporting infrastructure of virtuous company performance. Within this area, industrial policy must work in line with market conformity. Market conformity implies that policies do not distort or deviate from market

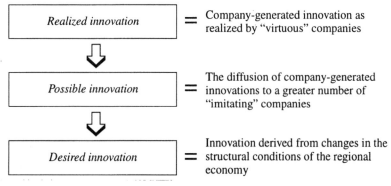

Figure 6.2   Levels of innovation

mechanisms, but limit themselves to strengthening the availability of a number of strategic factors, to lowering costs and speeding up the pace of adjustments.

	ECONOMIC AND INDUSTRIAL POLICIES	
Realized Innovation	*Objectives*	*Tools* → *impact on the learning region*
⇩⇦	Accompanying and supporting the diffusion of innovation	market conforming industrial policies → inward-looking learning by imitation and incremental innovation
Possible Innovation		
⇩⇦	The structural *upgrading* of the local economy	Structural investments → outward-looking learning for discontinuous change
Desired Innovation		

Figure 6.3   Areas for industrial policy

They are not simply hands-off policies, dismantling 'State failures' but have an active role in supporting change. Market conformity implies absence of *dirigisme*, but the risk of implicit *dirigisme* is present if policies are not correctly designed and implemented. In fact, market-conforming policies must be at the same time:

• intelligent (see above);
• systematic: they must be based on a wide range of tools (regulations, incentives, service infrastructures, etc.), as opposed to simplified one-policy strategies;
• constant and reliable: they must guarantee stability in governmental behaviour and policy content and a reliable quality of the policy management and implementation, which allows companies to include policies as a variable in their internal decision-making.

The policies for the 'desired innovation' have the objective of upgrading the conditions and opportunities of the regional system as a whole and must be considered as structural investments. They trigger outward-looking, radical learning processes that redefine actors, their behaviour and their opportunities. Therefore, learning may also imply forgetting past or decaying structures and habits. This is an obvious reason for resistance to these policies by conservative coalitions. The policies for 'desired innovation' are characterized by:

- their capacity to give a clear signal of positive discontinuity with the present situation by rejuvenating the collective assets of the production system;
- a focus on results, rather than on rules;
- the setting of medium and long-term objectives (i.e. accepting a possible absence of results in the short run);
- the acceptance of some calculated risk (see above);
- the ability to rank projects according to their feasibility level (*cantierabilità* as current bureaucratic jargon now, inelegantly although effectively, labels it in Italy);
- the ability to identify priorities, based on a political multiplier, i.e. their capacity to trigger new and consistent behaviour in a variety of actors;
- a distinctive and diffused project-making ability in order to respond to changing circumstances and seize windows of opportunity;
- the ability to engineer adequate (and often new) policy networks working as regional 'growth coalitions'. Within them a serious commitment of resources by various actors must be assured, together with their renunciation of opportunistic behaviour and the pursuit of short-term self-interest.

These policies are obviously aimed at opening up local systems to learning interactions and widening the number and quality of the participants. Localities (and the economic value of local embeddedness) are viewed as part of, rather than separate from, the global (cf. Amin and Thrift, 1994; and Rullani, 1997). This is indeed a central feature of both documents. While other experiences[19] in Europe appear to concentrate on the construction of internal networks, the main concern in Tuscany and Emilia-Romagna (where networks are a well-rooted historic heritage) is the connection between these and the extra-regional (national, European and, possibly, global) networks.

The opening strategies are both crucial and difficult. In Emilia-Romagna, in particular, where opening up implies (or may be perceived to imply) reduced weight being given to indigenous entrepreneurs, the need to counter protectionist resistance is clearly (and bravely) spelled out. The territorial identification of companies cannot turn into a policy trap: territorial development cannot be based only on 'local' companies. Inward investment policies (formerly an unknown item in these regions) are only one option here. A more general conceptualization may be offered by the matrix in Figure 6.4 (adapted from Pratofutura, 1996). The opening up of the local system

Exhibit 2				
The matrix of actors in local systems[1]				

Exhibit 2

The matrix of actors in local systems[1]

		local	> local
Source of competence	*exogenous*	Inward innovators	Displaced
	endogenous	Satellites	Outward innovators

Extent of the market

Note: Adapted from Pratofutura, 1996

Figure 6.4   Exhibit 2

either needs subjects making more extended use of indigenously developed competencies (outward innovators) or subjects importing exogenous competencies into the local system (inward innovators). They must be distinguished from subjects that are local in both competencies and range of action, as well as from subjects that have no linkage with the regional community. Identifying them is an essential ingredient of policy for learning regions.

The opening up of local economies also dramatizes the problem of consensus building. Emilia-Romagna, whose stable and integrated polity had been a major factor in economic success,[20] now seems unable to provide a substitute for old 'consociative' practices. The document hints at a renewed dialogue with the social actors and is filled with explicit statements about the government's renunciation of *dirigiste* temptations. But no clear picture emerges. Tuscany, on the other hand, shows an attempt to overcome practices of mere consultation with social partners within the framework of an updated version of neo-corporatism.

6.4.2   Rule-maker

An essential role of the regional government is to provide rules for inter-institutional co-ordination: in this respect regional governments must work out a balance between two alternative approaches. They may stress *ex ante* policy co-ordination, constraining the behaviour of other institutions and autonomous learning processes; or they may ride the tiger of policy pluralism, allowing for competing policies and networks and, of course, learning. In the latter case, they accept some of the costs of inefficiency and redundancy in exchange for greater readiness to exploit windows of opportunity in local and regional development. These costs may be partially offset by *ex post* co-ordination: fostering connections and synergy between autonomous initiatives, selecting and cutting financial support to failed ventures and so on. The alternative is clearly shown by the comparative analysis of the two documents. In Tuscany an intensive effort has been started in order to 'educate' sub-regional institutions in bottom-up planning, while regional government retreats and focuses on a limited number of specific tasks. The result, at least in the intentions made explicit by the PRS, may constitute a pioneering experience. Two kinds of programme (in obvious analogy with the European experience) are provided for:

- the PO (*programma-obiettivo*, programme-objective) is the framework for the allocation of resources according to the subsidiarity principle. Sub-regional programmes are the means for applying (competitively) for those funds;
- the PIR (*programma di iniziativa regionale*, regional initiative programme) includes actions that are not manageable according to the subsidiarity method and require at least a regional scale.

Tuscany now faces a harsh test. The project-making capacity of sub-regional authorities has been only partially tested, but non-governmental actors (like associations, chambers of commerce, local development agencies etc.) also require a substantial upgrading of their capacities. Inefficiency losses must be expected, at least in a transition phase. The strengthening of technical support therefore becomes a priority and Tuscany is now, in fact, reconsidering the opportunity for establishing a regional development agency (which does not exist at present) and strengthening the High Technology Network Agency (*Rete Regionale dell'Alta Tecnologia*). The Emilia-Romagna document, on the contrary, seems to be overwhelmed by worries about centrifugal initiatives by local entities. The opening premise can hardly be denied: inward-looking district policies have produced inward-looking initiatives, responding to local needs rather than to global competition. Trade fairs, airports, transport infra-structure and technology centres have reflected parochial interests more than international standards of excellence. They have been added to local networks without questioning their actual or potential positioning in the global ones.

The government of Emilia-Romagna, therefore, is being pulled into a vision of regional government and planning that sees its own legitimacy (and almost identifies itself) in the claim to control and order local pluralism. The concept of *Sistema metropolitano policentrico* (Polycentric Metropolitan System), developed by the regional territorial plan at the end of the eighties, once again shows its ambiguity. It recognizes territorial diversity, but gives the regional government the power to constrain it within predefined roles and 'vocations'. The issue of 'Bologna as capital' is a good example of a long and so far inconclusive tension between very lively local initiatives and regional centralism.

While Tuscany may have to face the costs of a phase of regional experimentalism, Emilia-Romagna is apparently embarking on a new attempt to subordinate local learning processes to a regional architecture. Past experiences (Bellini, 1989) and present conditions suggest that this is a Herculean task: it may turn out to be either destructive and frustrating for local network creativity or a useless exhibition of impotence in face of the many means localities can adopt to bypass regional constraints. Or both, of course.

6.5   CONCLUDING REMARKS

This paper has used the 'learning region' framework to reinterpret the role of regional governments in economic development. As a result, a number of issues have become better focused and analysed. An important feature of the learning region framework is an intelligent regional government. Such a government would adhere to the following principles:

1.   a sophisticated and updated interpretation of relevant scenarios where future developments are linked with the historical context of a region;
2.   continuous monitoring and evaluation of policies, which allows intelligent governments to accept risk-taking as an ordinary condition of policy-making, as opposed to subsidizing present behaviour;
3.   a substantial policy flexibility which focuses on the ability to manage a sufficient range of options, rather than on a precise strategy. Priority lies with the control and management of information flows.

The role of regional governments within the learning region is characterized by two main tasks and sets of problems. First, the animateur/engineer role in relation to inter-firm networks and policy networks. Linking these regional networks to supra-regional (international) networks is of particular importance and stresses the need for consensus building within the region. Secondly, the rule-making for inter-institutional co-ordination. Here, regional governments must strike a balance between the constraints of *ex ante* co-ordination versus the learning potential of policy pluralism (but accept some inefficiency losses), on the one hand, and *ex post* co-ordination fostering connections and synergies, on the other hand.

The regional (meso) level is a source of great potential for innovation, resulting from the diversity of a region, although it runs the risk of being ill-adapted to both the micro level of the firm and the pressures of internationalization. In conclusion, however, it may be useful to stress the need for consistency between regional governments as proactive participants in the learning regions' interactions and regional governments as learning organizations. One should be aware of the risk of superimposing rigid, formalized and hierarchical policy making on inherently dynamic and pluralist learning interactions. What is obviously inconsistent for updated theory may well be a persistent inertia in the reality of policy practice.

NOTES

1. I am especially grateful to Dr. Mario Agnoli, director of Confindustria Emilia-Romagna, and to Prof. Giuliano Bianchi, director of the Planning Department of the Regione Toscana, for inviting me to contribute to discussions within their respective organizations about the documents which are analysed in this paper. I am also indebted to Giuliano Bianchi for the analysis of the role and evolution of regional planning in Italy, as reported in Section 6.2. This analysis, and its relationship to the Tuscan case, is further elaborated in Bianchi and Bellini (1998).
2. Of course, 'planning' refers to the process and 'plan' to its result.
3. The concept of policy network seems especially adequate for describing a pattern of policy making that responds to territorial and functional fragmentation and provides problem-solving opportunities in the management of contemporary political economies (cf. Bellini, 1996b). Within a wider 'policy community', networks identify management structures that derive from 'the interaction of many separate but interdependent organisations, which coordinate their action through interdependencies of resources and interests. Actors, who take an interest in the making of a certain policy and who dispose of resources (material and immaterial) required for the formulation, decision and implementation of the policy, form linkages to exchange these resources. ... [N]etworks are characterised by predominantly informal interactions between public and private actors with distinctive, but interdependent interests, who strive to solve problems of collective action on a central, non-hierarchical level' (Börzel 1997, p. 5).
4. Regione Emilia-Romagna, *La regione globale. L'Emilia-Romagna nell'Europa del duemila. Scenari e opzioni strategiche per l'aggiornamento del Piano Territoriale Regionale*, Bologna, July 1997 (Italian text also available on Internet at: http://www.regione.emilia-romagna.it/ptr/).
5. The text of the plan is published in the Official Bulletin of the Regione Toscana.
6. The bibliography on Emilia-Romagna and Tuscany is abundant. Limiting ourselves to the references that can most usefully complement this paper, we suggest: on Emilia-Romagna: Leonardi and Nanetti, 1990; Cooke and Morgan, 1991; Cooke, 1996; Cossentino *et al.*, 1996; Bellini and Pasquini, 1998; on Tuscany: Leonardi and Nanetti, 1994; Bianchi, 1996; Varaldo *et al.*, 1997.
7. These are: Valle d'Aosta; Trentino–Alto Adige; Friuli–Venezia Giulia; Sicilia; Sardegna.
8. These planning experiences actually involved many of the best experts and economists of the time and were based on the use of sophisticated techniques. Indeed, during the 1960s,

      regional research institutes were established, again on the initiative of provinces and chambers of commerce. Some of these institutes have an outstanding record of scientific excellence. This is the case, in particular, of Tuscany's IRPET (*Istituto regionale per la programmazione economica della Toscana*).

9. Regional politics were actually dominated in some cases by issues, such as the ethnic question in Trentino-Alto Adige, that were obviously intractable.

10. In the case of Tuscany, however, it must be mentioned that a great effort was made (and a considerable amount of money was spent) between 1979 and 1984 on the construction of a powerful input-output model. This model has provided the regional government with useful analytical tools in crucial decisions.

11. A significant obstacle was created by the resistance of the Italian government (and the Ministry of Foreign Affairs) to the establishment of representative offices of the regions in Brussels, as well as to international activity by the regions as a whole. Learning about Europe was, of course, accelerated in those policy areas where the European jurisdiction was the strongest: some of the best experts on Brussels technicalities are still found among the *assessorati* for agriculture.

12. Par. 4.1.6 (author's translation).

13. In fact, the post-industrial hypothesis rests on fragile grounds: no real shift towards innovative and high value-added services to companies has been detected. On the contrary, personal services almost monopolize the tertiary sector and show low levels of competitiveness and productivity.

14. The following analysis draws both on Tuscany's new PRS and from a preparatory piece of research, the influence of which is explicitly acknowledged by the PRS itself: Varaldo *et al.*, 1997.

15. 'The owl of Minerva spreads its wings only with the falling of the dusk': quotations are of course from Hegel's *Philosophy of Right* (English version edited by T.M. Knox, Oxford 1967, pp. 12 f.).

16. Additionality refers to the ability of policies to cause individuals (companies) to behave differently from how they would have behaved in the absence of the policy.

17. 'There are dispositions apt to be attracted by the mere novelty of an undertaking; but these are not always the best calculated to give it success. To this it is of importance that the confidence of cautious, sagacious capitalists, both citizens and foreigners, should be excited. And to inspire this description of persons with confidence, it is essential that they should be made to see in any project which is new – and for that reason alone, if for no other, precarious – the prospect of such a degree of countenance and support from governments, as may be capable of overcoming the obstacles inseparable from first experiments.' (Report on Manufactures, in Alexander Hamilton's Papers on Public Credit and Finance, New York: The Liberal Arts Press 1957, p. 204)

18. A. Bonomi, 'Le Regioni, l'industria e la nuova gerarchia', *Corriere della Sera*, Economic Supplement, 23 March 1998 (author's translation).

19. Including those that make explicit reference to the 'learning region' concept. See, for instance, the partners of the ADAPT 'Learning Region' project, such as the Chemnitz area in Germany and the Graz area in Austria.

20. This has been traditionally labelled as 'Emilian Model': see Brusco, 1982.

REFERENCES

Amin, A. and N. Thrift (1994), 'Living in the global', in A. Amin and N. Thrift (eds), *Globalization, Institutions, and Regional Development in Europe*, Oxford: Oxford University Press.

Bellini, N. (1989), 'Il PCI ed il governo dell'industria in Emilia-Romagna', *Il Mulino*, **5**, pp. 707–32 (an abridged English version of the same essay is Bellini, N., 'The management of the economy in Emilia-Romagna: the PCI and the regional experience', in Leonardi and Nanetti, 1990).

Bellini, N. (1996a), 'Regional economic policies and the non-linearity of history', *European Planning Studies*, **4** (1), pp. 63–73.

Bellini, N. (1996b), *Stato e Industria nelle Economie Contemporanee*, Roma: Donzelli.

Bellini, N. and F. Pasquini (1998), 'The case of ERVET in Emilia-Romagna: towards a second-generation regional development agency', in H. Halkier, M. Danson and C. Damborg (eds), *Regional Development Agencies in Europe*, London: Jessica Kingsley.

Belussi, F. (1997), 'Le politiche knowledge-intensive per lo sviluppo dei sistemi produttivi territoriali', in A. Bramanti and M. Maggioni (1997).

Bianchi, G. (1982), 'L'esperienza di programmazione regionale in Italia: una breve rassegna critica', in M. Bielli and A. La Bella (eds), *Problematiche dei Livelli Sub-Regionali di Programmazione*, Milano: Franco Angeli.

Bianchi G. (1990), *Beautiful Music Badly Played: The Integrated Mediterranean Programmes: An Appraisal of Planning Design. Report prepared for DG XVI of the EC Commission*, Firenze: European University Institute.

Bianchi, G. (1996), 'Galileo used to live here. Tuscany hi-tech: the network and its poles', *R&D Management*, **26** (3).

Bianchi, P. and N. Bellini (1991), 'Public policies for local networks of innovators, *Research Policy*, **20**, pp. 487–97.

Bianchi, G. and N. Bellini (1998), 'La programmation du développement régional: des velléités á l'utopie réaliste. Le cas de la Toscane', *Pôle Sud* (forthcoming).

Börzel, T.A. (1997), 'What's so special about policy networks? – an exploration of the concept and its usefuless in studying European governance', *European Integration Online Papers*, 1997–016.

Bramanti, A. and M. Maggioni (eds) (1997), *La Dinamica dei Sistemi Produttivi Territoriali: Teorie, Tecniche, Politiche*, Milano: Franco Angeli.

Brusco, S. (1982), 'The Emilian Model: productive decentralisation and social integration', *Cambridge Journal of Economics*, **6**.

Cooke, P. (1996), 'Building a twenty-first century regional economy in Emilia-Romagna', *European Planning Studies*, **4** (1), pp. 53–62.

Cooke, P. and K. Morgan (1991), *The Intelligent Region: Industrial and Institutional Innovation in Emilia-Romagna, Regional Industrial Research Report no. 14*, University of Wales, College of Cardiff.

Cossentino, F., F. Pyke and W. Sengenberger (1996), *Local and Regional Response to Global Pressure: The Case of Italy and its Industrial Districts*, Geneva: ILO.

Grassi, M. and A. Cavalieri (1997), 'Politiche economiche per i sistemi locali: quale ruolo per il livello regionale nel binomio locale–globale', in A. Bramanti and M. Maggioni (1997).

Gregersen B. and B. Johnson (1997), 'Learning economies, innovation systems and European integration', *Regional Studies*, **31** (5), pp. 479–90.

Humphries, C. (1996), 'The territorialisation of public policies: the role of public governance and funding', in OECD, 1996.

Leonardi, R. and R.Y. Nanetti (eds) (1990), *The Regions and European Integration. The case of Emilia-Romagna*, London: Pinter.

Leonardi, R. and R.Y. Nanetti (eds) (1994), *Regional Development in a Modern European Economy: The Case of Tuscany*, London: Pinter.

Morgan, K. (1996), 'Learning-by-interacting: inter-firm networks and enterprise support', in OECD, 1996.

Morgan, K. (1997), 'The learning region: institutions, innovation and regional renewal', *Regional Studies*, **31** (5), pp. 491–503.

OECD (1996), 'Networks of enterprises and local development. Competing and co-operating in local productive systems', Paris.

Pratofutura (1996), *I Servizi per le Imprese nel Distretto Pratese*, Prato: Unione Industriale Pratese.

Rullani, E. (1997), 'Più locale e più globale: verso un'economia post-fordista del territorio', in A. Bramanti and M. Maggioni (1997).

Sabel, C. (1996), 'Learning-by-monitoring: the dilemmas of regional economic policy in Europe', in OECD, 1996.

Storper, M. (1995), 'The resurgence of regional economies, ten years later: the region as nexus of untraded interdependencies', *European Urban and Regional Studies*, **2** (3), pp. 191–221.

Trigilia, C. (1992), *Sviluppo Senza Autonomia*, Bologna: Il Mulino.

Varaldo, R., N. Bellini and A. Bonaccorsi (1997), *Tendenze e Vie di Cambiamento dell'Industria Toscana*, Milano: Franco Angeli.

7. In Search of a Regional Innovation Strategy for Flanders[1]

Ben Dankbaar and Jan Cobbenhagen

This paper discusses the issues and dilemmas of regional innovation policy in Flanders. After a brief discussion of the political, economic and social characteristics of Flanders, attention is focused on the specific problems of designing a technology transfer and innovation policy supporting SMEs in the Flemish environment. Flanders, like many similar regions, suffers from an 'embarrassment of choices', when it comes to technology transfer institutions and intermediaries aiming to support SMEs. Policy makers taking a fresh look at the problem of supporting innovativeness in SMEs are facing the choice between the construction of a completely new infrastructure or the utilization of the various existing pieces of infrastructure already available. Section 7.2 provides a brief overview of the major institutions involved and distinguishes between four types of actor which are active in this field: (1) civil service and policy makers; (2) technology producers and providers; (3) intermediaries; and (4) organizations of technology-users. Data derived from standardized interviews with representatives of these institutions provide insights into the opinions of these persons concerning the sources of technological knowledge and the technology transfer needs of SMEs in Flanders. The needs of Flemish SMEs with regard to the technological infrastructure are discussed in Section 7.4 on the basis of 45 interviews with small entrepreneurs from a wide range of sectors and all parts of Flanders. These interviews were carried out using an adapted form of the so-called 'repertory grid' method in order to uncover the priorities of the entrepreneurs. The methodology is briefly discussed in Section 7.3. In Section 7.5, finally, we compare the opinions of the intermediaries and those of the entrepreneurs concerning the needs of enterprises in relation to technological innovation. It seems that the intermediaries and the entrepreneurs have almost completely opposite estimations concerning the priority needs for support of SMEs. Section 7.6 provides a brief epilogue concerning recent developments in innovation policy in Flanders.

7.1   FLANDERS, A SPECIAL REGION

From the perspective of the European Union, Flanders is a region, because
it is a subnational geographical entity. Flanders is part of Belgium. The
word 'region', however, hardly conveys the sense of national identity that
the inhabitants of Flanders display in relation to their part of Belgium.
And indeed, after decades of 'language struggle', the Belgian state has
decomposed itself for most purposes of internal government into a French and
German-speaking part on the one hand (with the German speaking part as a
separate entity for language-related matters) and a Flemish (Dutch-speaking)
part on the other hand. The Belgian capital Brussels has remained a separate,
bilingual entity. The government of Flanders, however, also has its seat in
Brussels.

The dividing lines between the language groups are not just based on
language, but carry also a social and economic meaning, as the two parts of
Belgium have gone through quite different histories of economic
development. The Southern, French-speaking part (Wallonia) belonged to the
early industrializing regions in Europe, characterized as it was by large coal
and iron deposits. The Northern, Flemish-speaking part had its Golden Age in
the 16th century, but became a laggard in economic development over the
following centuries. The Industrial Revolution only began to have an impact
late in the 19th century and on a less intensive scale than in Wallonia. In the
course of the 20th century, however, structural change turned the tables in
Belgium. Wallonia became a troubled, crisis-ridden region. The coal mines
were closed one after another. The steel mills failed to modernize, the
engineering industry (also arms production) deteriorated. Unemployment
became endemic. In Flanders, on the other hand, the economy developed
quite propitiously. The era of mass production became most visible by the
introduction of a large number of car manufacturing operations. Belgium
(mainly Flanders) became the country with the highest number of
automobiles assembled per inhabitant per year in the whole world. Chemical
and pharmaceutical industries also developed remarkably and the harbour of
Antwerp boomed. Today, therefore, the dividing lines between Flanders and
Wallonia are also concerned with the question of who will be paying the bill
for the modernization of the Walloon industry. The willingness of the
inhabitants of Flanders to subsidize their less fortunate compatriots in the
South appears to be limited.

The territory of Flanders takes up approximately 40 per cent of Belgium,
but its population of almost 6 million stands for close to 60 per cent of the
total Belgian population. The working population of Flanders consists of
approximately 1.8 million wage earners and about 385,000 self employed.
Unemployment has been around 12.5 per cent in recent years according to

national definitions. The harmonized unemployment rates provided by Eurostat indicate less than 7 per cent for Flanders compared to over 10 per cent for the average of the European Union. Unemployment has been consistently lower than the average of the European Union in recent years and also considerably lower than in Wallonia. Flanders has five provinces: West Flanders (with Bruges as the major city), East Flanders (Gent), Antwerp (Antwerp), Flemish Brabant (Leuven) and Limburg (Hasselt). The middle part of Flanders, in particular, is highly urbanized with Antwerp, Ghent and Leuven as the most important cities. Brussels is not part of Flanders, but the social, economic and political impact of this metropolis on the surrounding region is obviously great.

In 1994, Flanders had 117,328 companies. Only 696 of them had more than 200 employees and more than a third of these were located in the province of Antwerp. Just over 25 per cent of the employed population worked in companies with less than 20 employees and another 40 per cent worked in companies with between 20 and 200 employees. Two thirds of the work-force therefore is employed in Small and Medium-Sized Enterprises (SMEs). Manufacturing accounted for approximately 27 per cent of employment in 1994. The five most important sectors in terms of employment were textiles and clothing (with a tradition going back to the 15th century), food and beverages, transport equipment, and chemicals and metal products.

Although one could argue that the Flemish economy is performing quite well if compared to other regions, it is obvious that unemployment is too high. Moreover, the government of Flanders is worried by the fact that mature sectors take up a disproportionally large part of employment in both manufacturing and services (mature sectors are defined as sectors having an average real growth of output between 0 and 2 per cent in the European Union). Only 15 per cent of employment is realized in so-called growth sectors (showing more than 3 per cent real growth at the European level). Ninety per cent of Flemish exports consist of goods and services from mature sectors. As such, this is not unusual. Other countries and regions in Europe also depend on mature sectors for most of their exports. However, competition in these markets is clearly increasing, not just following the completion of the European market, but also because of the increasing internationalization of markets and production activities. In this increasingly global competition the Flemish SMEs are clearly under attack. The Flemish government is worried that many of them, representing a large share of Flemish employment, will not survive unless they become more dynamic, more open to the use of new technologies and more innovative in their product offerings. It should be noted too, that Flanders has only very few indigenous large corporations. In contrast to its neighbour The Netherlands, where large home-grown multinational corporations such as Philips, Shell,

Unilever, or AKZO have dominated the economy for most of the century, the large mass production operations in Flanders are mainly subsidiaries of foreign multinationals. This means that decisions concerning expansion or contraction of these activities are taken outside Belgium. Many of these subsidiaries, like the car assembly plants, are pure manufacturing operations without research, development, or design functions attached. This is seen as a liability in a time where high-wage economies like Flanders are expected to be increasingly knowledge-intensive.

Understandably, the Flemish government is interested in improving the innovative performance of its economy. It is especially interested in providing support to the large number of SMEs, which are facing the double challenge of global competition and technological change. The investigation on which this paper is based was carried out for the Flemish government within the framework of a European Programme supporting the development of regional innovation and technology transfer strategies and related infrastructures (RITTS). The study focused specifically on SMEs. It is important to differentiate here between different types of SMEs (cf. Dankbaar, 1998). Although smallness by itself does bring some specific problems (less opportunity to spread risks; higher costs of capital) as well as advantages (usually quick decision making), it cannot be maintained that all small or medium-sized companies face identical problems. From the perspective of this paper, it is especially necessary to distinguish between, on the one hand, small technology-intensive companies, offering innovative products and often led by entrepreneurs with academic training, and on the other hand, small companies operating in traditional sectors, owned and managed by entrepreneurs with medium-level technical training. The first type of company does not need technology transfer support. These companies know the way to various sources of new technology. The second type of company may be in need of support, but may not be aware of that need or willing to call for outside help, if only because they consider their independence their main strength. Our investigation has concentrated on the latter category of SMEs.

7.2   THE TECHNOLOGY TRANSFER INFRASTRUCTURE OF FLANDERS

Flanders, like many similar regions with a long history of restructuring, has a large number of more or less specialized technology transfer institutions and intermediaries aiming to support innovation in SMEs. One would think that companies looking for help would not have any problem finding it. Help is being offered from every corner. The problem is, of course, that many companies aren't looking for help and the infrastructure seems to be unable to reach them. Policy makers taking a fresh look at the problem of supporting innovativeness in SMEs are facing the choice between the construction of a completely new infrastructure and the utilization of the various existing pieces of infrastructure already available. There are good reasons to take the latter road, if only because it is politically more feasible and potentially less costly. The disadvantage of using existing infrastructures, however, is that in the course of time different institutions and different agents have become successful in different parts of the country and different parts of the economy. Making use of the best in every province or sector would involve a choice of different institutions in each case, hardly a good precondition for an efficient and uniform policy execution.

Four major types of actor can be distinguished which are active in the field of technology transfer and innovation support in Flanders: (1) Civil service and policy makers; (2) Technology producers and providers; (3) Intermediaries; and (4) Organizations of technology-users. Figure 7.1 shows how they are related to the flow of technology to SMEs.

Technology suppliers are in the first place the institutions where new technologies are actually being produced by means of research and development: universities, independent (contract) research institutions and

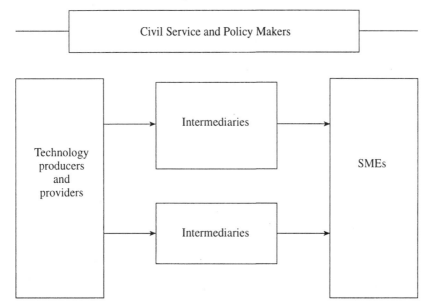

Source: derived from Bartels, 1993

Figure 7.1   Flows of technology to SMEs in the knowledge infrastructure

laboratories of large enterprises. Flanders has eight universities or institutes with a university status, the largest of which are located in Leuven, Brussels and Gent. All universities have their own knowledge transfer agency. There are two major independent research institutions: one focused on micro-electronics and the other focused on environmental technologies, new materials and non-nuclear energy. Recently, an institute for biotechnology research was created. Large enterprises and their R&D departments can be an important source of knowledge for SMEs. In their laboratories they employ people who can communicate with universities and operate on the frontiers of knowledge, but who are also able to translate and apply such knowledge to the needs of the enterprise. SMEs usually lack such personnel, several 'clusters' in which large companies share their technological know-how with smaller companies, suppliers or customers, in order to improve the innovative performance in their sector.

Among the technology suppliers we also count here educational institutions with limited research activities such as polytechnics as well as other training institutions, which are an important original source of knowledge, especially for SMEs which feel too far removed from the problems and issues dealt with in university research. Precisely to overcome this gap between universities and enterprises, the so-called Collective Centres were created by law shortly after the World War II. These are sectoral research centres, focusing on applied technological research, which are funded 50 per cent by government and 50 per cent by a compulsory levy on all companies in their sector. The Collective Centres are expected to focus on business needs, but they are physically located in universities. The three largest Collective Centres are the ones of the textile industry, the metal industry and the building industry. Attached to the Collective Centres are Technological Advisory Services, which focus on supporting (mainly) SMEs with regard to specific techno-logical problems. These Technological Advisory Services are funded for more than 80 per cent by government. They could also be treated as intermediaries, a category to which we now turn.

Intermediaries are institutions and organizations, which do not possess in-house research capacities but play a role in the process of knowledge transfer between technology suppliers and enterprises. Some of these organizations have a broader purpose, like the Chambers of Commerce, which perform various formal and administrative functions on behalf of the government, or the Provincial Development Agencies, which have been created to stimulate employment creation, especially in regions hit by structural economic change. Apart from these government created development agencies, there are also development agencies created by private initiative (but also receiving funding from government), the so-called Strategic Plans, which in some cases also offer technology search and partnering services. In other cases, the intermediaries have been founded precisely for the purpose of technology transfer and innovation support. The five Provincial Development Agencies support a separate technology transfer agency called the Technological Innovation Cell Flanders, which provides technological audit and search functions to individual companies. The Flemish Institute for Scientific and Technological Research in Industry (IWT) was created in 1991 in order to evaluate and finance research proposals coming from industry. It also has an advisory role to the government in relation to research proposals, where the actual funding decision is taken by the government. Moreover, it also provides advisory services to enterprises in the field of technology transfer, for example by evaluating and publicizing technologies becoming available from research supported by the European Union.

It is useful to differentiate these intermediary institutions from the organizations of the technology users themselves. In several sectors associations of employers exist, which also support technology transfer and innovation, for instance by organizing information meetings on specific technologies or by setting up networks between their members. Moreover, as representatives of their members they are also involved in the articulation of technological needs of their sectors through contact with government agencies, universities and of course the sectoral Collective Centres. The general (nonsectoral) employers' associations fulfil similar roles, both at the regional and the national level. These activities are a logical consequence from the fact that for many companies these associations are the first instance they turn to, if they have questions or problems to discuss.

Finally, it is important to note that policy makers and their civil servants are also important actors in this field. By their policies, they influence the activities of the other actors directly or indirectly, if not always with the desired effect. The Flemish government has formulated as its aim to increase spending on research and development in Flanders to 2 per cent of the gross regional product. Moreover, it wants to concentrate these means in a limited number of programmes in order to avoid too large a dispersion of efforts. Finally, it hopes to achieve a further regionalization of spending, that is, more influence on those research funds which are still controlled by the federal government.

In order to gather information on their activities and gain an understanding of their views on technology transfer and innovation in SMEs, 38 standardized interviews were carried out with representatives of the various institutions mentioned above. Although there are obviously differences between the institutions, their background and activities, some observations can be made on the basis of these interviews, which are valid for all of them.

- Even where the respondents considered technology transfer a task of

their organization, they considered their role as a source of technological knowledge for SMEs as relatively unimportant.

- Respondents supported the view that technology transfer was important
  to SMEs, but considered the SMEs themselves as the major obstacle to
  technology transfer. They think that SMEs are too much internally
  focused; that they don't know what is technologically possible; that
  they don't know their own needs; and that they lack important
  management skills especially in this field of knowledge acquisition and
  innovation.
- The respondents gave highest priority to the following needs of SMEs:
  - Making available technology applicable in a small enterprise
    setting;
  - Getting insight in the potential of available technology;
  - Finding candidates for technological partnership.

7.3   UNDERSTANDING THE NEEDS OF SMEs: A METHODOLOGY

In view of the fact that many actors in the technological infrastructure argue
that SMEs don't know their own needs, it is important to find out how the
leadership of SMEs views their needs, where they consider themselves to be
under competitive pressure, and if (and how) they would like to see government support them. Thus, after we had charted the technological infrastructure
of Flanders, we planned a series of interviews with small entrepreneurs from
different sectors and different parts of Flanders. Given the opinions prevailing
in the infrastructure we thought it particularly relevant to question these
entrepreneurs about their needs and priorities without unduly influencing their
answers. Of course, we were interested to find out what kind of technological
needs they had and if they saw a need for a particular type of support.
However, we also wanted to know if technology was high on their list of
priorities. We therefore looked for a method which would allow us to hear
about their priorities before we would inform them that we were interested
specifically in technology transfer.

We found this method in an adaptation of the so-called 'repertory grid'
method. This method was developed by Kelly in the 1950s, based on
'Personal Construct Theory' (Kelly, 1955). The axiomatic starting point of
this psychological theory is that each individual creates his or her own
representation of reality. Between individuals consensus can be reached on
aspects of reality, but never on reality as a whole. Kelly argued that the
constructs people use to come to grips with reality have a bipolar structure.
The repertory grid method was developed on the basis of this theory to elicit

the personal constructs from people and by doing so make their implicit knowledge (their 'mental maps' of the world) explicit. The methodology was first described comprehensively in the handbook by Fransella and Bannister (1977). The primary advantage of this method is that it does not impose any concepts, models or paradigms on the respondent. Disadvantage is that its theoretical foundations do not really allow for an aggregation of individual answers. Applications in social research have consequently been scarce, but interesting results were achieved in an investigation of factors influencing strategic decision-making in enterprises (cf. Huff 1990) and in mapping individual knowledge for expert systems at the University of Calgary (http://ksi.cpsc.ucalgary.ca). We have decided to adapt this methodology for our purposes and to allow for a careful aggregation of individual responses as described below.

In its adapted form, the repertory grid method has taken the following format. A representative sample of 1,500 Flemish SMEs was approached by mail with a one-page questionnaire, which asked for some basic information concerning the company as well as the names of its three most important customers, its three most important suppliers and its three most important competitors. The questionnaire could be returned by fax. The accompanying letter explained that this questionnaire was part of an investigation carried out on behalf of the Flemish government, but no further explanation was given concerning the focus of the investigation.

A total of 128 questionnaires were returned completed. Given that the response rate to postal questionnaires tends to be very low among SMEs, this was a quite acceptable response, which at any rate provided a good basis for the next step in the investigation. Out of the 128 companies responding, 45 companies were selected for in-depth interviews in such a manner that all five Flemish provinces, their main industries and all size classes were represented. Interview partners in all cases were leading managers of the companies, quite frequently the owner-manager.

Interviews were carried out according to a script detailing the exact wordings of each question, especially in the first part of the interview. In this first part, the respondents were shown sets of three cards with the names written on them of the three important customers, competitors and suppliers they had provided themselves. For every set, the respondent was asked to indicate which two of these companies were more similar than the third. No criterion was provided by the interviewer. The respondent almost never asked for one, but pointed out the two companies which according to his (we encountered no leading female managers in these companies) opinion were most similar. These two cards were than moved away a little bit from the third one, visualizing the distance. Then, he was asked to explain this choice: why was this company different from the other two. The exact wordings of the answers were carefully noted. Questioning started with the competitors, followed by the suppliers and then the customers. The choice of these three categories was based on results from earlier studies, which consistently point to competitors, suppliers and customers as the most important sources of new knowledge and ideas for small and medium-sized enterprises (Cannell and Dankbaar, 1996; Van der Meijden and Jacobs, 1995). In the case of the competitors, after they had been discussed a fourth card was put on the table with the name of the respondent's company. The respondent was asked where he would put his own company: was it more similar to the two competitors he had put together or was it more similar to the single one – and why.

After a first round of questioning concerning these three triplets of companies, it was revealed to the respondents that we were really interested in technology and technology transfer.[2] Thereafter, a second round of the 'card game' started, but now the questions were more specifically focused on innovation and technology. Again, attention was focused first on the competitors. Respondents had to indicate which two competitors were more alike than the third, if they would think of 1) technological capabilities; 2) openness for innovation; and 3) creativity. In each case, they were asked to explain their choice (and by doing so they also explained how they interpreted technological capabilities, openness for innovation and creativity). Furthermore, they were asked to rank their competitors and their own company according to innovative capacity, which was defined as the 'sum' of technological capability, openness for innovation and creativity. Respondents had to indicate what was the main criterion they had used in their ranking. They were also asked what measures they were currently undertaking to improve or maintain their position in that ranking.

Next, the respondents were invited to look at their three most important suppliers and indicate which two were more similar than the third, first in terms of innovative capacity and then in terms of knowledge transfer. After the latter question, it was also asked if thinking about knowledge transfer there were maybe other suppliers, which would be more important than the three mentioned on the cards (and if yes, why). Thinking about these suppliers, could they also indicate which of them was most alike to their own company (and why)? Finally, the same questions were asked concerning the customers as had been asked concerning suppliers. That concluded the first part of the interview. In almost all cases, respondents found this part quite interesting. They warmed up to the 'game' quickly and began to shuffle the cards around in answer to the various questions. Some even indicated that they actually had learnt something from this little game.

In the second part of the interview, a series of mainly open questions were asked. These questions concerned the company and its (innovative) performance; awareness of the Flemish technological infrastructure; awareness and uses made of various intermediaries; and the opinions of respondents concerning some of the generally recognized innovation needs of SMEs. Finally, the respondents could indicate what they would do to improve technology transfer to SMEs and to increase their innovative strength, if they headed the government of Flanders. The second part of the interview was evaluated in the usual way, but for the first part, obviously, a special approach had to be followed. In a first step, the repertory grid comparisons were grouped in three categories:

- General comparisons concerning the company and its environment;
- Comparisons related to innovation and technology;
- Comparisons related to knowledge transfer.

For each category, the key expressions used by the 45 respondents in their explanations of their choices in these comparisons were listed. This resulted in three long lists of characteristics and criteria. Three investigators subsequently analysed all three lists and independently from each other made a proposal to consolidate these criteria and characteristics into 10–15 dimensions per list. A dimension would be an expression covering the meaning of the various items included in it. Finally, these proposals were discussed and a single list of dimensions was determined for each category of comparisons. Further analysis took place using these dimensions and not the individual responses. These dimensions should provide us with insights, at an aggregate level, into the views and priorities of small entrepreneurs thinking about their most important partners in business, i.e. their customers, their suppliers and their competitors.

7.4   THE PRIORITIES OF FLEMISH SMEs

A not surprising but nevertheless significant result of the first 'unfocused' round of comparisons was that innovation and technology were not very prominent in the explanations of the respondents. When thinking about differential characteristics of competitors for instance, 22 per cent of the respondents mentioned items like R&D, product development, technical knowledge or originality (grouped under the dimension 'innovation & technology', cf. Figure 7.2). Much more frequently (51 per cent), they mentioned product-range and/or the markets on which the competitors were active (grouped under 'product/market') or specific characteristics of the companies like size, ownership or country of origin (49 per cent, grouped under 'firm characteristics'). The dimension 'market approach', including items like pricing policy, branding, aggressiveness, export-orientation, was

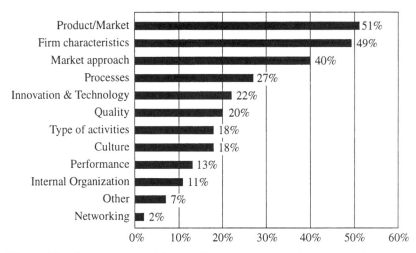

Product/Market	51%
Firm characteristics	49%
Market approach	40%
Processes	27%
Innovation & Technology	22%
Quality	20%
Type of activities	18%
Culture	18%
Performance	13%
Internal Organization	11%
Other	7%
Networking	2%

Figure 7.2   Categories used by small entrepreneurs when comparing their competitors

used by 40 per cent of the respondents. Technical capabilities like the machine park or level of automation (included under the dimension 'processes') were mentioned by just over a quarter of the respondents.

The 'internal organization' of the company and 'networking' (co-operation with others, vertical integration) were seldom mentioned as differentiating characteristics. Nor is one inclined to compare competitors in terms of performance parameters like growth, productivity, competitiveness, and so on. The dimension 'networking' deserves some more discussion. Networking was seldom mentioned to differentiate competitors from each other (only by 2 per cent of the respondents). There exists a quite extensive literature on SMEs and networking, which argues that external networking is essential for small enterprises, because they have no internal sources of technology and other kinds of knowledge. Networking, co-operation, and exchange of information with other companies provide them with essential know-how concerning their competitive environment (e.g. Piore and Sabel, 1984). The fact that networking is apparently not considered a differentiating element should not be interpreted as a rejection of the importance of networking. It does indicate that important competitors apparently do not differ very much in this respect. In the comparisons of important customers and important suppliers, the dimension 'networking' was much more frequently mentioned as a differentiating element: it was mentioned by 27 per cent of the respondents for the suppliers and by 24 per cent for the customers.

It is also notable that the entrepreneurs evaluate their competitors in terms of current products and market shares and much less in terms of capabilities (innovation, technology, quality) to compete in the future. This suggests a short-term orientation with only limited attention for innovation. A similar conclusion was drawn from the European (Eurostat) innovation-survey among Flemish companies. Maintaining and expanding market share and increasing product quality were considered the most important aims of innovation – rather than acquiring new markets or adding functionality (Debackere and Fleurent, 1994).

In the comparisons of suppliers and of customers the dimension 'technology and innovation' is again not very prominent. In comparisons of suppliers it was mentioned by 9 per cent of the respondents; in comparisons of customers, it was mentioned by 16 per cent. 'Quality' was relatively more important in the comparisons of suppliers, whereas customers were compared most frequently in terms of size, country of origin, ownership structure and other company characteristics. As noted, networking was considered a differentiating dimension by about a quarter of the respondents for both the suppliers and the customers.

Figure 7.3 shows the number of times a dimension was used in all the comparisons made before it was clear that the focus of the investigation was on technology transfer and innovation. Clearly, 'innovation and technology' is not unimportant and one cannot argue that the respondents were completely negligent of this dimension. On the other hand, the more traditional

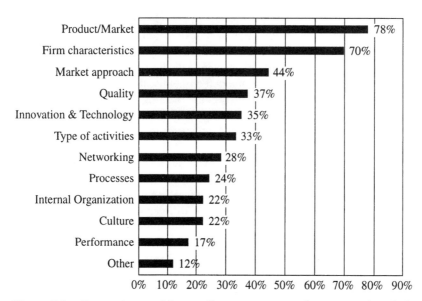

Figure 7.3   Categories used by small entrepreneurs when comparing their competitors, customers and suppliers

dimensions of product/market combination, market approach and firm characteristics were used more frequently. The implication could be that agencies wanting to draw the attention of these entrepreneurs should try to find an entrance point along these traditional dimensions. Supporting innovation in SMEs may have to start with thinking about current products, markets, quality, and marketing before a further step towards new products and new technologies can be fruitfully made.

Once the respondents had been made aware of the interest of the interviewers in innovation and technology, different dimensions were utilized in the comparisons. In comparisons regarding technological capabilities, attention was focused on various aspects of the production process (level of automation, machinery installed) and on particular know-how available to the companies. However, in comparisons with regard to overall innovative capacity respondents focused much less on processes (that is, current techno- logical capabilities) and know-how and much more on the specific product/market combinations and on the market approaches of the companies concerned. Apparently, the innovative capacity of competitors is not so much seen to be related to the mastery of technologies, but rather to good positioning on the market. The innovative capacity of customers, on the other hand, was more frequently discussed in terms of research, product or process innovation as well as in terms of specific characteristics of the companies such as size, vertical integration, or being part of a larger corporation, all of which give a measure for ease of access to knowledge and capital.

When thinking about the transfer of technology from suppliers and customers to their companies, the respondents emphasized that this was most important within the framework of long-standing relations with a limited number of suppliers and/or customers. Frequently, the transfer and exchange of information was organized in regular meetings. Large suppliers were organizing special information meetings for their customers. Generally, it appeared that technology transfer from suppliers to SMEs was more common than knowledge transfer from customers to SMEs.

To test their awareness of the existing technological infrastructure respondents were first asked to mention some institutions which could be of help in organizing for innovation or implementing new technologies. In their answers, the respondents usually did not differentiate between technology suppliers and intermediaries. Universities and polytechnics were mentioned most frequently (by about half of the respondents). The employers' associa- tions were mentioned by a third of the respondents, while about 10 per cent mentioned the Collective Centres and the IWT. Several organizations which see a role for themselves in the field of technology transfer, like the Chambers of Commerce, the federations of employers' associations, or the Provincial Development Agencies, were hardly ever mentioned, although the respondents were aware of their existence. Interestingly, the Collective Centres are known (because companies pay for them), but their transfer agents, the Technological Advisory Services, are not! The Technological Advisory Services and the Technological Innovation Cell Flanders were virtually unknown. Large technological institutes like VITO and IMEC were not mentioned spontaneously. The fact that universities and polytechnics were mentioned most frequently should not be interpreted as indicative of the use made of these institutions. They are simply associated with the presence of potentially useful knowledge, but our interviews as well as other investigations show that only a limited number of SMEs find a way to approach these institutions directly. Although this is often blamed on a lack of accessibility on the part of the technology suppliers, it may also be related to lack of interest or different priorities on the part of SMEs, as will be discussed in the next section.

7.5   DIFFERENT PRIORITIES: SMEs AND INTERMEDIARIES

The entrepreneurs were shown a short list of five needs for innovation management in SMEs, which are frequently mentioned in the literature. They could indicate the relative importance of these needs for their company on a five point scale ranging from not important to very important. The results were interesting in many respects.

- All five needs were considered unimportant or hardly important by at least 50 per cent of the respondents.
- The need considered most important was attracting technically qualified staff.
- The order of importance given to the five problems was almost exactly opposite to the order given to the same list by the intermediaries we had interviewed in the first stage of the investigation.

Figure 7.4 illustrates the last point.

Most interesting is the fact that more than 80 per cent of the intermediaries think that SMEs have major problems in acquiring insight in available technologies, whereas almost 80 per cent of the entrepreneurs think that this is hardly or not at all a problem. How should we interpret this finding? There is no reason to assume it is a peculiarity of the Flemish situation. Intermediaries and small entrepreneurs apparently have a somewhat different view of the needs of the latter. To some extent, our finding was already predicted by the intermediaries who argued that small entrepreneurs do not

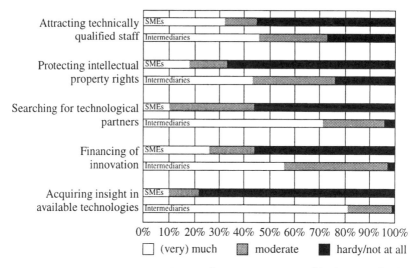

Figure 7.4   Importance given by small entrepreneurs and by intermediaries to five frequently mentioned needs of SMEs

know their own needs. The idea that SMEs don't know their own needs, especially in the field of technology transfer and innovation, is not particularly novel. Many observers have noted that the leadership of small enterprises is preoccupied with short-term problem solving and does not take the time to study relevant changes in the environment. Moreover, the leadership often lacks the formal education necessary to understand some of the new technologies. They are not much inclined to hire people who could understand them, if only because they feel somewhat uncomfortable employing people with a higher education than themselves. Small enterprises tend to be understaffed, but at the same time they are also less inclined than larger firms to call in outside consultants to make up for the lack of internal competencies. Small and medium-sized enterprises, so the argument goes, are therefore not aware of relevant technologies and may underestimate the threat arising from such technologies to their competitive position. On the other hand, if the leadership of SMEs is not aware of the potential threats presented by new technologies, then these threats are apparently not felt in current business. The entrepreneurs we interviewed were mostly quite successful in keeping their business going. Wouldn't they know, if the short-term survival of their companies were threatened? And if the threat is still some time away, should they bother? Why (and how) would a small enterprise without internal research or development functions have to anticipate threats that may arise in the future?

One argument for taking a longer-term perspective would be that the reaction time left may be too short once these threats are taking the form of actual competition on the market. However, there is no reason to assume that important new competitors with new technologies will appear out of nowhere – and if they do, they will probably be large companies or companies with a completely novel technology. In both cases there is no reason to assume that SMEs can adequately prepare for such an onslaught. In fact, even large companies find it difficult to be aware of radical new technologies that threaten their established products or processes. The large Swiss watch manufacturers, for instance, were almost all taken by surprise when Japanese manufacturers introduced microelectronics in watches.

So, who is right? The intermediaries, who say that SMEs need support in the acquisition of new technologies? Or the entrepreneurs, who see much less need for such support? And, one may add, does it make sense to spend money on supporting companies, if their leadership sees no need for support? If no support is needed, the money will be wasted; but if support is needed and the leadership of the company does not understand this, the money will be wasted as well. Why spend public money on companies with failing leadership? Such companies will not survive anyway. It is part of the dynamics of an economy that the life expectancy of companies and especially of small companies is not eternal. Before concluding, however, that all actions in the field of innovation support and technology transfer can be eliminated, it is useful to return to our interviews with the Flemish entrepreneurs. It is true that they saw less need for support than the intermediaries, but they did not say that there was no need for action.

- They did not see a great need for an expansion of the existing technological infrastructure, but they would be pleased if the infrastructure became more accessible and above all less complex. It should be noted that the people complaining about complexity of the infrastructure are the same who often know only part of it – and many of them have never actually tested the accessibility. Nevertheless, all parties appear to agree that some streamlining and maybe better marketing of the infrastructure would be useful.
- Opinions are strongly divided concerning the need for financial support for innovation. Some entrepreneurs argue that a real entrepreneur with a good project will always find a financier. Others see a real problem here, but would prefer fiscal measures supporting innovation instead of subsidies for innovation projects. Subsidies are seen as something for large companies, which have the capability to deal with the bureaucracy of applying for subsidies (whereas fiscal measures could be left to the accountant and the bank). Others again would favour a well functioning venture capital market. Flanders does not have an

adequately functioning venture capital market at the moment and the fiscal regime appears to be adverse to investing in start-up companies.

• Most importantly, the interviews showed clearly that, in the eyes of the entrepreneurs, innovation in SMEs is not just and not mainly a question of technology. Many SMEs have been started by entrepreneurs with considerable technological competence in a certain field. Their short-comings – and therefore reasons for failing in innovation – are to be found in the field of marketing, general management and organizational competencies or knowledge of legal arrangements. Some entrepreneurs would favour government support for advisory services for SMEs in these more generic fields of business administration. And indeed, if awareness of technology is less of a problem than an understanding of marketing, why would government support of innovation be limited to technology transfer? In the neighbouring country The Netherlands, the so-called innovation centres, which were set up in the late 1980s to support innovation in SMEs, were recently merged with centres providing general 'first line' business services to SMEs. Setting up a similar network of support centres – or asking existing intermediaries to set up such services – would probably be helpful in Flanders too.

7.6   EPILOGUE

In the summer of 1997, the Flemish government published a white paper outlining its policies in support of technological innovation (Van den Brande, 1997). The white paper differentiates between economic innovation and technological innovation. Economic innovation consists of 'all activities in which existing and/or new elements of knowledge are creatively applied or combined for the improvement of existing or the development and introduc-tion of new products and services, processes, or organizational methods, thereby realizing or maintaining added value' (Van den Brande, 1997, p. 14). The white paper emphasizes that technological innovation covers only a part of economic innovation. It concerns 'only those innovations in which scientific-technological research and development or the creative application of technologies play an essential role' (ibid.). The white paper then concentrates on technological innovation. Because of this focus, the point that most SMEs may need support for innovation in other areas than technology receives only very limited attention. The government argues on the contrary that it wants to start the construction of a co-ordinated policy in support of innovation in the admittedly limited field of technological innovation. It notes that Flanders has an excellent research infrastructure and a well-developed set of intermediary institutions, which may require some streamlining. The white paper then concentrates on the role of the Flemish Institute for Scientific and Technological Research in Industry (IWT), which will play a central role in all government efforts to support technological innovation in Flanders. As noted above (section 7.2), the IWT is especially focused on the evaluation of project proposals for technological research and to a lesser extent on technology transfer. Obviously, the IWT can play an important role in technological innovation, but it is not clear that it can be a good starting point for a policy supporting 'economic innovation'. For most SMEs, the IWT is too much technology-centred and far removed from their everyday concerns. From that perspective, the construction of a Flemish policy in support of innovation in SMEs has not yet started.

NOTES

1. This paper is based on work done under contract for the Flemish government and the European Commission within the framework of the RITTS Programme (Regional Innovation and Technology Transfer Strategies and Infrastructures). Partners in the project were the Maastricht Economic Research Institute on Innovation and Technology MERIT (co-ordination), the Vlerick School of Management, and the Study Centre on SMEs of the Catholic University of Brussels. The project was documented in two reports: Cobbenhagen *et al.* (eds) (1996a) and Cobbenhagen *et al.* (1996b).
2. In a try-out with several versions of the methodology in different companies, it was established that it was necessary to introduce our own focus fairly early into the interview in order to avoid uneasiness on the part of the respondents ('where is this leading up to') as well as annoying repetitions in later stages of the interview.

REFERENCES

Bartels, C.P.A. (1993), 'Interventies in de kennisindustrie', in: *Economisch Statistische Berichten*, **78**, pp. 840–44.

Brande, L. Van den (1997), *Memorie van toelichting bij het ontwerp van decreet betreffende het voeren van een beleid ter aanmoediging van de technologische innovatie*, Brussels.

Cannell, W. and B. Dankbaar (eds) (1996), *Technology Management and Public Policy in the European Union*, Oxford: Oxford University Press.

Cobbenhagen, J., B. Dankbaar and A. Wolters (eds) (1996a), *De Vlaamse technologische infrastructuur vanuit de KMO-optiek bekeken. Rapportage fase 1 van het RITTS project Vlaanderen*, UPM, Maastricht.

Cobbenhagen, J., B. Dankbaar and A. Wolters (1996b), *Kiezen voor innovativiteit. Beleidsaanbevelingen voor een KMO-gericht innovatieweefsel in Vlaanderen, eindraportage van het RITTS project Vlaanderen*, MERIT, Maastricht.

Dankbaar, B. (1998), 'Technology management in technology-contingent SMEs', *International Journal of Technology Management*, **15** (1/2), pp. 70–81.

Debackere, K. and I. Fleurent(1994), *Resultaten van de Eerste Innovatie-Enquête in Vlaanderen, Onderzoeksrapport opgemaakt in opdracht van het IWT*, Katholieke Universiteit Leuven, Leuven.

Fransella, F. and D. Bannister (1977), *A Manual for Repertory Grid Technique*, London: Academic Press.

Huff, A.S. (ed.) (1990), *Mapping Strategic Thought*, Chichester: John Wiley & Sons.

Kelly, G.A. (1955), *The Psychology of Personal Constructs*, New York: Norton & Company.

Meijden, R. Van der and D. Jacobs (1995), 'Waar haalt het MKB zijn kennis vandaan?', *Economisch Statistische Berichten*, **80**, pp. 93-6.

Piore, M. and C. Sabel (1984), *The Second Industrial Divide*, New York: Basic Books.

Porter, M.E. (1990), *The Competitive Advantage of Nations*, New York: The Free Press.

PART THREE

Learning and Collaboration in Practice

8. Learning, Innovation and Proximity: An Empirical Exploration of Patterns of Learning: a Case Study

**Leon Oerlemans[1], Marius Meeus[1]
and Frans Boekema[2]**

8.1 INTRODUCTION

A growing body of theoretical research is addressing the importance of learning in the organizational and technological renewal of firms, and therefore in their efforts to improve competitiveness (Daft and Huber, 1987; Levitt and March, 1988; Huber, 1991; Dodgson, 1993; Blackler, 1995; Dodgson, 1996). In these discussions, regions are thought to have important features for facilitating innovation too (Florida, 1995; Cooke *et al.*, 1997; Morgan, 1997). This paper reviews literature on organizational learning and networks, learning regions as systems of innovation, and the role of proximity in the transfer of information and knowledge.

Literature on organizational learning and regional systems of innovation takes as a point of departure the embeddedness or relational perspective on innovation. Moreover, in studies on proximity the existence of embeddedness is often taken for granted. But, is embeddedness always as important for innovation as it is assumed to be? And is proximity really of importance in systems of innovations? In this paper, these questions are explored empirically. After a brief discussion of theoretical literature on organizational learning, economic networks, and spatial proximity, the paper focuses on the empirical exploration of patterns of learning in a specific Dutch region. Learning organizations are depicted as problem-solving actors. In coping with innovation problems, actors participate in different kinds of networks. Finally, the spatial dimension of these networks is investigated.

8.2 ORGANIZATIONAL LEARNING AND ECONOMIC NETWORKS

Conceptions of organizational learning are omnipresent. Not only has organizational theory addressed the issue, but a range of other academic disciplines (for example, industrial economics, strategic management, and psychology) have also studied it. A number of reasons can be suggested why the study of organizational learning is so fashionable at present (Dodgson, 1993). First, learning is seen as a key to competitiveness. Learning enables organizations to develop structures and systems that are more adaptable and responsive to change. Second, and partly related, is the deep influence that rapid technological change has on organizations. There is an increasing need for firms to learn to do things in a new, and often drastically different, way. Third, the concept of learning has a broad analytical value.

Both within and between disciplines there is rarely any agreement as to what learning is, and how it occurs. Various fields of literature tend to examine the outcomes of learning, rather than inquire as to what learning actually is and how these outcomes are achieved. Learning, in the sense it is used here, relates to firms, and comprises both processes and outcomes. In general terms (Huber, 1991), someone/something learns if the range of its potential behaviours is changed through the processing of information. More specifically for organizations, it can be described (Dodgson, 1996) as the ways firms build, supplement, and organize knowledge and routines around their competences and within their cultures, and adapt and develop organizational efficiency by improving the use of these competences. Competences are the focused combination of resources within a firm, which define its business activities and comparative advantage. This definition of organizational learning contains a number of important assumptions (Dodgson, 1993):

- Learning has positive consequences even though the outcomes of learning may be negative. Here, it is important to note that firms learn by making mistakes and solving problems. Morgan (1997) also stresses the problem-solving capacity of learning organizations.
- Although learning is based on individuals in the work-force of the firm, it is assumed that firms can learn.
- Learning occurs throughout all the activities of the firm. It occurs at different speeds and levels. Encouraging and co-ordinating the variety of interactions in learning is a key organizational task.

How do firms learn? A major mechanism by which firms learn about technology is through their internal R&D efforts. They also learn, of course, from a wide range of other internal functions, particularly from marketing and manufacturing and from the interactive interactions between these functions. Furthermore, learning has both an 'internal' and 'external' component. External links, with customers, suppliers, and other sources of information and knowledge, are critical in assisting a firm's learning processes.

The argument that external links are important for firms as proposed by literature on organizational learning, can also be found in literature on economic networks. The main difference between these two bodies of literature is that in the former the accent is on the importance of these links for the 'learning processes' of firms, whereas in the latter the emphasis is on the formation of network structures and their 'impact on the innovation process'. The network structures enable innovating firms to perform in a more efficient way.

The economics network approach, especially as developed by Håkansson (1987, 1989, 1992, and 1993) and Håkansson and Snehota (1995), provides us with a framework to analyse the relationship between learning, innovation and networks. Håkansson's economic network model contains three main elements: actors, activities, and resources. Actors perform activities and possess or control resources. They have a certain, but limited, knowledge of the resources they use and the activities they perform. Their main goal is to increase their control of the network. Actors in networks can be studied at different levels, from individuals to groups of firms. Two main types of activities are distinguished in the network model: transformation and trans-action activities. Both are related to resources because they change (transform) or exchange (transact) resources through the use of other resources. Transformation activities are performed by one actor and are characterized by the fact that a resource is improved by combining it with other resources. Transaction activities link the transformation activities of the different actors. These exchanges result in the development of economic (network) relations between actors. There are several types of resource: physical (machines, raw materials, and components), financial and human (labour, knowledge, and relations). Furthermore, resources can be classified according to the degree of organizational control. In the case of internal resources the firm has hierarchical control. External resource providers control external resources. As a consequence, resources are heterogeneous, i.e. their (economic) value depends on the other resources with which they are combined.

Despite Håkansson's claim that resources or knowledge bases are heterogeneous, and internal and external, he does not specify which bases he is referring to. If we assume that innovation is a knowledge-intensive process, we must determine which 'knowledge bases' (Dosi, 1988, p. 1126) innovators can use. Smith (1995, pp. 78–81) systematizes the attributes of, what he calls, a 'modern view' on technological knowledge. One of these attributes is that technological knowledge is differentiated and multi-layered. At least three different knowledge bases can be discerned. First, there is the general (scientific) knowledge base. This base is highly differentiated internally and of varying relevance for industrial production and innovation. Secondly, knowledge bases exist at the level of the industry or product field and entail shared understandings of technical functions, performance characteristics, use of materials, and so on, for products and processes. This knowledge and these practices shape the performance of firms in an industry. Thirdly, the knowledge bases of firms are highly localized and specific. They tend to comprise one or more technologies and practices that they understand well and that form the basis of their competitive position. This firm-specific knowledge base is not only technical, but also concerns the way in which technical processes are interwoven with other firm activities. These include identifying market opportunities, financing, purchasing, and marketing new products and processes.

The fact that knowledge bases of (industrial) firms are multi-layered has two important consequences for the use of Håkansson's economic network model. Firstly, it means that although individual innovating firms are competent in specific areas, their competence is nonetheless limited. In other words, innovating firms use their specific knowledge bases to innovate but they can easily run into problems. The solution of these problems may lie outside their area of expertise. Therefore, they must be able to access and use new internally and/or externally generated knowledge (learning) to solve these problems. Secondly, the multi-layered and heterogeneous nature of knowledge bases makes it necessary to distinguish several actors and institutions inside and outside the firm in which knowledge is embodied. Internal resources are embodied in the transformation (R&D, production) and transaction (purchase, marketing/sales) functions of the firm. Outside the firm, at least three groups of actors can be distinguished: the public and private knowledge infrastructure, and the production chain. The public knowledge infrastructure consists of organizations such as universities and colleges for professional and vocational training. These knowledge bases are mainly of a general (scientific) kind. Trade organizations, consultants, and intermediaries such as Chambers of Commerce and regional Innovation Centres populate the private knowledge infrastructure. The first two have technological knowledge mainly related to the industry or product field. The last two can be seen as information brokers. They are able to give general and specific information on innovation and business related issues, but they are also able to bring parties into contact with each other. The third and last group is called the production chain. Suppliers, buyers, and other firms such as competitors are part of this group. The technological knowledge embodied in these actors is also mainly related to the industry and product field.

The linking of learning, innovation, and networks hinges on the heterogeneity of resources and resource mobilization. According to Håkansson (1993), the effects of heterogeneity are that knowledge and learning become important. How should the firm handle these heterogeneous resources? In answer to this question, Håkansson cites Alchian & Demsetz (1972, p. 793) who state that 'efficient production using heterogeneous resources is not a result of having better resources, but knowing more accurately the relative performance of the resources'. In other words, it is not only necessary to have resources, but also to know how to use them.

This knowledge can be acquired in two ways: internally and/or externally. Learning to use internal resources can be accomplished in several different ways, for example through R&D activities or learning by using or doing. The external mobilization of resources can be labelled 'learning by interacting' (Lundvall, 1988, p. 362), that is, firms can use the knowledge and experience of other economic actors.

To make use of external resources, firms need to exist within structures that make these learning processes possible and efficient. According to Håkansson, economic network relations produce structures characterized by stability and variety. First, scarce external resources are more easily mobilized through stable relations with other economic actors. Second, stable relations in networks enable innovating firms to gather knowledge and to learn how to use heterogeneous resources innovatively and efficiently from other actors. Third, the stability of economic network structures provides a basis for variety. This variety offers new opportunities for innovation.[3]

The economic network approach makes it clear that firms can supplement their innovation process by using external resources. They can acquire knowledge supporting their innovation processes, through the use of their economic network relations.

Although the relational view on learning and innovation processes is important in the organizational learning literature and in the economic network approach, the spatial dimension is often left implicit. So, in order to focus on the link between learning, innovation, and proximity, these literatures have to be connected. This link can be found in the work of Lundvall on systems of innovation and in the work of Maillat on 'milieux innovateurs'.

8.3   SYSTEMS OF INNOVATION, 'MILIEUX INNOVATEURS' AND PROXIMITY

To make this link clear, one must go into the concept of RIS. A RIS can be divided into three parts that make up the term: Regional, Innovation and

System. Before discussing the regional or spatial dimension, we shall first explore the concept of the innovation system.

Innovation can be defined as the process by which firms master and put into practice product designs and manufacturing processes that are new to them (Nelson and Rosenberg, 1993). Defined in this way, it is clear that innovation is a process. In this process new knowledge or new combinations of old knowledge are embodied in products and production processes and possibly introduced into the economy. Put in a simple way, innovation is the result of learning processes. Learning leads to new knowledge and firms use this knowledge in an attempt to improve products and production processes. As Lundvall (1992) stated, there is now growing support for the view that innovation is an interactive or a relational process: between firms and the knowledge infrastructure, between the different functions within the firm, or between users and producers. The interactive characteristics of the innovation process are the link with organizational learning.

In system theory, a system consists of a number of discrete elements and the relationships between them. A system of innovation therefore comprises elements of importance to innovation and the relationships amongst them. Florida (1995) describes the basic elements of a system of innovation: (1) a manufacturing infrastructure, (2) a human infrastructure, (3) a physical and communications infrastructure, (4) a capital allocation system and financial market. These infrastructures can facilitate the innovation processes of firms.

The relationships between the elements in a system of innovation are the linkages that can be specified in terms of flows of knowledge and information, flows of investment funding, flows of authority and other arrangements such as networks, clubs, and partnerships. As Cooke *et al.* (1997) state, these linkages or interactions are clearly a social process in which institutions are of importance. Consequently, innovation is shaped by a variety of institutional routines and social conventions (Morgan, 1997).

What is the regional or spatial dimension of these systems of innovation? In theoretical literatures several answers to this question are proposed. One of these answers refers to the relation between proximity and the type of knowledge exchanged (Storper and Harrison, 1992; Cooke *et al.*, 1997). Knowledge is thought to be partly codified and primarily tacit. The argument is that tacit knowledge is highly personal and specific, hence it is not easily codified and communicated. Learning organizations interact with their environment. This has become essential as more and more firms externalize business functions. Where externalization involves interactions at great distances, codified knowledge can be exchanged reasonably satisfactorily. But innovation is intimately bound up with tacit knowledge exchange. This is difficult to achieve at a distance. It is of importance to understand why regional systems of innovation are a valuable feature of innovation-based competitive advantage.

A similar line of thought is developed by Lundvall (1992), who studies the relationship between the character of technological change and the spatial interactions. Three types of technological change are discerned, namely stationary technology, incremental innovation, and radical innovation that are each associated with specific patterns of spatial interaction between users and producers.

In the case of stationary technology, the technical opportunities as well as the needs of users are fairly constant. There are available norms, standards, and terminologies giving a near complete description of the technology involved. In other words, knowledge is highly codified. Such a high degree of codification means that communication between users and producers can be performed over long distances. If this is the case, industries virtually become footloose.

For incremental innovation, codes and channels of communication must be flexible in order to include technological opportunities and changing user needs. Recurrent changes in product specifications, functions, and qualities of artefacts constrain standardization. Consequently, codification of knowledge is more difficult. This means that messages are relatively complex and information cannot easily be translated. In this case space will play a role. The proximity of advanced users plays an important role in the adaptation process of an artefact to local conditions. Such industries, often a part of national industrial complexes, or clusters, are not footloose. Comparative advantages are often based on spatial proximity.

In the case of radical innovation, codes developed to communicate a constant, or a gradually changing, technology become inadequate. Producers who follow a given technological trajectory will have difficulties in evaluating the potentials of the new paradigm. Users will have difficulties in decoding the communications coming from producers, developing new products built according to the new paradigm. The lack of standard criteria for sorting out what is the best paradigm implies that 'subjective' elements in the user–producer relationships – like mutual trust and even personal friendship – will become important. These subjective elements are not easily shared across regional borders. So, here spatial proximity is extremely important for user–producer interaction.

In sum, the more radical the process of technological innovation, the less codified knowledge is. The more tacit the knowledge communicated, the more important is spatial proximity between user and producer. So, there is a positive relationship between the level of tacitness of knowledge and the importance of spatial proximity.

A comparable line of thought on the relationship between innovation and proximity is developed in the '*milieux innovateurs*' approach. The work of Maillat (1991) is of particular interest. Maillat argues that there are links between some features of the innovation process and the local environment. The importance of the local environment for the innovation process depends on the type of innovation involved. In addition, the innovation strategies applied by firms influence the character of the relation with the environment.

Regarding the type of innovation, the local environment is of little importance for firms developing incremental innovations. The resources needed for this kind of innovation are easily found within the firm. Firms with radical innovations develop more links with the local environment. Mostly, external resources are also needed to realize this type of innovation.

Maillat also postulates relations between the type of innovation strategy and the local environment. He distinguishes two kind of strategies: the exploitation of an already existing technological trajectory and 'technology creation'. In the first case, innovation is a process in which an already existing technology is used. For firms using this innovation strategy, the local environment is 'an external datum whence the firm derived its inputs' (Maillat, 1991, p. 111). In the second case, the local environment is an essential part of the innovation process of the firm. Because the outcomes of this kind of innovation are uncertain or even unknown, Maillat argues (1991, p. 111):

> indeed, the creation of technologies presupposes that the environment becomes an essential component of innovation, that these various resources be used and combined to generate a new form of localised production organisation. The enterprise is then no longer isolated in a territory which represents to it only an external component, it helps to create its environment by setting up a network of partnership-style relations, both with other firms ... and with public and private training and research centres, technology transfer centres and local authorities.

If we compare the lines of reasoning of Lundvall and Maillat some differences and similarities come to the fore. The main difference between Lundvall and Maillat concerns the assumed links between the characteristics of the innovation process and proximity. Lundvall stresses the interaction component in the system of innovation, that is, the relation between the nature of the knowledge exchanged and proximity. Moreover, Lundvall focuses on a specific kind of relation, namely between users and producers. Maillat, on the other hand, takes a more resource-based view on the relation between innovation and space. Depending on the type of innovation or strategy involved, other or more (external) resources are needed. The local environment is mainly viewed as a resource base, but relations can develop between a wide variety of (local) actors. Both assume a similar relation between innovation and proximity. In short, they assume that the more radical innovations are, the more important proximity is. Although Lundvall and Maillat differ in their opinion about the relation between incremental innovation and space, they agree on the relation between radical innovation and proximity. In our empirical section about the relation between innovation and proximity, we return to these issues.

8.4   RESEARCH QUESTIONS

The main aim of this paper is an empirical exploration of patterns of learning in a specific Dutch region. Answers are sought for the research questions mentioned below:

1.   If learning organizations are depicted as problem-solving actors, it is obvious to assume a relation between the number of innovation problems and the results of innovations. So, to what extent do innovation problems influence innovation results?
2.   Learning has both an internal and external component. To what extent do internal and external knowledge bases as elements of the system of innovation contribute to the results of innovations?
3.   Organizations learn by coping with (innovation) problems. We assume that different problem levels of the innovation process are associated with different patterns of learning. This raises the following question: To what extent are the relations between internal and external contributions on the one hand, and the results of innovation on the other, influenced by different levels of innovation problems?
4.   Innovating organizations learn through their external relations. Proximity is thought to be of importance in these learning processes. Is proximity indeed of importance in these innovative relations?

8.5   METHOD

Our study used a mailed questionnaire to obtain information on innovation processes from manufacturing and industrial firms with five or more employees in the region of North Brabant (a province in the southern part of the Netherlands). The data gathering took place between December 1992 and January 1993.

The data was collected in one of the most industrialized regions in the Netherlands. In 1992, the total number of jobs in manufacturing was roughly 210,000; the manufacturing sector share of employment was 28.8 per cent (19.5 per cent for the Netherlands).

The population of firms in the region consists of a mix of small, medium, and large enterprises. Furthermore, the manufacturing sector has a relatively high R&D and export performance (Meeus and Oerlemans, 1995). Because technological activity is an important issue in this paper, industrial firms were grouped according to Pavitt's taxonomy (1984). Oerlemans (1996) applied his criteria to the responding firms.[4]

Table 8.1 Population and sample divided into Pavitt sectors

Pavitt sector	Population	% population	% sample
Supplier dominated	1,028	33.5	25.7
Scale intensive	1,261	41.1	36.1
Specialized suppliers	417	13.6	21.4
Science based	363	11.8	16.8
Total	3,069	100	100

Table 8.1 shows that the sample is a fairly reliable representation of the population of industrial firms in the region of North Brabant. The maximum deviation between the proportions in the population and in the usable response is within 8 percentage points. The mean deviation between the percentages in the sample and in the response is 6.4 percentage points.

8.6 INNOVATION PROBLEMS AND INNOVATION RESULTS

For our first research question the model depicted in Figure 8.1 is used as our model of analysis. As was stated before, we expect that more innovation problems are associated with poorer results of innovation.

The dependent variable in this model is 'results of innovation'. It contains a count of the number of performance improvements due to product and process innovations (see Table 8.2) achieved by a firm during the period 1987–1992.[5] This variable is calculated as the sum of the scores of the items divided by 8. A higher score indicates better innovative performance. Four independent variables were used. Two of them indicate latent knowledge deficiencies: LKD1 and LKD2. LKD1 measures the number of innovation problems distinguished by their causes (for example, exceeding time schedules, bad timing, or insufficient marketing efforts). The variable LKD2 indicates the number of stages in the innovation process that were problematic

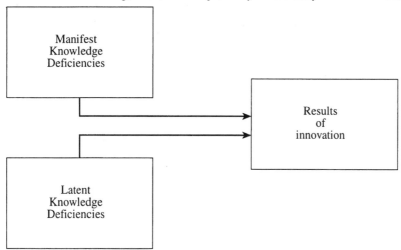

Figure 8.1   Knowledge deficiencies and results of innovation

(for example, economic or technical feasibility). Higher values of these variables signify more innovation problems or more problematic stages in the innovation process, respectively. These variables are labelled latent knowledge deficiencies because we assume that real or manifest knowledge deficiencies are hidden behind the innovation problems mentioned by firms. After all, problems would not occur if the knowledge bases of the firms were sufficient in quantitative and qualitative terms.

The two other independent variables are labelled manifest knowledge deficiencies. On the one hand it concerns shortages of skilled workers, and the lack of technical knowledge on the other. Both variables are coded as dummies. The value 1 is assigned if these knowledge deficiencies constrain innovative activity. If this is not the case, the value of the variables is 0.

Using multiple regression analysis, the relationship between the dependent and the independent variables is investigated. The result of this analysis is presented in Table 8.3.

The results of the estimation only signify a partial confirmation of our expectations. Only the variables 'shortages of skilled workers' and 'lack of technical knowledge' show the expected negative relationship with innovation results. In other words, only variables indicating manifest knowledge deficiencies have an impact on innovative performance.

The percentage of variance explained of the estimation is extremely low (3 per cent). Moreover, the magnitude of the beta coefficients is small and their statistical significance is poor. So, it can be concluded that the obvious assumption regarding the negative relationship between innovation problems and innovative performance is not empirically obvious at all.

Table 8.2   Measurements of the variables used for research question 1

Variable	Descriptions	Indicator
	Dependent variable	
IR	Innovation results	Product and/or process innovations resulted in: ● cost price reduction ● quality improvement of products or processes ● increased production capacity ● delivery time improvement ● sales increase ● profit increase
	Independent variables	
LKD1	Number of innovation problems by nature (latent knowledge deficiency)	● exceeding time planning ● product deficiencies ● technical production deficiencies ● exceeding budgets ● bad timing ● wrong partners ● reaction of competitors ● insufficient market introduction efforts
LKD2	Number of innovation problems by stage (latent knowledge deficiency)	● idea formation ● economic feasibility ● technical feasibility ● technical realization ● implementation ● introduction and production
MKD	Manifest knowledge deficiencies	1. Shortage of skilled workers (dummy) 2. Lack of technical knowledge (dummy)

Our analysis shows that latent knowledge deficiencies – the problems innovating firms encountered in the period 1987–1992 – did not constrain their innovation results. Our interpretation of these results is that innovating firms,

Table 8.3   OLS estimates with innovation results as the dependent variable
and latent and manifest knowledge deficiencies as independent
variables

Independent variables	Beta
Latent knowledge deficiencies:	
LKD1	0.04
LKD2	0.06
Manifest knowledge deficiencies:	
Shortage of skilled workers	−0.10
Lack of technical knowledge	−0.11
R^2	0.03
Adj. R^2	0.02
F value	2.21
Sign. F	0.068

however difficult it may be, are able to produce positive innovation outcomes.
As learning organizations, they are capable of solving their problems. In the
light of this interpretation the question emerges as to how these firms solve
their problems and where they obtain the necessary resources.

8.7   COPING WITH KNOWLEDGE DEFICIENCIES: THE USE OF INTERNAL AND EXTERNAL KNOWLEDGE BASES

Our second and third research question concern the relationships between the
use of internal and external knowledge bases as elements of the system of
innovation, and their impact on the innovative performance of firms. The
conceptual model in Figure 8.2 is used to answer these questions. The model
can be considered an empirical application of Håkansson's economic network
model.

Again the variable 'innovation results' is used as the dependent variable.
Furthermore, six independent variables are included in our analyses (see Table
8.4). Two of them describe the use of internal knowledge bases (transformation (TF) and transaction (TA) function of the firm). Three external
knowledge bases are discerned: public (EC1), private (EC2), and business

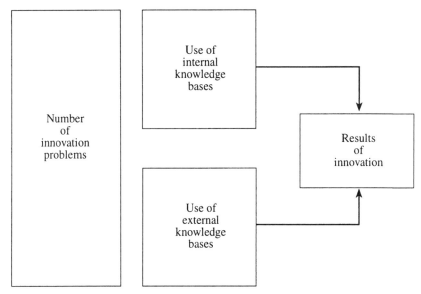

Figure 8.2   The use of internal and external knowledge bases and results of innovation

(EC3) knowledge bases. These five variables are measured in the same way. Firms were asked how often in the past five years external organizations thought up ideas for, or made an important contribution to, the realization of innovations.[6] Higher values of these variables indicate a more intensive use of the knowledge base involved. The sixth independent variable is 'technology policy'. It describes the total number of technology policy instruments used by a firm and can be interpreted as an external financial resource stimulating innovation provided by a government, and being part of the national system of innovation. The higher the score on this variable, the more technology policy instruments are used. The number of innovation problems (LKD1) is used as a moderating variable.[7] With a rank procedure, innovating firms are divided into three subgroups: firms with low, medium, and high levels of innovation problems. In this way, it is possible to make separate estimations for subgroups.

In Table 8.4, different groups of actors who influence the innovation process were distinguished on theoretical grounds. Subsequently, the question was addressed whether these theoretical dimensions also exist empirically. In order to answer this question, factor analysis was applied which resulted in the three factors presented in Table 8.5.[8]

Factors EC1–EC3 represent contributions to the innovation process by the public and private knowledge infrastructure, and the production chain. In

Table 8.4   Measurement of variables used for research questions 2 and 3

Variable	Description	Indicators
	Moderating variable	
LKD1	Number of innovation problems	see Table 8.2
	Dependent variable	
IR	Innovation results	see Table 8.2
	Independent variables	
TF	Use of knowledge base of the transformation function	• R&D function • Production function
TA	Use of the knowledge base of the transaction function	• Marketing/sales function • Purchase function
EC1	Use of public knowledge bases	Contributions to the innovation process by (technical) universities and colleges for professional and vocational education
EC2	Use of private knowledge bases	Contributions to the innovation process by intermediaries (Innovation Centres and Chambers of Commerce) and the private knowledge infrastructure (trade organizations, National Centre of Applied Research [TNO], private consultants)
EC3	Use of business knowledge bases	Contributions to the innovation process by important buyers, suppliers, and competitors
TP	Technology policy	Number of technology policy instruments used by a firm

short, we can conclude that the results of this factor analysis empirically confirm the initial categorization. Factors EC1–EC3 were used as independent variables in further regression analyses.

Table 8.5   Results of factor analysis on the use of external knowledge bases

Factors and items	Factor coefficients	Labels of knowledge bases
Factor 1 (EC1):		
Technical universities	0.78	
Other universities	0.74	Contributions of the public
Colleges	0.74	knowledge infrastructure
MBO	0.58	
Factor 2 (EC2):		
Trade organizations	0.70	
Regional Innovation Centres	0.66	Contributions of private
Chambers of Commerce	0.66	knowledge infrastructure
National Centre of Applied Research (TNO)	0.59	
Consultants	0.49	
Factor 3 (EC3):		
Important buyers	0.73	Contributions of the
Important suppliers	0.72	production chain
Competitors	0.66	

To investigate research question 2 and 3, four OLS models were estimated, one for the total response and three for the different levels of innovation problems. Once more, estimations are produced using multivariate regression analysis with the model in Figure 8.2 as the point of departure. As can be seen in Table 8.6, all models are significant as indicated by the F-values and their levels of significance. The percentages of variance explained varies between 11 per cent for the model with firms having medium problem levels in their innovation process, and 27 per cent for the model with firms having a highly problematic innovation process.

The model that includes all responding firms shows that the use of both internal and external knowledge bases are positively related to results of innovation. The higher the contributions of the transformation function (internal knowledge base), the contributions of the private knowledge infrastructure and the production chain (external knowledge bases), the more positive the results of innovation. Therefore, the analysis shows that an additive combination of the use of internal and external knowledge bases results in a better innovative performance, stressing the importance of including network variables in the analysis of innovation.

Furthermore, it becomes clear that the estimations made for subgroups of

Table 8.6   *OLS estimates with innovation results as the dependent variable and the use of internal and external knowledge bases for the innovation process as independent variables: a comparison between different levels of innovation problems*

Independent variables	Problem levels in innovation process			TP (n = 216)
	Low (n = 54)	Medium (n = 60)	High (n = 145)	
Internal knowledge bases:				
Transformation (TF)	0.46***	−0.05	0.03	0.26****
Transaction (TA)	0.11	0.32**	0.21***	0.07
External knowledge bases:				
EC1	−0.12	−0.17	0.01	−0.02
EC2	0.16	0.18	0.22***	0.18**
EC3	0.21	0.02	0.37****	0.24****
TP	−0.05	−0.08	0.18***	0.10
R^2	0.22	0.11	0.27	0.19
Adj. R^2	0.20	0.08	0.25	0.17
F value	13.19	5.56	12.84	16.017
Sign. F	0.001	0.022	0.000	0.000

Notes:
* $p < 0.10$
** $p < 0.05$
*** $p < 0.01$
**** $p < 0.001$

firms distinguished by the number of innovation problems encountered differ strongly regarding the use of internal and external knowledge bases. Firms with a few innovation problems only use their internal transformation function to achieve better results. The second group, firms with medium problem levels, utilize the knowledge bases embodied in the transaction function to obtain a better innovative performance. The same is true for firms with high problem levels, the third group distinguished, though in this group the contributions of the private knowledge infrastructure, the production chain and the use of technology policy instruments are also positively related to innovative performance.

An interesting pattern emerges from these analyses. The more problems firms encounter in their innovation processes, the more these innovation firms take an external orientation. In other words, the system of innovation is especially of interest for firms with highly problematic innovation processes.

Next, it is interesting to examine which specific internal and external knowledge bases are positively related to the results of innovation. In order to perform this analysis, we used the individual items of the statistically significant independent variables and correlated them with results of innovation. As a measure of association we used the Spearman rank correlation. The coefficients and their significance are presented in Table 8.7.

For innovating firms with a low level of innovation problems, we see in particular that the contributions of the production function are positively correlated with the results of innovation. The R&D function is also of importance, but to a much lesser extent. The transaction function made

Table 8.7   Spearman rank correlations between the results of innovation and the use of specific internal and external knowledge bases

Level of innovation project problems		
Low	Medium	High
Items Transformation	*Items Transaction*	*Items Transaction:*
R&D (0.25*)	Purchase (0.38**)	Purchase (0.11)
Production (0.49***)	Marketing (0.17)	Marketing (0.13*)
		Items EC2:
		Trade organization (0.13)
		Innovation Centres (0.16*)
		Chamber of Commerce (0.01)
		TNO (0.15*)
		Consultants (0.22***)
		Items EC3:
		Important buyers (0.20**)
		Important suppliers (0.31***)
		Other firms (0.21**)

Notes:
* $p < 0.10$
** $p < 0.05$
*** $p < 0.01$

positive contributions to the results of innovation for firms with medium problem levels. Within this function, the contributions of the purchasing function to the innovation process proved to be positively related with results of innovation. The marketing function also has a positive tendency, but is not significant statistically. For firms with highly problematic innovation processes, the utilization of internal knowledge bases is not enough to solve their problems. They have to obtain external resources too. Consultants, buyers, other firms, but especially suppliers become involved in the innovation process of these firms.

Our empirical findings enable us to formulate two conclusions. First, our analyses make clear that the number of problems that firms encounter in their innovation process is a factor of importance. The patterns of relations and learning in the system of innovation are strongly influenced by the different problem levels. Second, Von Hippel's claim about the importance of buyers, the so-called lead-users, for the innovation process is differentiated. Important buyers are indeed making positive contributions, but it turns out that suppliers are even more influential.

Until now we have focused on patterns of relations and learning without paying attention to the spatial dimension of the system of innovation. In the next section, this issue is dealt with.

8.8   SPATIAL PROXIMITY IN THE SYSTEM OF INNOVATION

As was stated in the previous section, innovating firms learn through their external relations. Spatial proximity is thought to be of importance in these learning processes. Is proximity indeed of importance in these relations? To answer this fourth research question, three approaches are used. First, we investigate the spatial distribution of buyers and suppliers who influence the innovation process. In this way, we have an indication of the importance of localized ties within the (regional) system of innovation. Second, we look at a specific characteristic of these relations: the transfer of knowledge. As was argued by Lundvall, precisely this feature of interaction between actors in the system of innovation is thought to have an important effect on the spatial distribution of innovative relations. Third, we investigate the relation between radicalness of innovations and spatial proximity. This analysis is based on the arguments of Lundvall and Maillat regarding the relation between the type of innovation and proximity.

The variables used to answer research question 4 are presented in Table 8.8. First, an important remark has to be made. In this section, the analysis is focused on a specific group of relations of innovating firms. This pertains to

Table 8.8 Measurement of variables used for research question 4

Variable	Description	Indicators
TS	Type of supplier most important for innovation	(1) raw materials; (2) components; (3) machines & tools; (4) consultants
TB	Type of buyer most important for innovation	(1) consumer; (2) retail/wholesale; (3) industrial user
LS	Location supplier	(1) Southern part of the Netherlands;
LB	Location buyer	(2) Elsewhere in the Netherlands; (3) Abroad
KT	Knowledge transfer	(1) never; (2) sometimes; (3) regularly; (4) often; (5) always
TI	Type of innovation	(1) no innovations; (2) process innovation; (3) product innovation
LI	Level of innovation	(1) incremental; (2) radical

the relations with other economic actors that are, in the view of the innovating firm, most important to the innovation process. Six variables are used in the analysis.

In the previous section, it was shown that suppliers and buyers are especially important external knowledge bases for innovating firms. To study the role of these economic partners more in depth, we asked the innovating firm several questions regarding the specific type of actors involved and various features of their network relations. First, we asked what kind of supplier (TS) or buyer (TB) was most important for the innovation process. Four types of suppliers (TS) were distinguished: suppliers of raw materials, product parts and components, machines and tools, and consultants. As regards the most essential buyers for the innovation process, three types were discerned: consumers, retail/wholesale, and industrial users. Second, we asked the innovating firm to indicate the spatial location of the buyer or supplier involved. Three choices of response were provided: the southern part of the Netherlands, elsewhere in the Netherlands, and outside the Netherlands.[9] Third, the transfer of knowledge between the innovator and economic actors in the system of innovation is believed to have an important influence on the spatial embeddedness of relations in the system of innova-tion. Therefore, we asked the innovation firm to what extent knowledge transfers occurred between supplier and buyer on the one hand, and the innovating firm on the other. Fourth, the spatial distribution of buyers and suppliers is supposed to be influenced by the type and level of innovation produced by the innovating firm. Therefore, we asked questions about the type of innovations (product or process innovations) and the level of the innovations (incremental or radical) produced by the firms.

Let us first look at the spatial distribution of suppliers and buyers essential to the innovation process (Table 8.9). It is clear that suppliers of machines and tools are mentioned most often as the most important supplier contributing to the innovation process. Approximately 46 per cent (125/273) of the innovating firms named this type of supplier. Suppliers of product parts and components come second (about 29 per cent). Industrial users dominate the group of buyers influencing the innovation process. About 58 per cent of the innovating firms considers this type of buyer the most important for their innovation processes.

Table 8.9   Spatial distribution of suppliers and buyers essential to the innovation process

Type of supplier	Location of supplier		
	SN	EN	AB
Raw materials (n = 54)	29.6%	35.2%	35.2%
Components (n = 79)	43.0%	22.8%	34.2%
Machines (n = 125)	27.2%	36.0%	36.8%
Consultants (n = 15)	53.3%	46.7%	0.0%
Total (n = 273)	33.7%	32.6%	33.7%

Type of buyer	Location of buyer		
	SN	EN	AB
Consumer (n = 13)	38.5%	61.5%	0.0%
Retail/wholesale (n = 104)	26.9%	53.8%	19.2%
Industrial user (n = 160)	48.8%	26.3%	25.0%
Total (n = 277)	40.1%	38.3%	21.7%

Notes:
SN = Southern part of the Netherlands,
EN = Elsewhere in the Netherlands
AB = Abroad

With regard to the spatial distribution of the suppliers, it appears that they are more or less equally distributed over the three geographical areas distinguished. This means that one out of three suppliers is located in the southern part of the Netherlands. The relations with suppliers of product parts and components and consultants in particular show signs of spatial concentration. About 53 per cent of the consultants and 43 per cent of the suppliers of components and parts are located in the southern part of the Netherlands. However, for the largest group of important suppliers (machines and tools) proximity seems to be less important.

As can be seen in the lower part of Table 8.9, buyers who are prominent in the innovation process are more spatially concentrated than suppliers are. Approximately 40 per cent of these buyers are located in the proximity of the innovating firm. This percentage is even higher for industrial users. Nearly 50 per cent of this type of buyer is located in the southern part of the country.

It can be concluded from this analysis that the spatial dimension of innovative relations is indeed of importance. A large number of suppliers and buyers can be found in the proximity of the innovating firm. Our findings stress the importance of particular elements in the (regional) system of innovation for technologically active firms.

As was argued by Lundvall, the transfer of knowledge between actors in a system of innovation is supposed to be sensitive to geographical distance. Thus, the obvious choice is to investigate the relation between knowledge intensity of innovative relations on the one hand, and the spatial distribution of innovative relations on the other. The results of this analysis are presented in Table 8.10.

First, a comparison between relations with buyers and relations with suppliers regarding the extent of knowledge transfer shows that relations with suppliers are more knowledge intensive. Forty-two per cent of the firms that have innovative relations with suppliers state that deliveries of suppliers are 'often or always' associated with the transfer of knowledge. The percentage for the innovative relations with buyers is about 25 per cent.

Second, innovative relations with buyers and suppliers located in the southern part of the Netherlands are neither more nor less knowledge intensive than the relations with buyers and suppliers located in the two other geographical areas distinguished in our analysis. So, there seems to be no relation between the extent of knowledge transfer and the proximity of buyers and suppliers important for innovation.

Perhaps, this result has to do with the fact that we did not make a specification, as Lundvall and Maillat propose, of the character of the technological change involved. After all, a consequence of their line of reasoning is that the importance of proximity for innovation depends on the technological opportunities and the needs of users. Using Lundvall's ideas empirically, it is possible to formulate two expectations concerning the relation between the type and level of innovations and proximity.

In the case of firms with incremental process and product innovations, a large proportion of the innovative relations with suppliers and buyers should be found in the southern part of the Netherlands. Because of restrictions in the

Table 8.10   *Spatial distribution of suppliers and buyers essential to the innovation process and the extent of knowledge transfer*

Knowledge transfer	Location supplier			Total
	SN	EN	AB	
Sometimes	26.1%	25.3%	20.0%	23.8%
Regularly	29.3%	34.5%	38.9%	34.2%
Often	44.6%	40.2%	41.1%	42.0%

Knowledge transfer	Location buyer			Total
	SN	EN	AB	
Sometimes	35.4%	49.5%	38.3%	41.4%
Regularly	37.2%	29.5%	31.7%	33.1%
Often	27.4%	21.0%	20.0%	25.5%

Notes:
SN = Southern part of the Netherlands
EN = Elsewhere in the Netherlands
AB = Abroad

standardization process and the importance of tacit knowledge, proximity plays an important role in the process of the adaptation to local conditions of a product or process. If we apply the arguments of Maillat, the opposite should be the case. Due to the fact that the resource base of firms with incremental innovations is sufficient, the local environment is not important for these firms.

The role of proximity becomes even more important in the case of firms with radical product and process innovations. As a result of a lack of standard criteria for evaluating technological opportunities and user needs, so-called 'subjective' elements, like trust, become important. Subsequently, the majority of suppliers or buyers should be located in the proximity of the innovating firm.

The table shows that there are no differences between firms with incremental and radical process innovations with regard to the spatial distribution of suppliers central to their innovation process. The same is true for the relations of such firms with buyers. As regards firms with product innovations, some differences can be noted. Although the percentages of firms

Table 8.11 *Spatial distribution of suppliers and buyers essential to the innovation process: a comparison between types and levels of innovation*

Location of suppliers	Level of innovation			
	Process innovations (n = 230) (P^2 = 0.39, sign. = 0.823)		Product innovations (n = 214) (P^2 = 1.76, sign = 0.416)	
	Incr. (n = 187)	Rad. (n = 43)	Incr. (n = 164)	Rad. (n = 50)
SN	33.2%	32.6%	35.4%	34.0%
EN	34.2%	30.2%	29.9%	22.0%
AB	32.6%	37.2%	34.8%	44.0%
Location of buyers	Process innovations (n = 226) (P^2 = 0.13, sign. = 0.939)		Product innovations (n = 226) (P^2 = 2.18, sign. = 0.336)	
	Incr. (n = 178)	Rad. (n = 48)	Incr. (n = 164)	Rad. (n = 62)
SN	38.2%	35.4%	36.0%	25.8%
EN	37.6%	39.6%	40.2%	48.4%
AB	24.2%	25.0%	23.8%	25.8%

Notes:
SN = Southern part of the Netherlands
EN = Elsewhere in the Netherlands
AB = Abroad
Incr. = Incremental innovations
Rad. = Radical innovations

with suppliers located in the southern part of the Netherlands are nearly equal, firms with radical product innovations in particular, show a high percentage of connections with suppliers outside the Netherlands. A comparison of firms with incremental or radical product innovations and their relations with buyers shows that a relatively high proportion of the buyers of firms with incremental product innovations are located in the proximity of the innovator.

In sum, there are some differences between incremental and radical process or product innovators regarding the spatial distributions of their buyers and suppliers important for innovation, but the overall picture does not lead to a confirmation of Lundvall's and Maillat's ideas about the relation between the character of technical change and the interactions in space. The expected importance of proximity for firms with radical innovations in particular is not found.

8.9   CONCLUSIONS AND DISCUSSION

In this paper, learning organizations were depicted as problem-solving agents. The obvious negative relation between the number of innovation problems and results of innovation (question 1) was not confirmed. Our interpretation of this result was that learning organizations were able to cope with these problems in such a way that their innovation outcomes were not hampered.

Next, the ways in which firms coped with these innovation problems was investigated (questions 2 and 3). Using an empirical application of Håkansson's economic network model, evidence was found that a combination of the use of internal and external knowledge bases improved innovation results. So, the importance of the relational perspective on innovation processes was confirmed empirically. But, the estimations proved to be sensitive to the amount of innovation problems encountered by firms. Higher levels of innovation problems were associated with the utilization of more, and a more diverse set of, external knowledge bases contributing to the innovation process. These findings stress the fact that the embeddedness or the relational perspective on innovation should not always be taken for granted. The strong emphasis in present day literature on the importance of inter-organizational relations for the economic performance is mitigated by our empirical findings. The innovative performance of firms is not always influenced by the extent to which firms are embedded. More particularly, firms with low levels of innovation problems proved to be utilizing internal knowledge bases only.

Our findings concerning the importance of proximity in systems of innovation were somewhat puzzling. On the one hand, a large number of the innovative relations with buyers and suppliers most important to the innovation process were found in the proximity of the innovating actor. As a consequence of this result, one can conclude that proximity is indeed of importance. On the other hand, it turned out that the assumptions of Lundvall and Maillat were not confirmed. First, innovative relations with buyers and suppliers located in the southern part of the Netherlands were just as knowledge intensive as relations with buyers and suppliers located in other areas. Second, the expected importance of proximity especially for firms with radical product and process innovations was not found.

From these findings one can conclude that proximity is indeed of importance for the innovating firms in our research, but variables other than the one proposed by Lundvall and Maillat influence the spatial distribution of innovative relations in the system of innovation. Research by Oerlemans *et al.* (1998, pp. 36–43) has shown that firm characteristics, such as firm size, were better predictors of the spatial distribution of innovative relations, than the extent of knowledge transfer. Smaller firms were more spatially embedded than large firms. Such results indicate that the development stage that a firm is in has greater influence on its composition of spatial relations than the features of its innovation process. Therefore, future research should have a greater focus on the life cycle of the firm and its relation with spatial embeddedness.

NOTES

1. Faculty of Technology Management, Eindhoven University of Technology, P.O. Box 513, 5600 MB, Eindhoven, The Netherlands.
2. Faculty of Economics, Tilburg University, P.O. Box 90153, 5000 LE, Tilburg. Faculty of Policy Sciences, University of Nijmegen, P.O. 9108, 6500 KH, Nijmegen, The Netherlands.
3. The variety argument of Håkansson is a variation on Granovetter's idea of weak ties. In his famous article 'The Strength of Weak Ties' (1973), Granovetter argues that actors receive most new (innovative) information through their weak ties with other networks.
4. The taxonomy consists of four sectors

Pavitt sector	Typical industries
Supplier dominated	Textiles; Leather goods and footwear; Furniture; Paper and board; Printing
Scale intensive	Food; Metal products; Glass; Cement; Transport vehicles
Specialized suppliers	Machinery; Instruments; Opticals
Science based	Chemicals; Plastics; Electronics

5. Firms were asked to judge these performance improvements on a Likert scale with values ranging from (1) 'very little' to (5) 'very much'. The highest possible score of this compounded variable was 8, the lowest 0.
6. Firms were asked to judge the impact of these knowledge bases on the innovation process on a Likert scale with values ranging from (1) 'never' to (5) 'always'. Regarding the internal knowledge bases, we distinguished functions instead of departments because a large part of our population of firms consisted of SMEs.
7. In this analysis one of the two variables describing latent knowledge deficiencies is used as a moderating variable. The main reason for this is that the variable LKD1 gives us the best indication of the difficulties during the innovation process. In our view, the variation in problems is a better indicator for this level of difficulty than the stages of the innovation process in which they occur.
8. The three factors were found using a varimax rotated principal components analysis. The KMO measure of sampling adequacy was 0.767. Bartlett's Test of Sphericity was 1008.38 (sign. 0.0000). The cumulative percentage of variance explained was 51.5 per cent.
9. The southern part of the Netherlands is a region containing three provinces: Noord-Brabant, Zeeland, and Limburg.

REFERENCES

Alchian, A. and H. Demsetz (1972), 'Production, information costs, and economic organization', *American Economic Review*, **62** (5), pp. 777-95.

Blackler, F. (1995), 'Knowledge, knowledge work and organizations: an overview and interpretation', *Organization Studies*, **16** (6), pp. 1021-46.

Cooke, P., M. Gomez Uranga and G. Etxebarria (1997), 'Regional innovation systems: Institutional and organisations dimensions', *Research Policy*, (26), pp. 475-91.

Daft, R. and G. Huber (1987), 'How organizations learn: A communication framework', *Research in the Sociology of Organizations*, (5), pp. 1-16.

Dodgson, M. (1993), 'Organizational learning: a review of some literatures', *Organization Studies*, **14** (3), pp. 375-94.

Dodgson, M. (1996), 'Learning, trust and inter-firm technological linkages: some theoretical associations', in R. Coombs, A. Richards, P.P. Saviotti and V. Walsh (eds), *Technological Collaboration. The Dynamics of Cooperation in Industrial Innovation*, London: Routledge, pp. 54-75.

Dosi, G. (1988), 'Sources, procedures, and microeconomic effects of innovation', *Journal of Economic Literature*, **XXVI**, pp. 1120-71.

Florida, R. (1995), 'Toward the learning region', *Futures*, **27** (5), pp. 527-36.

Granovetter, M. (1973), 'The strength of weak ties', *American Journal of Sociology*, **78** (6), pp. 1360-80.

Gregersen, B. and B. Johnson (1997), 'Learning economies, innovation systems and European integration', *Regional Studies*, **31** (5), pp. 479-90.

Håkansson, H. (1987), *Industrial Technological Development: A Network Approach*, London: Croom Helm.

Håkansson, H. (1989), *Corporate Technological Behaviour: Co-operation and Networks*, London: Routledge.

Håkansson, H. (1992), 'Evolution processes in industrial networks', in B. Axelsson and G. Easton (eds), *Industrial Networks: A New View of Reality*, London: Routledge.

Håkansson, H. (1993), 'Networks as a mechanism to develop resources', in P. Beije, J. Groenewegen, O. Nuys (eds), *Networking in Dutch Industries*, Leuven/ Apeldoorn: Garant/SISWO, pp. 207-23.

Håkansson, H. and I. Snehota (1995), *Developing Relationships in Business Networks*, London: Routledge.

Hippel, E. von (1988), *The Sources of Innovation*, New York, Oxford: Oxford University Press.

Huber G.P. (1991), 'Organizational learning; the contributing process and the literatures', *Organizational Science*, **2** (1), pp. 88-115.

Katz, D. and R. Kahn (1966), *The Social Psychology of Organizations*, New York: John Wiley.

Levitt, B. and J. March (1988), 'Organizational learning', *Annual Review of Sociology*, (14), pp. 319-40.

Lundvall, B-Å. (1988), 'Innovation as an interactive process: from user-producer interaction to the national system of innovation', in G. Dosi, C. Freeman, R. Nelson, G. Silverberg and L. Soete (eds), *Technical Change and Economic Theory*, London: Pinter Publishers, pp. 349-69.

Lundvall, B-Å. (1992), 'User-producer relationships, national systems of innovation and internationalisation', in B-Å. Lundvall (ed.), *National Systems of Innovation: Towards a Theory of Innovation and Interactive Learning*, London: Pinter Publishers, pp. 45-67.

Maillat, D. (1991), 'The innovation process and the role of the milieu', in E. Bergman, G. Maier and F. Tödtling (eds), *Regions Reconsidered: Economic Networks, Innovation and Local Development in Industrialized Countries*, London/New York: Mansell Publishing Limited.

Meeus, M. and L. Oerlemans (1995), 'The competitiveness of firms in the region of North Brabant', in P. Beije and H. Nuys (eds), *The Dutch Diamond: The Usefulness of Porter in Analyzing Small Countries*, Leuven/Apeldoorn: Garant/SISWO, pp. 223–56.

Morgan, K. (1997), 'The learning region: institutions, innovation and regional renewal', in *Regional Studies*, **31** (5), pp. 491–503.

Nelson, R. and N. Rosenberg (1993), 'Technical innovation and national systems', in R. Nelson (ed.), *National Innovation Systems: A Comparative Analysis*, Oxford: Oxford University Press.

Oerlemans, L. (1996), *The Embedded Firm: Innovation in Industrial Networks (in Dutch)*, Tilburg: Tilburg University Press.

Oerlemans, L., M. Meeus and F. Boekema (1998), 'Innovation: some empirical explorations of spatial embeddedness', in J. van Dijk and F. Boekema (eds), *Innovation in Firms and Regions (in Dutch)*, Assen: Van Gorcum, pp. 31–61.

Pavitt, K. (1984), 'Sectoral patterns of technical change: towards a taxonomy and a theory', in *Research Policy*, **13** (6), pp. 343–74.

Smith, K. (1995), 'Interactions in knowledge systems: foundations, policy implications and empirical methods', in *STI Review*, (16), OECD, pp. 69–102.

Storper, M. and B. Harrison (1992), 'Flexibility, hierarchy and regional development: The changing structure of industrial production systems and their forms of governance in the 1990s', in *Research Policy*, (20), pp. 407–22.

9. Learning in Non-core Regions: Towards 'Intelligent Clusters'; Addressing Business and Regional Needs

Arnoud Lagendijk

9.1 INTRODUCTION

While the significance of learning-oriented agendas as crucial elements of a regional development policy is generally accepted, the practical implementation of such agendas remains an open issue. This bears particularly on non-core regions. More than core regions, these areas need appropriate policies to overcome obstacles to learning and to find new ways of mobilizing regional resources. While the direction and forms of such policies are still under discussion, there is already quite a pool of experience from which lessons can be drawn. In recent years, there has been a proliferation of policy initiatives targeting non-core regions, with particular emphasis on the development of SMEs. Many initiatives are geared to improving the innovative capacity and learning capabilities of SMEs, both through technology transfer and the facilitating of new forms of interaction among firms, and between firms and other regional agencies.

This chapter presents the results of a study on innovative forms of regional support for SME development in non-core regions, inspired by the 'cluster' concept. The study formed part of the European ADAPT project (CORE), in which research was carried out through direct regular contact with regional support agencies participating in the ADAPT programme. The main aim of the research programme was to discover how cluster-oriented forms of business support improve the way SMEs contribute to regional development. Both the dimensions of business learning and policy learning featured in the project. Since the focus is on practical forms of learning, this chapter will pay less attention to the regional knowledge infrastructure (which has been covered in Part I of this book).

The chapter is structured in four further parts. Section 9.2 introduces the main theoretical issues, followed by a section setting out the policy background and dilemmas. Section 9.4 introduces the methodology underlying the research proforma. Section 9.5 presents a summary of the case study results and is followed by the conclusion.

9.2 THE PERIPHERALITY DILEMMA IN A REGIONAL LEARNING AGENDA

While the term seems to be less in vogue than in previous decades, the problem of peripherality is still an actual and pressing issue in regional development. Over the last two decades, regional analysis has highlighted the factors underpinning the success of core regions and, even more impressively, the way in which certain regions have cast off their marginal position and turned into 'new industrial spaces'. What is implicit, and sometimes explicit, in much of the literature is that these cases present general role models for regional development. Following this idea of addressing peripherality, regions should emulate the example of Emilia-Romagna or Baden-Württemberg, while the most ambitious regions may find inspiration in Silicon Valley.

Examining the successes of these role models has obviously made a great contribution to the study of regional economic development. It has paved the way for a different approach to regional economic development, building on such concepts as the social embedding of economic activities, the role of proximity in interactive learning processes, the spatial embedding of innovation systems, and the significance of regional governance systems in building new associational forms of economic development (cf. Storper, 1997b; Healey, 1997). Altogether, a creative, institutionalist perspective of regional development has emerged with a strong appeal, not only to academic researchers, but also to the policy community. Indeed, one of the results of recent developments has been a fundamental change in the way regional development initiatives are designed and implemented, ushering in a new generation of regional policy. Key words of the new generation are the shaping of learning capabilities and 'relational assets' (Amin, 1999), associated, *inter alia*, with support to clusters of SMEs and the combining of public and private efforts into regional partnerships. One may add to this the notion of 'reflexive' knowledge, that is, the knowledge possessed by regional actors about the development and position of their own regional business system (Storper, 1997a; Gibbons *et al.*, 1994). Strategic regional development is increasingly reliant on the application of reflexive knowledge.

It is important that non-core regions, however, should treat 'role models' with great caution. The cultural and political embedding of regional economies is a crucial factor in improving the relational infrastructure of a region and accumulating reflexive knowledge (Camagni, 1991). Only when regional actors are able to open themselves to new forms of doing things, overcoming petty rivalries and developing some kind of collective strategic vision, does an agenda of building 'relational assets' stand a chance. For non-core regions, changing cultural and political habits and attitudes is often seen as the most difficult hurdle to overcome in breaking the chains of peripherality (Putnam, 1993; Grabher, 1991). This point applies, in particular, to the older industrial areas, which already exhibit strong traditions of economic organization. To quote Rehfeld (1994, p. 198): 'The question of economic restructuring does not only present itself as an economic problem, but also as a question of the appropriateness of the actual political and socio-cultural routine and strategies.' While the examination of role models may show the kind of 'soft' factors on which success is built, it teaches less about changing 'inappropriate' forms of culture.

Highlighting the deeper dimensions of change and learning also pinpoints the most controversial issue in the regional development debate, that of the 'locking in' of peripherality in cultural and political structures. The core question is to what extent, and at what level, regions are able to mould their socio-cultural fabric through institutional processes. One answer to this question is given by Sabel (1992, pp. 216–17) when he denounces any 'paralysing acceptance of history as destiny'. Sabel contends that trust and collaboration can be nurtured through the deliberate creation of dispute-resolving procedures and institutions. The common culture and historical binding of a local community might be revealed or 'discovered' by story-telling and networking between local actors in a more systematic way, creating what he calls 'studied trust'. The issue of the manipulation of under-lying social and cultural structures, however, remains highly controversial, as shown, for instance, by the heated discussions about the concept of 'social capital' (Ingham, 1996; Putnam, 1993).

Besides culture, there is another fundamental element of 'lock in' that bears on the issue of peripherality. Incentives to economic restructuring and learning agendas need not only to be facilitated by changes in routines and attitudes, but also to be triggered and pulled by an awareness of economic opportunities and strategic direction. This points to another, more structural, dimension of the peripherality problem, the lack of an existing basis of economic specialization to serve as a basis for future strengths and expansion. Indeed, for many non-core regions, even the more prosperous ones, the problem is that 'they do a lot of things without doing anything special' (Steiner, 1997, p. 19). In Steiner's view, specialization is therefore the only way to overcome the 'globalization trap', that is, outrunning the risk of being outcompeted across the board. For old industrial areas, finding new directions presents a major and continuing challenge to regional development. Hence, learning has a strong strategic element. Institutional capacity should be geared not only to increasing the orientation and interaction of regional actors towards learning, but also to frame learning processes in a strategic context.

Peripheral regions thus face a daunting development task. To put it briefly, they need to build parallel, but linked, trajectories in which subtle changes in orientation and behaviour at the micro (actor) and meso (organizational) level are combined with incentives to more structural changes at the meso-macro level. Fortunately, this observation is not just a theoretical one. The past two decades have seen a proliferation of innovative regional initiatives in which changes in micro/meso behaviour are pursued within a view to improving the regional economic structure and giving it a measure of specialization. This chapter will focus on one concept that has featured in these initiatives, that of 'clusters', as applied to the development of SMEs in the context of European regional development.

Cluster approaches are interpreted here as follows. Through drawing upon recent insights into the relationship between innovation and the relational aspects of the economy (Porter, 1990; Jacobs, 1997), cluster approaches are able to bring together a notion of economic restructuring at the macro-economic level with concepts of networks, 'governance' and systems of knowledge accumulation at the micro/meso level. Restructuring then refers to shaping or reshaping the regional specialization within a relational perspective, that is, with emphasis on the role of linkages between businesses and with the wider regional support infrastructure.

9.3 INTERTWINING POLICY AND BUSINESS LEARNING: TOWARDS INTEGRAL AND CLUSTER-ORIENTED SUPPORT

This study will focus on cluster initiatives in the context of regional support to local firms, with special reference to SMEs. Adopting a cluster perspective presents a major challenge to policy makers. Changing routines, building trust and 'relational assets', as well as framing business support in a strategic context cannot be achieved overnight. Indeed, it is not only business behaviour which needs to become more learning-oriented in a relational context, policy-making itself also needs to change its own routines and perspectives on the basis of reflexive knowledge about its own practices. This section will therefore start by setting out the current state of business support to SMEs and indicate how regional cluster approaches can bring improvements. The role of clusters will be formalized in a regional competitiveness model, in which a key role is played by the concept of 'club goods'. Defined as locally rooted assets improving business performance, 'club goods' reflect the link between business dynamics and regional development. More specifically, 'club goods' occupy a bridge position between the business support structure and client groups of related businesses. Hence, 'club goods' are crucial to the intertwining of policy and business learning, as cornerstones of 'Learning Regions'.

The Policy Dilemma: A History of Ineffective Regional Business Support

Within the context of regional support to SMEs, cluster-oriented approaches present an innovative step in policy development, but in order to understand their introduction and appeal, we need to take into account the way this policy field has been developing over the past decade. In effect, despite a proliferation of support initiatives over the last decades and an accumulation of knowledge stemming from research and evaluation, the effectiveness of most business support is still questionable. Various authors have pointed to a continuing mismatch between the providers and clients of business support. Aspects which have incurred much criticism are the standard, non-customized nature of much support, the lack of sophistication and credibility among providers, the emphasis on 'quick fixes', the bias towards technical solutions rather than towards addressing organizational and managerial deficits, and the risk-averse attitudes of most service providers (Morgan, 1996; Shapira *et al.*, 1995; Hutchinson *et al.*, 1996; Burgess, 1997). Even worse, in countries with a long history of support measures, such as the UK and Germany, increasing disillusionment with the support sector by SMEs has led to a kind of support fatigue (Hassink, 1996). Support agencies were increasingly facing the fact that they somehow had to sell their service, not in the sense of commercial sales, but merely finding clients who showed at least initial interest in their services. In response to such persistent failures, various governments have undertaken the first steps towards reshaping and even rationalizing the business support sector. This has happened, for instance, with the Dutch Business Innovation Centres.

Why has it been so difficult to increase the effectiveness of business support? An important factor has been the initial organization of the support sector and the kind of philosophy employed. The provision of support started with a strong emphasis on technology transfer and demonstration, following a 'technology push' model. These support measures suffered from two handicaps: a lack of understanding of SMEs as organizations and a lack of proper demand identification.

The first handicap can be attributed to a general lack of understanding of the organizational and management capacities of SMEs and the problems they may face in adapting to the requirements of new technology. While the innovation deficit was acknowledged, the specific behavioural context of

SMEs tended to be overlooked (OECD, 1993; Monck *et al.*, 1988). The idea thus emerged that technology transfer should form part of an integral strategy of business modernization, which included management, organizational change, skills upgrading etc. The first initiatives which tried to follow such an approach involved the deployment of innovation consultants in programmes such as the UK *Enterprise Consultancy Initiative*, the French *Aides au Projet d'Innovation* and the German *Unternehmensberatungen für KMU*. While these initiatives took a more managerial view of innovation, they failed to tailor support to the organization of the SME, and they tended to offer little more than 'quick fixes' (Burgess, 1997). In particular, these initiatives continued to be grafted onto 'large firm' models and strategies.

A specific problem with the technology-led approaches was that they failed to give small firms a sense of direction. Rather than focusing on business development as the bottom line of support provision, each agency focused narrowly on its own specific mission: technology transfer, skill development, innovation support and so on. Whereas large firms have the capacity to assess their market position, to develop a growth strategy and accommodate their innovation strategy accordingly, SMEs often lack such strategic learning capabilities. A key problem with SMEs is that they are not able to articulate what their needs are for long-term survival and growth (Brusco, 1992), although they may be able to express some immediate wants. Without a strategic concept of business development, the inclination to see technology and innovation as universal solutions to the problems of SMEs may even be harmful:

> Innovation, broadly perceived, is not the sole preserve of successful, growing firms. Nor is it necessarily good in itself. It can either open doors into new areas of the market place or help firms to lock themselves in. It can be linked with an outward-looking, diversifying approach to market development, but it can also represent the struggles of firms to keep alive an enclosed and shrinking market. In the latter case, it can be argued that innovation merely stretches the period of decline and the market adaptation which is required. ... What matters is not so much innovation itself, but where it leads. Unless these small firms can connect their innovative efforts to wider markets beyond their depressed region, or to new technology, these efforts may lead nowhere (White *et al.*, 1988, pp. 108–9).

In a more general context, some serious claims have been made that Europe, apart from clinging on to a technology-push approach, suffers from a 'productivity cult' while it lacks a strategic approach to innovation (European Commission, 1995). The allusion to a 'productivity cult' refers to the fact that much energy appeared to have been devoted to improving activities and technologies that, however successful these improvements had proved to be, were fundamentally obsolete and applicable only in mature markets. Accordingly, what was needed, was a support sector with proper diagnostic skills and the provision of 'economic intelligence', at the level both of the firm and of the wider economy. In terms of the content of service provision, this meant that there is a need not only to shift from routine to more specialized services, but also to provide a more organizational and managerial orientation. In the European Green Paper on innovation, the seriousness of the situation was expressed as follows:

> one of the weaknesses of European innovation systems is the inadequate level of organisational innovation. This serious shortcoming makes it impossible to renovate models which are now inefficient and which are unfortunately still being applied in a large number of businesses. The same applies to effective innovation-oriented formulae for business management (European Commission, 1995, p. 19).

A related problem was that support agencies and policy makers seemed to lack a proper understanding of the cognitive and communicative routines of SMEs, and the same could be said of most of the academic approaches (Gertler, 1996). Scott *et al.* (1996, p. 95) found evidence for the communication gap in their study of UK small and medium-sized manufacturing firms (SMMEs):

> even where SMMEs actively identify deficiencies in their in-house technical capabilities, there is often – particularly in owner-managed firms – uncertainty about, or resistance to, outside help. This problem is compounded by a lack of adequate communication channels for the transmission of aid.

To add to this picture, Curran and Blackburn (1994) observed that owner-managers tended to rely more on 'word of mouth' as a source of knowledge about business improvement rather than formalized information structures. To reach firms, their communication routines and patterns should clearly be taken into account.

The problems of inadequate integration have been further compounded by the way in which support has been financed and evaluated. The frequent need to show quick results has also forced the agencies to opt for less risky, i.e. less innovative, forms of support. To quote Bellini (1998, p. 24): 'Evaluation "imposed" on service providers triggers defensive and instrumental attitudes: complying with formal requirements is often more important than exploitation of the learning potential of the evaluation procedures.'

Towards Integral Support Structures

The need for more strategically informed and tailored modes of support for SMEs, to improve communication between service providers and their clients, and for organizational and financial streamlining called for more integrated support structures and inspired ideas about moving to them. An integral approach should go beyond the mere transfer of technology and emphasize the upgrading or modernization of the business as a whole, and take account of the specific business culture and management style. In their study on modernization programmes focused on SMEs, Shapira *et al.* (1995, p. 78) indicated what kind of strategy is most appropriate and how this should be organized:

> From the perspective of a small or midsized customer, modernisation programmes should be 'seamless', offering a full range of expertise and resources. Modernization programmes can seek to do this by providing a range of different kinds of expertise or services themselves, or – perhaps more feasible – developing strong linkages and co-ordination with other service providers.

Different models have been developed to accommodate the call for improved business support. One development with a strong technological focus was the development of RTACs (Regional Technology Advisory Centres) (Charles, 1997). Although RTACs appear in many different forms and approaches, the common parameter is that they act as an intermediary between SMEs and technology providers. Their emergence can be seen in the light of the shift towards more demand-led innovation policies for SMEs. Advice on technology transfer thus comes with a package of auditing, diagnosis and support in other areas such as funding and assistance with organizational change. Some RTACs (for instance, in certain French and Spanish regions) perform a role as 'one-stop-shops', as points of referral to other forms of business support. Some even act as strategic co-ordinators within the wider regional network of business support. Thus RTACs appear to support integration at two levels: at the client level by offering access to an integral support package, and at the regional level by improving the integration and supervision of the regional support structure.

The performance of RTACs varies widely. Some have been able to develop services on a more commercial basis, but most activities depend on public subsidy. One problem which RTACs face is that, while they have become more demand-led, many of their services tend to be highly generic. Once SMEs have embarked on a process of upgrading, their demands quickly shift from generic support to meeting more sector-specific, special needs. They also shift from solving immediate technological and organizational problems to becoming more linked to marketing issues (Devins, 1996). In particular, helping SMEs to find a sense of long-term direction requires a basis of intelligence gathering, 'technology watch' and 'marketing watch'. Especially when firms successfully adopt measures of modernization and upgrading, they will need more sophisticated, i.e. less generic, forms of support. This insight forms the basis for a more sector or cluster-based approach to business support, linked to the idea that, at a regional level, a certain degree of targeting may be pursued. Smallbone's (1997, p. 133) study of SME support gives an illustration of some of the benefits as well as the caveats of sectoral differentiation:

> a policy of targeting at the levels of sectors to support growth is not recommended if this means focusing on firms in some sectors to the exclusion of firms in others ... At the same time, there may be a case for prioritising certain types of activity over others because there are a priori reasons for suggesting there is greater public benefit in terms of contribution to economic development [for instance, if strong market growth is expected] ... Nevertheless, some of the support that firms need requires sectoral differentiation and agencies must build up locally relevant expertise, not least to establish a basis of credibility with client firms (Smallbone, 1997, p. 133).

How could such a differentiated approach be organized in practice? While the general parameters of a sector or cluster-based approach are generally accepted, authorities themselves often lack the knowledge and organizational capabilities to pursue such a policy. Totterdill's (1995) analysis of the development of local industrial policy in the UK, for instance, concludes: 'The relative sophistication of sectoral strategies, needing specialising knowledge and vocabulary, presents a real obstacle for many local authorities.' A key problem is thus a quality mismatch between much service provision and business needs (North *et al.*, 1997).

Rather than following a conventional support model, sector and cluster-based approaches for SME support are interpreted along associational lines (Devins, 1996). The role of the government thus becomes one of facilitating and part-financing the setting up of specific knowledge-oriented service centres, often in collaboration with other organizations such as Chambers of Commerce and business associations. According to the European Commission, however, such associational trends are still hard to find.

> Determined collection, sharing (co-operation between firms, pooling of resources with public authorities) and protection of strategic information are still too rare in Europe. Social and professional divides, fear of competition and deliberate secrecy make collaboration between firms and authorities a difficult matter. Individual and collective attitudes therefore need to change if economic intelligence is to gain a foothold (European Commission, 1995, p. 30).

Towards 'Intelligent Clusters' in Regional Development: A Model

To improve the way business support can contribute to regional development, policies need to adopt new perspectives that are especially geared to improving relational assets in the region. Besides improving means of communication and the development of collective initiatives and resources, these assets should serve to improve the learning capabilities of firms as well as support organizations and the policy community. One aspect of this learning is that support activities should be framed in a strategic perspective of regional development. Only in that way, can a perspective of modernization and 'intelligence gathering' be developed that helps to improve communication between business support organizations and their clients, as well as the quality of the supply and absorption of services provided.

One way of promoting such a regional learning perspective is by using a cluster approach, as suggested here. As we stressed before, clusters link the micro/meso level of communicating and networking among firms and regional organizations with the meso/macro level of economic specialization and building institutional capacity. Figure 9.1 gives a model of how cluster approaches can provide a bridge between the local supportive infrastructure and groups of firms working in related industries (besides other forms of institutional support to regional development). The crux of this model is the development of 'club goods', that is, of assets that are accessible and beneficial to specific groups of businesses and organizations in a locality.

In the context of cluster-based regional development, 'club goods' can be characterized as follows:

- The most important 'club goods' are of an associational nature, stemming from shaping relational assets, institution building and gathering 'economic intelligence'; these assets underpin the institutional capacity for reflexive and strategic action.
- 'Club goods' also include assets of a more conventional nature, such as the specialization of the labour market and dedicated infrastructure
- Although they relate to business performance, 'club goods' are essentially regional assets. They are rooted in the regional social and economic structure, accessible only (easily and naturally) to local actors.
- 'Club goods' are the product of institutional dynamics and self-organization. The cluster dimension is important because it helps to focus communication and learning among regional actors. 'Club goods' sustain the collective learning capabilities of regional clusters. This makes 'intelligent clusters', in which firms, business support and other regional organizations work together to improve their collective assets, i.e. their club goods. These actions may include a process of shaping and promoting a cluster identity as part of the region's economic profile.

A core issue is how can such cluster-based 'club goods' be nurtured,

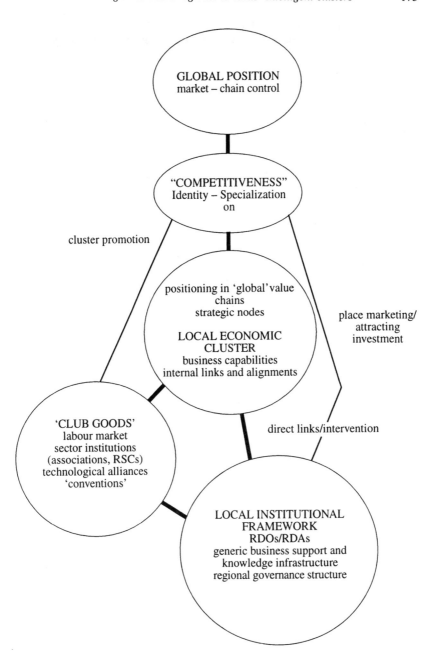

Figure 9.1   Club goods underpinning cluster competitiveness

especially in peripheral regions? This is the central question that will be addressed now, on the basis of empirical observations in the remainder of the chapter.

9.4 METHODOLOGY OF POLICY ANALYSIS

The empirical analysis focuses on regional initiatives in peripheral areas aimed at building relational assets and improving learning capabilities through the use of cluster approaches. The analysis falls into three sets of questions. An overview is provided in the Research Pro Forma (Table 9.1).

The first question is: how have the policy initiatives been inspired and developed? Although regional actors may be enticed by the idea of creating self-governing, self-sustaining institutions, putting this into practice presents a major challenge. Old policy-making routines have to be changed and this will often meet resistance (Peter and Van Nispen, 1998). Targets, objectives and methods appropriate to the local institutional and economic context need to be found and articulated. Finally, there are specific aspects of cluster approaches that need to be addressed, such as the way firms can participate (composition, openness), the role of mediators in shaping relational structures and building trust, and the way clusters are monitored and sustained in time.

Secondly, how have firms participated and benefited from cluster approaches? The key question here is whether cluster approaches have helped to overcome the problems of mismatch and lack of focus that characterized much of business support in the past. Three types of benefit will be distinguished: direct benefits to individual business performance, the building of relational assets in the context of inter-firm interaction, helping firms to learn from each other, and changes in communication and interaction with support organizations.

Thirdly, to what extent have cluster initiatives made a more sustainable contribution to regional development? This bears on the issue of shaping regional 'club goods' through the anchoring of cluster benefits within the regional socio-economic structure. A core task here is to understand the way interactive learning processes are nurtured. Another interesting issue is to what extent the cluster approach has reached out to sectors beyond those initially targeted: the theme of demonstration effects. A related issue is how specific cluster initiatives are, or have become, part of a strategic vision of the future of the region, particularly its specialization within the global economy. Finally, a more pragmatic question is: how, beyond the policy initiative itself, have the cluster approaches contributed to a more cost-effective form of business support, for example, by achieving higher rates of self-financing.

The case studies for the analysis are located in four regions: Tyneside (NE

Table 9.1 The Research Pro Forma

Themes	Questions
Policy cycle	
Conception and launching	*Where did policy makers find the inspiration for the cluster initiative? What was the regional economic background? What cluster approach is pursued (framework conditions, network building, etc)?*
Role of support agencies and funding regimes	*What are the funding conditions for clustering initiatives? What kind of institutional arrangements (partnerships, networks) underpin the cluster initiatives?*
Cluster mapping and audits	*How were targeted clusters selected? What was the quality and depth of the analysis? To what extent do business actors participate in the cluster analysis?*
Setting objectives	*Given the policy context and problem analysis, how are objectives and methods developed? What are the possibilities for changing the objectives and methods?*
Implementation	*How has the implementation succeeded in practice? What is the role of mediators?*
Cluster composition	*To what extent are the clusters 'open' versus 'closed'? Are there geographical constraints on business participation?*
Evaluation and monitoring	*How are clusters evaluated and monitored? How is the data used?*
Business development perspective	*How do firms see their benefits from clustering?*
Direct benefits: improving business capabilities through clustering	*To what extent do firms see improvement of business capabilities due to clustering? To what extent are these individual benefits; to what extent are they part of network building? What resources have businesses spent on cluster initiatives?*
Business networking: obtaining benefits from collaborating with other firms	*What are the practical and cultural obstacles to collaboration? What relational assets have been built up among firms? What kind of corrective institutional capacity assists this process?*

Table 9.1　(continued)

Themes	Questions
Institutional networking: obtaining benefits from local institutions	*To what extent has policy-induced clustering improved the image of and engagement with the local public sector and regional business association?*
Regional policy perspective	*How should cluster initiatives be arranged to optimize regional benefits?*
Anchoring cluster benefits to the regional economy: shaping 'club goods'	*What regional assets are developed through clustering wholly or partially independently of the business firms involved? To what extent are the assets of a 'classical' (labour, knowledge centres, infrastructure) or a more intangible nature (knowledge, 'conventions', identity)?*
Demonstration effects	*How have clustering benefits accrued to the wider regional economy, i.e. other firms in similar or in other sectors? How have policy makers addressed pilots and the issue of sustainability?*
Embedding of cluster initiatives in regional specialization strategies	*Have cluster initiatives formed part of integrated programmes or do they 'stand alone'? How do the initiatives contribute to regional specialization?*
The learning dimension of clusters and 'learning regions'	*What has been the knowledge orientation of clustering? What have been the wider learning implications at the regional level?*
Effectiveness of regional business support	*To what extent has the cluster approach contributed to more cost-effective ways of regional business support?*
Conclusion: aligning business and regional interests	*To what extent have actors in the policy/support domain been able to attune initiatives to the regional interest?* *To what extent have businesses become committed to the regional cause?*

England), Aragon (Spain), Hessen and NRW (Bergisches Land), both in Germany. The regions present cases of peripheral development or restructuring (only the latter in the case of Hessen). The policy initiatives employ a relational perspective, in which changes at the business level are bridged with structural change in the regional economy. Some cases reflect more standard types of policy initiatives, geared to providing certain types of support for a limited period; others are of a more associational nature, supporting processes of institution-building. Table 9.2 summarizes the case studies. Further details of the case studies and the method of selection and research can be found in Lagendijk (1999).

The methodology for exploring the case studies is based primarily on interviews with representatives of firms and regional agencies, plus additional desk research of policy and regional development material. The data was gathered between September 1996 and October 1998. The results will be presented following the categories of the Research Pro Forma as shown in Table 9.1.

Table 9.2   A case study overview

Region	Targeted sectors	Cluster aims	Organization
NE of England	Automotive	Embedding of foreign investors	ASSA, public–private partnership
Hessen, NRW	Automotive (networking)	Securing/anchoring of established activities	Public business support organization (RKW)
NE of England	Marine offshore	Revitalization of marine industries	Industry association (NOF)
Aragon	Wine	Modernization of the wine industry	Regional development agency (IAF)
NRW (Bergisches Land)	Chemical industry	Focus groups for collective strategies	Regional development agency (Regionalburo)
NE England	Various sectors	Joint marketing and other activities	North Tyneside Real Service Centre (public)

9.5 SUMMARY OF CASE STUDY RESULTS

a. The Development of the Policy Initiatives

Conception/launching: While the various case studies showed considerable variation in objectives, cluster approaches and implementation, most are somehow grafted onto the work of Porter. What is interesting is how the general (Porterian) concept of clusters has been locally interpreted and translated into practical initiatives. In the Tyneside case, for instance, a Porter-based recommendation of cluster-oriented approaches, combined with experience gained in 'Central Italy' (particularly Emilia Romagna), inspired the establishment of an innovative organization geared to the facilitation of business clusters among SMEs (the North Tyneside Real Service Centre, RSC). Another application on Tyneside was developed with the aim of attracting and servicing foreign investors, especially through the regional development agency (NDC = Northern Development Company). Here, the cluster concept, particularly through its supply chain dimension, underpinned the development of 'value added' embedding strategies. The German case studies concentrated on the way clustering could contribute to structural improvements in the regional economy through a relational perspective. In particular, they endorsed the idea that innovation could be stimulated by nurturing collaborative attitudes and collective learning processes. Thus, in nearly all cases, a specific threat (relocation, ongoing rationalization, business closures) or clear opportunity (embedding investors, move to quality wine) triggered off the cluster initiative.

Support agencies and funding regimes: The agencies that initiated the cluster projects vary from 'pure' public sector (Aragon), partnership arrangements (IAT, RSC), to business associations with public support (Tyneside offshore). Overall, the research confirms the idea that a public/private mix will generally provide the best support arrangement. Public sector participation is vital for funding, for the embedding in regional policies and facilitating demonstration effects, while private sector participation is important for creating commitment, encouraging bottom-up initiatives and customization of support. Funding regimes showed a similar degree of variation. Many initiatives relied on short-term, project-based funding. While this is understandable, given the innovative nature of the cluster approach, not all initiatives seem to have had sufficient time to develop and show their impact. Viewed from a policy cycle perspective, therefore, cluster initiatives suffer from the fact that most results become manifest only in the medium to long term, long after the time when new funding has to be applied for.

Cluster mapping and audits: Most cluster initiatives were not preceded by in-depth regional analysis (comparable with Porter's cluster mapping). Some grew from bottom-up in response to specific needs or opportunities (Tyneside); others developed their core themes and targets through self-auditing (Bergisches Land). Audits played a role in the acquisition of funding (RSC), or strategic reevaluation (NOF). In general, the results endorse the idea that ongoing learning and feedback, with a strong participatory role for business, is a more appropriate approach than a linear scheme, in which policy design is based on *ex ante* identification of 'business needs'. Specific SME audits were carried out by the RSC and in Bergisches Land, which helped to tailor the initiatives to their client groups.

Setting objectives: Tracing cluster objectives revealed a much more varied and dynamic picture than initially envisaged. The variation in objectives is particularly striking. While none of the case studies fails to mention regional competitiveness, and all somehow invoke a notion of the benefits from relational assets, there is less clarity about specific goals. This is due primarily to the fuzziness of the cluster concept and the innovative character of the initiatives. Cluster-oriented ideas are employed to serve specific regional purposes, such as preventing relocation, improving local linkages, facilitating inter-firm learning etc. In translating the fuzzy notion of clustering into concrete initiatives, however, the setting of priorities largely reflects the context in which projects are developed, and the specific ideas of the decision makers at the point of planning. Variations stem from context conditions (including terms of funding and evaluation), as well the specific preferences of the initiators.

The explorative and often arbitrary nature of setting objectives is confirmed by the way objectives appear as moving targets. The RSC has shifted from an intensive process of cluster building to more emphasis on facilitating and more generic forms of business support. The Aragonese case shifted from creating new limited companies as local leaders to a more gradual process of concentration. In Bergisches Land, the initial objective of creating regional assets by linking two sectors was overtaken by the priority of facilitating inter-firm learning. In all these cases, the fact that firms were engaged on a longer term basis contributed to these changes and learning processes.

Implementation through brokers: To achieve their – albeit often moving – targets, the initiatives generally rely strongly on the input of brokering and expert contributions. Brokering is especially important for developing the relational dimension of regional economic development. The present study has provided ample evidence of the crucial role of brokers. A distinction can be made between the clusters geared to associational strategies and 'institution building' at industrial/sectoral level, and to more network and learning-oriented initiatives. For the first category, the associational initiatives, the role of initiators from the sector itself has proved to be crucial (ASSA, NOF), either as triggers or even as coaches throughout the project. The same applies to the local wine regulators in Aragon.

In the case of the successful networking/learning initiatives, brokers and experts with an industrial background also proved to be most effective (Bergisches Land). The RSC has been able to thrive with the help of public sector brokers. This can be explained in part by reference to the specific type of knowledge these brokers embodied, knowledge that facilitated effective public partnerships and guidance with grant application. Even here, support was sought from the industrial sector. The first RSC clusters were assisted by industrial figureheads as independent advisors. Where no appropriate mediators with a business background were available, as in some of the German cases, projects had difficulties in creating commitment and trust among participating businesses. This again endorses the significance of the nature and quality of brokering.

Cluster composition: The nature of cluster composition is closely related to the nature of the cluster initiative. The associational initiatives are membership-based and generally open to all the firms in relevant sectors within a demarcated area. The spatial restriction was especially noticeable in Aragon, where the initiatives were geared to four specific areas in the larger region, and where the aim was to involve all the firms in those areas, but none outside. The Bergisches Land initiatives were open to all local SMEs in the enrolment phase, but were subsequently closed. The RSC clusters, on the other hand, are closed. Changes in RSC cluster membership are subject to contractual stipulations and incur transaction costs, manifesting a contractual process of changing the cluster memberships. However, the RSC clustering service is in principle open to all kinds of SMEs in the area, with no strict application of territorial boundaries.

Evaluation and monitoring: The organization of evaluation also depends on the nature of the initiative. There is only one case where evaluation is largely informal, based on the generally observed sectoral performance, namely, the Aragonese wine cluster. The institutional/associational initiatives, and the RSC, are obliged to make evaluations for public funding bodies. The RSC and NOF are also strong in self-monitoring and producing regular reports for the wider public. The German projects are evaluated in depth after the end of the projects, both to account for the expenditure and to draw lessons for future initiatives. The results, however, also show how much the process of evaluation, including some of the initiatives themselves, is geared towards the evaluation processes and standards. This applies especially to the way networking is translated in terms of numbers of participants, meetings, and so on, and to the translation of the competitive position of firms into product inquiries made etc. In some cases, notably the RSC, there was a tension between the more qualitative nature of self-monitoring, and the more quantitative external evaluations. It is obvious that, for this kind of initiative, more thought should be given to evaluation methods that really contribute to improvements in cluster approaches.

b. Business Development Perspective: How do Firms see their Benefits from Clustering?

Businesses can benefit from cluster initiatives in three ways:

1. direct benefits to individual firms,
2. collective benefits stemming from business networking, and
3. benefits stemming from interaction with support organizations.

Direct benefits: Through participating in cluster initiatives, firms may be able to improve their existing business capabilities. All the case studies confirm this, although with considerable differences in type and extent of improvements. Improving labour skills is an important result, which is shared by ASSA, NOF, the chemical industry in the Bergisches Land, and, in limited cases, by the RSC. Quality and environmental certification is supported in nearly all cases. Marketing at firm level shows advances in the RSC clusters and the Aragonese wine cluster. Quality improvements feature in the Aragonese case, the RSC clusters, and the German automotive clusters. In the same case studies, a variety of managerial issues was also dealt with. Surprisingly, innovation does not appear as a prominent issue, although attention is paid to technological issues in almost all cases. This is manifested most strongly in the NOF, which also pays attention to procurement issues.

Some of these benefits represent almost purely individual gains, in the sense that clustering has been instrumental in business-level modernization, with certification (e.g. ISO 9000-13000) as the clearest example. Other benefits, such as skills improvement and management changes, combine individual benefits with cluster effects. This means that there are spillover effects to other cluster members or even to the wider regional economy, and that the benefits would be reduced if the cluster disappeared. Cluster effects are most prominent in the case of marketing. While firms may again draw individual lessons from their cluster experiences, marketing efforts generally involve using the cluster and its regional embedding as a brand image. Such collective gains depend on the clustering dimension, as shown most clearly in the cases of the RSC and Aragonese wine DOCs.

While collective benefits are referred to by brokers, policy makers and cluster analysts, it is essential for participating businesses to obtain individual benefits. For SMEs, in particular, 'hard' benefits are the main justification for their investments and commitment. The study confirmed that, in general, firms appear to be more interested in learning from other firms or engaging in collective lobbying than in contributing to collective cluster assets. From an SME perspective, an important aspect of clustering appears to be the social encounter with peer firms or firms in related businesses in order to improve individual business performance. The emphasis on inter-firm learning for individual benefits even occurred when the initiatives were initially grafted onto a (trade) linkage model (Bergisches Land, some RSC clusters). While the primary investment made by the business thus consisted of time and some administrative loads, returns are counted in terms of improved business performance or products. In addition, in some case studies (Aragon, some RSC clusters), firms have benefited from grants won through the cluster.

Business networking: The second level of business benefits consists of those gains that stem from, and are dependent on, inter-firm collaboration. This includes three types of results:

1. Starting with the emphasis on inter-firm learning, the creation of a social network and relational assets reflects such a benefit. In areas characterized by rather individualistic business attitudes, such as the North East and Bergisches Land, building trust and social networking among SMEs emerged as crucial outcomes of the cluster initiatives.
2. Another type of benefit which has emerged from the case studies and also from the associational initiatives (NOF, ASSA), is the building of a collective lobbying position. In practice, the position of SMEs appears to be less strong than that of larger firms.
3. Closer to the original cluster philosophy is the forging of new supply linkages and the shaping of a common identity, as shown by most of the RSC clusters. The NOF also presents a new approach to supply chains as part of a new contracting regime in the offshore industry. The Aragonese wine sector presents a somewhat deviant case in this respect, since changes in the production chain are framed within a transition from co-operative to more rationalized and concentrated forms of production.

To what extent these advantages will endure remains an open question, particularly in the cases of more temporary initiatives. With the RSC, it is hoped that the organization will obtain a more permanent status. This would allow it to help business clusters to address problems that may arise in the future, for example, as a result of opportunistic behaviour. In this way, the organization could help to sustain the level of social capital accumulated in the region.

Institutional networking: Cluster initiatives have brought firms closer together and they have also forged links between the private and public sectors. In what respects have these links served business needs? In particular, has the support sector managed to improve its reputation among the business sector? The results are quite mixed in this respect. On the one hand, there are some good examples of improved links and reputation. The most prominent cases here are the RSC and the Bergisches Land (chemical industry), although in the latter instance, the public sector remained partly concealed behind intermediaries. The benefits to firms consisted of access to information about other forms of support and assistance to grant applications. Public–private links have also been developed through ASSA and the NOF, which were able to build on already existing links. On the other hand, the automotive initiative in Bergisches Land and the Aragonese wine initiative are cases where some of the firms still regard the regional support sector with suspicion.

We can give a final judgement on this question only when the exact intentions of the regional support agencies are known, and this is the issue to which we now turn.

c. Regional Policy Perspective: How should Cluster Initiatives be Arranged in Order to Optimize Regional Benefits?

Anchoring cluster benefits to the regional economy: shaping 'club goods': Regions will particularly benefit from cluster initiatives if the latter produce a kind of 'sediment', that is, nurture assets or 'club goods' that may serve wider purposes than the cluster alone. Practical examples of such assets are training facilities, infrastructure, support centres and industry associations. Less tangible assets are the stock of cluster-related knowledge diffused in the region, commitment of regional actors to support certain economic activities, and contributions to the regional economic identity (Figure 9.1). The case studies include good examples of both categories. Shaping identities is part of all the initiatives and has succeeded most in the cases of Aragon and the marine activities in the North East (both NOF and RSC). In the latter case, the development of institutions in itself presents a valuable 'club good' that can be used by a variety of actors. Improvements in the labour market were observed for all the initiatives in the North East, where there is perceived to be a general skills shortage in the region, and for chemical production in Bergisches Land. Contributions to infrastructure improvements have been more limited and largely indirect, notably through the interventions of core firms and associations in the automotive and offshore industries (in the latter case, the contribution to the infrastructure is manifested primarily through the arrest of further dismantling of harbour-related activities).

Demonstration effects: Beyond their own remits, have cluster developments infected the wider regional economy with collaborative and associational attitudes? This does indeed seem to be the case in all the regions. In the North East, this 'infection' is institutionalized in the form of the RSC, which has gradually extended its sectoral coverage, while the organization receives much attention from policy actors all over Europe. Similarly, the NOF acts as a role model for comparable initiatives in other sectors, including those outside the region. In Aragon, policy makers have embraced the cluster approach and further initiatives are expected in other indigenous sectors.

The survival of existing clusters and cluster-related institutions remains a sensitive issue. Cluster facilitators generally try to avoid failures, since, apart from posing evaluation problems, they are expected to tarnish the image of clustering and the brokering agencies. For the benefit of both the firms and the region, however, failures should be accepted and even expected. The study has shown that continued assistance geared to cluster survival may lead to a situation where client firms become the 'babies' of the facilitating organization. Facilitating clustering should stand at arm's length from the participating firms and continued assistance should be offered only at the instigation of business. Evaluations should focus less on the benefits for individual firms and have more eye for wider regional effects and the innovative nature of the cluster initiatives.

Embedding of cluster initiatives in regional specialization strategies: The cluster case studies discussed here present predominantly 'stand alone' initiatives, which are not part of wider cluster policies. Where facilitating clustering has been extended to other sectors, as in the North East, it reflects an emergent pattern rather than a predefined strategy. In nearly all cases, however, the cluster initiatives are part of other forms of regional policy. Institution building in the North East, for instance, is closely associated with the attraction and embedding of foreign investors. The support to the wine sector in Aragon is part of a rural development policy. Indeed, even for the RSC, the focus on clustering emerged only after the local council had already started to anchor SMEs in the local economy. Nevertheless, by embarking on clustering, all these cases developed an orientation towards networking, inter-firm learning and regional specialization. In most cases, this link contains a defensive element, that is, the aim behind clustering is to bind existing firms to the region. The German initiatives, in particular, take such a position. The

North East and Aragonese cases, on the other hand, are more growth oriented, although they remain close to existing regional strengths. A further trend towards diversification may be expected in the future, in which the ambition to nurture new strengths may grow.

The learning dimension of clusters: Clusters have been described as a specific level of social interaction and governance which allows for new forms of learning. Rather than a binary world characterized by a support sector and business clients, cluster initiatives embody an associational level with its own learning dynamics. The nature and depth of this dynamic may vary. When clustering is geared towards 'institution building' or an associational process, this intermediate level manifests itself as such. In other cases, social interaction and learning are supported by the facilitating of clustering, structured in regular meetings, workshops, and so forth.

The extent to which learning is part of cluster dynamics depends both on the design of the initiative and the kind of chemistry emerging during the project. Projects conceived in a top-down way, where initiators leave little room for knowledge creation and reflexivity during the project, will obviously tend to be less self-adaptive than initiatives with a strong learning-orientation. A lack of learning orientation was illustrated, for instance, in the Aragonese case, where policy makers changed the project only when confronted with strong protests from within the targeted business sector. A positive learning curve could be observed with the RSC. While the initial projects were based on strong premises about the aim and means of clustering, a more open and qualified approach emerged over time, in which more was left to the client firms. The Bergisches Land, finally, showed a marked difference between a less successful project, in which much knowledge had been acquired before-hand, and a more effective project where knowledge gathering had mostly been part of the project itself. While this had been born out of necessity, rather than deliberate policy design, it gave firms the opportunity to have a greater share in the project and, therefore, a greater commitment and reflexivity.

To what extent have the initiatives supported regional learning agendas? Different answers can be given to this. In general, cluster initiatives are seen as innovative forms of regional policy and are praised for the way they support new forms of business engagement. In this sense, all the initiatives seem to have contributed to policy learning and to greater awareness of the specific knowledge needs of SMEs in the regional economy. Among firms, the initiatives have helped to change business attitudes, notably towards more openness to other firms and even support agencies. More specifically, clusters have formed bridges between firms and knowledge centres, which has contributed to the tailoring of support services to business needs. The problem of monitoring cluster initiatives remains, together with the reliance on short-term financing. This appears to limit the extent to which initiatives can be innovative and learning effects can spill over to the regional economy.

Cost-effectiveness of regional business support: Cluster initiatives, with the facilitating of networking and 'institution building' as a primary investment, are a cheap form of business support. With the exception of Aragon, where substantial amounts were initially spent on business transformation, this has been borne out by the various case studies. In some cases, such as the industry associations, self-financing covers a substantial part of the costs. Moreover, since they generally involve contacts between public, private and other actors, cluster arrangements appear to be a fruitful basis for grant applications, as shown in particular by the RSC. Thus not only do cluster initiatives impose a low burden on the local public purse, but they may also lever out additional sources of income.

Besides the pecuniary benefits, the cluster initiatives have proved to be effective forms of assistance, not only to facilitate clustering, but also as a vehicle for other forms of business support. The latter is particularly evident where clustering does not so much present a goal as a method of business support (learning-oriented clusters). Cluster-related institutions, such as the RSC and NOF, act as effective brokers between client firms and the wider environment of business support and grant provision. In this way, cluster-oriented 'institution building' appears to be a welcome complement, rather than a threat to existing forms of business support.

9.6   CONCLUSION

In an associational, reflexive perspective on economic development, learning forms an intrinsic part of the complex institutional arrangements under-pinning regional development. Within such a setting, learning is interactive, taking place between businesses, regional agencies, educational organizations and knowledge centres. Learning may also be seen as proactive, that is, linked to a notion of structural change and the shaping of regional specialization. Finally, from an institutional perspective, learning takes place at various levels and through multiple loops, bringing about minor modifications in economic activities, as well as more fundamental changes in underlying routines and forms of behaviour. The crux of 'learning regions', in this view, is the intertwining of business learning and policy learning, underpinning a recursive and reflexive style of collective learning. In a regional development context, the benefits of interaction become manifest in the shaping of 'club goods', i.e. assets beneficial to specific firms and organizations and anchored to the regional socio-economic structure.

The institutional arrangements highlighted in this chapter stem from the development and adoption of regional cluster concepts. Clusters have been presented as the associational vehicle for linking different forms of learning (business and policy). It is important to reiterate the strategic dimension of this process. Clusters do not refer here to the process of animating spatial-economic agglomerations that need only a catalyst to spring up and grow naturally. While such phenomena can be observed in core regions, non-core regions face particular problems of cultural and structural lock-in, which will generally prevent new or revived forms of economic agglomeration from emerging naturally. Regional actors in non-core regions often need to fight hard to align the interests of firms with those of the region, in order to create a basis of trust and commitment in which firms are prepared to co-operate. The case studies discussed here illustrated how cluster initiatives in old industrial areas were triggered by the aspiration to increase the embedding of indigenous firms in the region, through nurturing various kinds of 'club goods', averting pending relocation of economic activity and facilitating inter-firm learning within a regional context. Other strategic goals revealed by the case studies included the embedding of foreign investors and the creation of economies of scale and scope between SMEs, notably in the area of marketing. In all these cases, a clear link could be observed between changes at the micro–meso level (business behaviour and interaction) and targeted structural change at the regional economy level.

Lastly, the policy learning dimension has been introduced against a background of poor policy performance in the past, notably in the area of business support. The case studies provide some interesting insights into how performance has been improved and what lessons can be learnt for the future. In particular, the research endorses the notion that linear and unfocused forms of business support need to be complemented, if not replaced, by more interactive forms of support framed within a strategic context. Interaction here refers to the role of brokering, which makes firms more committed to learning through interaction with other firms and agencies. It may also include focused 'intelligence gathering' that provides firms with new strategic insights and improves the articulation of business needs. These processes can be focused, framed and facilitated, as suggested here, by adopting a cluster perspective. The strategic context refers to embedding initiatives within a notion of where a regional economy is going, in terms of its economic specialization (which may be seen in terms of cluster maps), the nature of regional competitiveness and its links with the global economy (for example, role of foreign investors). Only by providing a strategic focus, can the nurturing of learning process in interactive settings – as in 'intelligent clusters' – be expected to make a genuine contribution to regional (as distinct from 'business') development.

ACKNOWLEDGEMENTS

The work for this chapter was funded under the European Programmes ADAPT (Core Project). The author wishes to acknowledge the support given by these programmes and the co-operation of the CORE participants. The author also wishes to thank the volume editors for their valuable comments.

REFERENCES

Amin, A. (1999), 'An institutionalist perspective on regional development', *International Journal of Urban and Regional Research*, **22** (forthcoming).

Bellini, N. (1998), *Services to Industry in the Framework of Regional and Local Industrial Policy*, Paper presented at the OECD Conference on Innovation and Territory, Modena, 28–29 May.

Brusco, S. (1992), 'Small firms and the provision of real services', in F. Pyke and W. Sengenberger (eds), *Industrial Districts and Local Economic Regeneration*, Geneva: International Institute for Labour Studies, pp. 177–96.

Burgess, J. (1997), *Supporting innovation in SMEs. A pan-European perspective*, ISPIM Conference, San Sebastian, October.

Camagni, R. (1991), 'Local "milieu", uncertainty and innovation networks: towards a new dynamic theory of economic space', in R. Camagni (ed.), *Innovation Networks. Spatial Perspectives*, London: Belhaven Press, pp. 121–44.

Charles, D. (1997), *'Regional Support Infrastructures for Small and Medium Sized Firms: an International Comparison of Regional Technology and Advisory Centres* (Series Working Paper), Centre for Urban and Regional Development Studies at the University of Newcastle, Newcastle upon Tyne.

Curran, J. and R. Blackburn (1994), *Small Firms and Local Economic Networks. The Death of the Local Economy?*, London: Paul Chapman Publishing.

Devins, D. (1996), 'The Use of External Advice by New and Established SMEs. Some Survey Evidence', in M.W. Danson (ed.), *Small Firm Formation and Regional Economic Development*, London: Routledge, pp. 161–88.

European Commission (1995), *Green paper on innovation*, Brussels: European Commission.

Gertler, M.S. (1996), 'Worlds apart – the changing market geography of the German machinery industry', *Small Business Economics*, **8** (2), pp.87–106.

Gibbons, M., C. Limoges, H. Nowotny, S. Schwartzman, P. Scott and M. Trow (1994), *The New Production of Knowledge*, London: Sage.

Grabher, G. (1991) 'Netzwerke – ein Ansatz für den Umbau des Montankomplexe im Ruhrgebiet?', in J. Hilbert, M. Kleinaltenkamp, J. Nordhause-Hanz and B. Widmaier (eds), *Neue Kooperationsformen in der Wirtschaft. Können Konkurrenten Partner Werden?*, Opladen: Leske & Budrich, pp. 147–70.

Hassink, R. (1996), 'Technology transfer agencies and regional economic development', *European Planning Studies*, **4** (2), pp. 167–84.

Healey, P. (1997), *Collaborative Planning: Shaping Places in Fragmented Societies*, London: Macmillan.

Hutchinson, J., P. Foley and H. Oztel (1996), 'From clutter to collaboration – business links and the rationalization of business support', *Regional Studies*, **30** (5), pp. 516–22.

Ingham, G. (1996), 'Some recent changes in the relationship between economics and sociology', *Cambridge Journal of Economics*, **20** (2), pp. 243–75.

Jacobs, D. (1997), 'Knowledge-intensive innovation: the potential of the cluster approach', *The IPTS Report*, **16**, pp. 22–8.

Lagendijk, A. (1999), *Good practices in SME cluster initiatives. Lessons from the 'core' regions and beyond*, Newcastle upon Tyne, CURDS, University of Newcastle.

Monck, C.S.P., P.R. Quintas, P. Wynarczyk, R.B. Porter and D.J. Storey (1988), *Science Parks and the Growth of High Technology Firms*, London: Croom Helm.

Morgan, K. (1996), 'Learning-by-interacting. Inter-firm networks and enterprise support', in *Networks of Enterprises and Local Development. Competing and Co-operating in Local Productive Systems*, Paris: OECD, pp. 53–65.

North, J., J. Curran and R. Blackburn (1997), 'Quality and small firms: a policy mismatch and its impact on small enterprise', in D. Deakins, P. Jennings and C. Mason (eds), *Small firms. Entrepreneurship in the 1990s*, London: Paul Chapman, pp. 112–26.

OECD (1993), *Small and medium-sized enterprises: technology and competitiveness*, Paris: OECD.

Peter, B.G. and F.K.M. Van Nispen (eds) (1998), *Public policy instruments: evaluating the tools of public administration*, Cheltenham: Edward Elgar.

Porter, M.E. (1990), *The competitive advantage of nations*, London: Macmillan.

Putnam, R. (1993), *Making democracy work: civic traditions in modern Italy*, Princeton, N.J.: Princeton University Press.

Rehfeld, D. (1994), 'Produktionscluster und räumliche Entwicklung - Beispiele und Konsequenzen', in W. Krumbein (ed.), *Ökonomische und politische Netzwerke in der Region: Beitrage aus der internationalen debatte*, Münster, Hamburg: Lit. Verlag, pp. 187–205.

Sabel, C.F. (1992), 'Studied trust: building new forms of co-operation', in F. Pyke and W. Sengenberger (eds), *Industrial districts and local economic regeneration*, Geneva: International Institute for Labour Studies, pp. 215–50.

Scott, P., B. Jones, A. Bramley and Brian Bolton (1996), 'Enhancing technology and skills in small and medium-size manufacturing firms: problems and prospects', *International Small Business Journal*, **14** (3), pp. 85–98.

Shapira, P., J.D. Roessner and R. Barke (1995), 'New public infrastructures for small industrial modernization in the USA', *Entrepreneurship and Regional Development*, **7**, pp. 63–84.

Smallbone, D. (1997), 'Selective targeting in SME policy: criteria and implementation issues', in D. Deakins, P. Jennings and C. Mason (eds), *Small Firms. Entrepreneurship in the 1990s*, London: Paul Chapman, pp. 127–40.

Steiner, M. (ed.) (1997), *Competence Clusters*, Workshop report, Graz and A1- Ring Austria, November 21-22, 1996, Graz: Leykam.

Storper, M. (1997a), 'Regional economies as relational assets', in R. Lee and J. Wills (eds), *Geographies of Economies*, London: Arnold, pp. 248–59.

Storper, M. (1997b), *The Regional World*, New York: Guildford Press.

Totterdill, P. (1995), 'Local authority sectoral networks: towards a model of industrial policy', *Local Economy*, **10** (4), pp. 365–8.

White, M., H.-J. Braczyk, A. Ghobadian and J. Niebuhr (1988), *Small Firm's Innovation: why Regions Differ*, London: Policy Studies Institute.

10. Interactive Learning within a Regional Innovation System: a Case Study in a Dutch Region

Marius Meeus[1], Leon Oerlemans[2] and Jules van Dijck

10.1 INTRODUCTION

Local and regional governments in Europe and the US are now more active in technology policy than they were 20 years ago. This new regionalism can be seen as a response to a paradoxical consequence of globalization – the growing importance of the locality as a site for innovation. In order to preserve the competitiveness of regions there has been a proliferation of programmes intended to attract high-tech firms from outside the region, for example by laying out science parks, to stimulate start-ups in newly emerging industries by means of incubator labs, or to facilitate the transfer of knowledge to regional firms (Tödtling, 1994). For this reason regional technology policy and regional innovation systems have become an important issue.

Many researchers consider the interaction between regional actors to be decisive for a dynamic regional development, with the stock of production factors and the economic and technology policy initiatives facilitating this interaction (Maillat, 1991; Cooke *et al.*, 1997; Nelson, 1993; Bergman *et al.*, 1991; Tödtling, 1994). Interactions between regional actors indicate that firms and institutional actors are utilizing their regional resources and policies (Håkannson, 1989; Oerlemans *et al.*, 1998). The basic idea behind regional innovation systems is that proximity makes specific resources more readily available. On the other hand, compared to relationships on a larger spatial scale, local relationships between firms and institutional actors (local universities and research laboratories) facilitate the utilization of resources because of cultural homogeneity (Lundvall, 1992; Morgan, 1997).

This alternative explanation of regional economic performance made relationships and networks an important variable on the research agendas of organization theory, institutional economics, and systems of innovation but, at the same time, raised a number of questions. The literature of innovation systems either lacks theoretical rigour or applies a naive, unidirectional approach in which institutional differences explain differences in innovative behaviour and performance (Nelson, 1993). More refined explanations, like Lundvall's interactive learning theory (Lundvall, 1992, 1993) in which innovating firms draw on their institutional environments have never been tested thoroughly. Studies of dynamic regions with intensive networking tend to be rather 'euphoric' and descriptive (Illeris and Jakobsen, 1990; Tödtling, 1994, p. 327). In most economic research, networks are treated as an exogenous variable. Approaches like transaction cost economics, which internalize networks, are seldom explored empirically. Moreover, the proxies used to measure relationships or networks represent economic exchange rather than networks. This is the case with the research on spillovers (Verspagen, 1997a, 1997b; Harabi, 1997) and input–output analysis (DeBresson and Andersen, 1996; Dalum, 1992; Fagerberg, 1992). In most organizational literature on networks the regional dimension is not a relevant variable, while there is a tendency to treat innovation networks and strategic alliances as equivalents. The fad of network research produced an enormous literature, which is very fragmented and also rather uncritical. This partly explains the strong bias towards descriptive accounts of strong linkages and the benefits of local co-operation, whereas the underutilization of local resources, the drawbacks of networks and weak ties are generally neglected.

In this paper we put forward an explanation for interactive learning in innovation networks based on the complexity of innovative activities. We concentrate on two related aspects of interactive learning in innovation networks in one specific regional innovation system: the variety and strength of relationships between innovating firms with distinct regional actors. Our study deals with the innovation system of one Dutch high-tech region, the province of North Brabant.

The patterns of interaction are regional up to a certain point. At least the firms whose behaviour was investigated are located in one specific region. Where external resources are acquired outside the region, they spill over into Brabant's local economy. The actor set involved is also mainly regional, with some exceptions (Dutch Centre for Applied Research/TNO, consultancies, competitors). About 33 per cent of the supplier relations assisting the innovating firms' innovation processes are located in North Brabant, while approximately 42 per cent of the customers are located in North Brabant.

Our paper adds to the growing body of literature on regional innovation systems, interactive learning and networks and performs several functions. First, whereas much empirical literature focuses on the dyadic relations of innovating firms with their competitors and the universities, or their customers or suppliers, we concentrate on the interaction of innovating firms with a broad set of actors. There are few empirical studies available that address regional patterns of interaction and relationship between innovating firms and a broad variety of actors (Håkansson, 1987, 1989; van der Knaap and Tortike, 1991; Krolis and Kamann, 1991; Cooke *et al.*, 1997). Secondly, while most network research applied in innovation studies does not present explicit theoretical explanations for the existence of networks or the level of interactive learning (Meeus and Oerlemans, 1993), we advance an alternative theoretical explanation for the strength and variety of external linkages between innovating firms and regional actors, based on the complexity perspective (Hage and Alter, 1994; Lundvall, 1992, 1993). Thirdly, compared with most innovation systems literature that investigates the effects of institutional arrangements on the innovative performance of a nation's firms, we internalize the innovation system by analysing how firms utilize their external resource bases. Finally, our empirical exploration of the validity of the complexity argument adds to our understanding of the antecedents of connectivity in regional innovation systems.

The structure of our paper is as follows. We first describe our theoretical framework. The central theoretical notions are the regional innovation system, the relation between networks and interaction, and two theoretical perspectives: the resource-based theory of the firm and a theory of interactive learning. This yields a research model and a set of hypotheses on the relationship between levels of interactive learning and the complexity of innovative activities. The next section describes the research design, including the sample, measurement and analyses. We then describe our results. Finally, we discuss these results and derive some theoretical and policy inferences, and give some suggestions for future research.

10.2 THEORETICAL FRAMEWORK

The central idea behind the concept of regional innovation systems is that the innovative performance of regions does not exclusively depend on the individual innovative performance of companies and research institutions. It also depends on the way in which these organizations interact with each other and with the public sector in the production and distribution of knowledge. Innovative enterprises function in a shared, institutional context. In this sense, they are dependent on, contribute to, and make use of a joint knowledge infrastructure. This infrastructure is viewed as a system that creates and distributes knowledge, uses this knowledge to achieve innovation, and thus generates economic value (Gregersen and Johnson, 1997, p. 482). In other words, the main function of a regional system of innovation relies on the development of regional innovation networks.

Networks involve the flow of resources among positions that reveal ties. These resource flows are enabled by the interaction between the actors involved. There are several theoretical explanations for interaction patterns. In general exchange theory, fluctuations in the value of interaction rewards determine the formation and longevity of links, together with the number of internal resources available for obtaining external resources. In the context of innovation, these resources are primarily defined in terms of money facilitating investments, a physical and technological infrastructure, a stock of knowledge, information and human skills enabling an organization to transform inputs into outputs and decision making. Innovation therefore draws on a large number of heterogeneous resources, which are not easily acquired (Håkansson, 1987).

Our theoretical explanation of these flows of heterogeneous resources and interaction in networks and innovation systems builds on the resource-based theory of networks (Pfeffer and Salançik, 1978) and the theory of interactive learning (Lundvall, 1992). Both approaches build on the complexity perspective, which implies basically that growth of knowledge yields more elaborate production and innovation processes. Inherent in complexity is the dilemma of co-ordination and co-operation, the need to build external linkages and control many discrete activities (Hage and Alter, 1994). Both of these approaches, however, share a knowledge-based perspective of the firm, which assumes that organizations can more easily accumulate knowledge and utilize it than can individuals or markets. Markets do not accumulate knowledge; they provide the invisible space connecting knowledgeable actors.

Although very implicit, the innovation systems approach posits a resource-based innovative firm behaviour, usually referred to as the technological capabilities of a nation's firms (Nelson, 1993). The central tenet is that, the higher the environmental dynamics, the more complex the innovative activity, and the more a firm has to draw on its internal and external environment in order to acquire all the knowledge resources conducive to innovation. Consequently, firms have to monitor actively their resource bases, particularly their knowledge base (embodied and disembodied), as well as their financial position, and decide how to solve their resource deficits. In that context, the intensification of existing relationships or the formation of new linkages with other firms, institutional actors like universities or venture capitalists, are considered as behavioural alternatives which facilitate innovation strategies. The competence of each regional actor to complement the resource base of the innovating firm can be evaluated. Thus, the interaction between innovating firms and a broad range of firms and institutional actors is the corollary of their need for heterogeneous resources (Håkansson, 1987; Lundvall, 1992; Hage and Alter, 1994; Tödtling, 1994).

Another related, although less implicit, notion in the literature on innovation systems is interactive learning. Learning is conceived as a process in which all kinds of knowledge are recombined to form something new. The interactivity of this learning relates to its dependency on the communication between people or organizations possessing different types of required knowledge. Basically, Lundvall's (1992) account of interactive learning clarifies: 1) how technological and market dynamics pressurize firms to innovate their processes and products, and 2) how this innovation process impels firms to interact forward and backward in the production chain. In Lundvall's theory innovation is conceptualized as an informational commodity (Cohendet *et al.*, 1993), and innovation profits are interpreted in a Schumpeterian way as transitory. In this view, the acquisition and protection of information is essential in order to innovate and profit from the innovation, which explains both the emergence of linkages and the importance of control.

Lundvall's starting point is that a broader range of technological opportunities and a higher changeability of user needs generate a higher rate of innovation. Since innovation is, by definition, the creation of qualitatively different, new objects and new knowledge, the chances and threats of technological opportunities, as well as changing user needs have to be evaluated in order to know whether they can be translated into new product/ process features. Particularly when a firm intends to innovate its processes or products, this feasibility check demands close co-operation between users and producers, because users provide the required information for the producers. This has two related consequences:

1. a higher rate of innovation generates more intense patterns of interaction between users and producers; and
2. a higher level of innovation (incremental/radical) affects the complexity of knowledge exchange.

It is especially radical innovations which erase existing communication codes between user and producers. New codes have to be developed on a trial and error basis, and this requires intensive interactions between users and producers as compared with incremental innovations. All these consequences are more easily assimilated with partners in the vicinity of the innovating firm.

The link between interactive learning and the resource-based perspective of innovation is straightforward. Higher rates and levels of innovation not only compel firms to interact with their customers and suppliers to check the feasibility of their innovation plans, but also force them to monitor and evaluate their resource base in order to determine their internal capabilities for implementing the innovation project. Thus, the central premise of our argument is that the higher complexity of an innovation project makes the detection of internal resource deficits more probable and therefore enlarges the chances of building external relationships. Firms have at least two alternatives for adapting their levels of interactive learning: they can either intensify the existing relationships (strength), or they can extend the number of relationships (variety) in order to complement their resource shortages. Thus our general research question is as follows: to what extent does the complexity of innovative activities affect the level of interactive learning between innovating firms, other firms and institutional actors within a region?

10.3   TOWARDS A RESEARCH MODEL

Our dependent variable is defined as the level of interactive learning between the innovating firms and the regional actors. Since we discerned two strategies for complementing innovation-induced resource deficits or shortages, the level of interactive learning is specified as: the strength and the variety of the linkages of the innovating firms with regional actors.[3] The strength of a relationship is defined as either the frequency of regional actors' active participation in, or contribution of ideas to, the innovation process of the innovating firm. The variety of relationships is defined as the number of different regional actors involved in the innovating firms' innovation projects.

What kinds of actors can be discerned within a region that could complement the resource deficits of the innovating firm or provide information on technological opportunities and changing user needs? The empirical literature supplies a broad variety of actors interacting in the innovation process. The key interactions involved are those between component and system producers, upstream and downstream firms, universities and industry, and government agencies and universities and industries (Nelson, 1993). Pavitt (1984) and Von Hippel (1976) stressed the role of suppliers and users. There is ample evidence that innovating firms co-operate with institutional actors like universities and higher vocational education in the knowledge infrastructure (Höglund & Person, 1987; Van Dierdonck, 1990; Mitchell, 1991). This also applies to relationships between competitors (Von Hippel, 1987; Kleinknecht and Reijnen, 1992; Hagedoorn and Schakenraad, 1992). Cooke *et al.* (1997) presents one of the most complete descriptions of the regional actor set contributing potentially to the innovation projects of innovating firms, including: firms in the production chain, intermediaries and the public knowledge infrastructure[4] (see Figure 10.1).

The independent variable in our research question is defined as the complexity of innovative activities. This raises another important theoretical issue affecting the measurement of the level of complexity of innovative

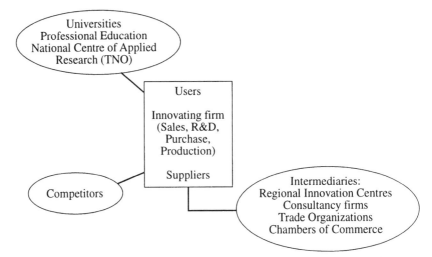

*Figure 10.1   Actor sets within a regional system of innovation (adapted from
Cooke et al., 1997)*

activities (see Figure 10.2). Hage and Alter (1994) define complexity as a
broad social issue in terms of the proliferation of knowledge, which makes
production and innovation processes more elaborate and requires a broader
variety of resources. Lundvall (1992) has a macro, as well as a micro
explanation of the complexity of innovative activities. At the macro level,
technological dynamics and changing user needs generate higher innovation
rates. The rate of innovation is particularly effective at a sectoral level (Pavitt,
1984; Cohen and Levin,1989; Baldwin and Scott, 1987). A micro explanation
of complexity of innovative activities is the level of innovation, defined in
terms of the radicalness of an innovation (Lundvall, 1992; Maillat, 1991).
Finally, the complexity of innovative activities can be measured at different
phases of innovation, with distinct types of search behaviour, which draw on
distinct resource bases (Mezias and Lant, 1994; Cyert and March, 1963).

10.4   HYPOTHESES

Pavitt (1984) showed that innovation rates differ widely between different
sectors because of distinct technological dynamics. Following Lundvall
(1992), this implies a different level of complexity of innovative activities in
these sectors. Pavitt also described the variety of relationships of the
innovating firms with external actors, as well as the contributions of internal
departments to their innovative activities. His findings do indeed confirm that

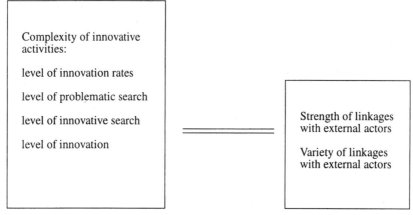

Figure 10.2   A research model of the relation between the complexity of innovative activities and the relationships of innovating firms with regional actors

the firms in the sector with the highest innovation rates had the largest variety of actors involved in their innovations.

The supplier-dominated firms can be found in traditional sectors of manufacturing, and in agriculture, construction and many professional, financial and commercial services. They are generally small and their in-house R&D and engineering capabilities are weak. Consequently, these sectors make only a minor contribution to their process or product technology and have relatively low innovation rates. Their main sources of technology are linkages with their suppliers and with big users. The scale-intensive producers are found in food products, metal manufacturing, shipbuilding, motor vehicles, and glass and cement. They produce a relatively high proportion of their own process technology, to which they devote a high proportion of their innovative resources. Innovating firms are relatively big and have a relatively high level of vertical technological diversification into equipment related to their own process technology. Scale-intensive firms acquire their technology from external and in-house suppliers and some internal departments. The specialized suppliers – mechanical and instrument engineering firms – produce a relatively high proportion of their own process technology too, but the main focus of their innovative activities is the manufacture of product innovations for use in other sectors. Innovating firms are relatively small. Specialized suppliers acquire their technology from their users and product design. The science-based industries are to be found in chemicals, oil and electronics. These firms are relatively large and have a high R&D intensity, which is done in-house. They produce a high proportion of their own process technology, as well as a high proportion of product innovations that are used in other sectors. Science-based firms have their internal R&D, production engineering, in-house suppliers and public science as technology sources.

Because of higher technological dynamics and rapid changes in user needs, the science-based and specialized industries generally have higher innovation rates. Higher innovation rates make the occurrence of internal resource deficits more probable. Innovating firms in the supplier-dominated and scale-intensive industries therefore interact less frequently with the actor set than innovating firms in science-based industries and specialized suppliers. This yields hypotheses 1a and 1b:

H1a   Supplier-dominated and scale-intensive innovating firms have weaker relations with the regional actor set than innovating firms in science-based industries and specialized suppliers.

H1b   Supplier-dominated and scale-intensive innovating firms have a smaller variety of relationships with the regional actor set than innovating firms in science-based industries and specialized suppliers.

In innovation research, the nexus between complexity and regional linkages is often indicated by the contrast between incremental and radical innovation. Lundvall (1992, 1993) and Maillat (1991) gave similar accounts for the relation between the level of innovation and the emergence of linkages. Maillat (1991) argues that the importance of the local environment for innovation is dependent both on the type of innovation and on the firms' innovation strategy. For incremental innovators, the local production environment is of little importance. According to Maillat, the resources necessary for incremental innovation can, in many cases, be found in the firm itself. Radical innovators, however, develop more relations with the local production environment if they have an insufficient supply of internal resources for realizing this type of innovation. We therefore infer that innovating firms implementing radical innovations have a higher probability of internal resource shortages and face higher uncertainties and are therefore more inclined to develop new linkages or intensify existing ones. Accordingly we hypothesize:

H2a   Innovating firms implementing radical innovations have stronger relationships with the regional actors set than innovating firms implementing incremental innovations.

H2b   Innovating firms implementing radical innovations have a larger variety of relationships with the regional actors set than innovating firms implementing incremental innovations.

Complexity has different meanings at different stages of the innovation process and it also impacts in different ways on the formation of linkages. At the pre-innovation stage complexity pertains to innovative search activities (Mezias and Lant, 1994). Innovative search increases as the firm becomes wealthier relative to other firms in the population. Firms' innovative searches are aimed at the monitoring of innovation possibilities for their products or processes, either looking at new technical findings or at new market needs. There are uncertainties about markets and technologies. These uncertainties, which are induced by both types of information, trigger an internal and external assessment of the capabilities needed to incorporate these new technical findings into an efficient process or product. If the internal resource base is insufficient, the alternative option is to draw on external resources. Because innovative search deals with the processing of relatively new and unused knowledge, it probably gives rise to more processing problems and therefore increases the likelihood of internal knowledge shortages, which in turn enlarges the probability of the emergence of external linkages. Hence, innovating firms with lower levels of innovative search activities interact less frequently with the actor set than firms with higher levels of innovative search activities. We therefore hypothesize:

H3a   Innovating firms with lower levels of problematic search activities have weaker relationships with the regional actor set than innovating firms with higher levels of problematic search activities.

H3b   Innovating firms with lower levels of problematic search activities have a smaller variety of relationships with the regional actor set than innovating firms with higher levels of problematic search activities.

Operational deficiencies are detected at the start of the implementation of an innovation-specific search, which is the point where a problematic search begins. The notion of problematic search is derived from Cyert and March (1963, pp. 79, 120). By problematic search, Cyert and March mean a search that is stimulated by a problem (usually a rather specific one) and is directed towards finding a solution to that problem. Problematic search increases by the amount by which performance is below aspiration level. Firms with this type of search consider those changes that alter the status quo only slightly. Since the solution of product deficiencies pertains to an existing product, it is probably concerned with codified knowledge. Where the problems are well defined and the knowledge required is not internally available, a higher level of interaction with external actors can be expected. However, it is well known that the solution of operational technical problems is often very troublesome and relies on untraceable tacit knowledge and tinkering. If the problems are ill-defined, knowledge deficits cannot be defined either. In that case we expect that problems be tackled in a trial and error mode internally, because building links outside the firm is not very effective. Hence we infer that innovating firms with lower levels of problematic search activities interact less frequently with the actor set than firms with higher levels of problematic search activities, but subject to the condition that the problems to be solved are well defined. Our hypotheses read as follows:

H4a   Innovating firms with lower levels of innovative search activities have weaker relations with the regional actor set than innovating firms with higher levels of innovative search activities.

H4b   Innovating firms with lower levels of innovative search activities have less variety in the relationships with the regional actor set than innovating firms with higher levels of innovative search activities.

10.5   RESEARCH DESIGN

Sample

A survey was conducted among industrial firms with five or more employees in North Brabant (a province in the southern part of the Netherlands). The data gathering took place between December 1992 and January 1993.

The data gathering was performed in a region with characteristic features. This region is one of the most industrialized regions in the Netherlands. In 1992, the total number of jobs in manufacturing was roughly 210,000; the share of manufacturing in the total employment of the region was 28.8 per cent (the Netherlands, 19.5 per cent). The population of firms in the region consists of a mix of small, medium-sized and large enterprises. About 84 per cent of the responding firms have 100 or fewer employees. Moreover, the manufacturing sector has shown a relatively high R&D and export performance (Meeus and Oerlemans, 1995). Because technological activity is an important issue in this article, industrial firms were grouped according to Pavitt's taxonomy (Oerlemans, 1996).

Our sample (see Table 10.1) is a reliable representation of the population of industrial firms in North Brabant, with sample strata and population strata deviating within limits of 8 per cent. The mean deviation between the percentages in the sample and in the response is 6.4 percentage points.

Analyses

In this paper we restrict our analyses to descriptive, exploratory analyses

Table 10.1 Population and sample divided into Pavitt sectors

Pavitt sector	Population	% population	% sample
Supplier dominated	1,028	33.5	25.7
Scale intensive	1,261	41.1	36.1
Specialized suppliers	417	13.6	21.4
Science based	363	11.8	16.8
Total	3,069	100	100

testing the bivariate relations between four different indicators of the complexity of innovative activities and the strength and variety of external linkages. Because of the level of measurement of our variables – ordinal rank scores – we will apply only non-parametric analyses.

We used two non-parametric statistical tests. The first was the Mann–Whitney U test, which is the most popular of the two-independent-samples tests. It is equivalent to the Wilcoxon rank sum test and the Krusskal–Wallis test for two groups. Mann–Whitney tests whether two sampled populations are equivalent in location. The observations from both groups are combined and ranked, with the average rank assigned in the event of ties. The number of ties should be small relative to the total number of observations. If the populations are identical in location, the ranks should be randomly mixed between the two samples. The number of times a score from group 1 precedes a score from group 2 and the number of times a score from group 2 precedes a score from group 1 were calculated. In Tables 10.2 and 10.4 this test is abbreviated as 'M-W'. The second test was the Krusskal–Wallis H-test. This is a non-parametric equivalent to one-way ANOVA. It tests whether more than two independent samples are from the same population. Assuming that the underlying variable has a continuous distribution and requires an ordinal level of measurement, the null hypothesis is that k related variables come from the same population. For each case, the k variables are ranked from 1 to k. The test statistic is based on these ranks. In Tables 10.2 and 10.4 this test is abbreviated as 'K-W'.

10.6 RESULTS

We shall first review the outcomes of our descriptive analyses, after which we shall describe the results of testing hypotheses H1a–H4a about the strength of external relationships. Lastly, we review the results of testing hypotheses H1b–H4b about the variety of external relationships.

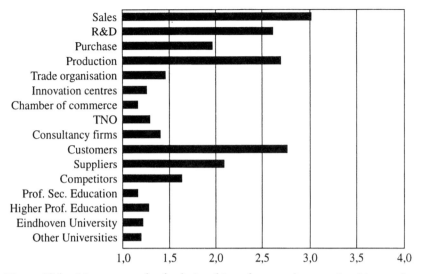

Figure 10.3 *Mean strength of relationships of external actors (and internal*
actors) with the innovating firms in North Brabant in terms of
the frequency (n=402)

Descriptive Statistics

Our general finding (Figure 10.3), is that the innovation process of the local firms seems to be affected most by internal departments, customers and suppliers. Neither the intermediary organizations, nor the public knowledge infrastructure have strong relations with the innovating firms. We accordingly infer that the innovating firms underutilize their environment within this specific regional innovation system.

Our findings gave very weak support to hypothesis 1a (Table 10.2, column 1/1a). This proxy of the complexity of innovative activities does not induce stronger relationships with many regional actors. Only four of the twelve actors have significantly different mean ranks: trade organizations, Eindhoven University of Technology, customers and suppliers. Our hypothesis on the strength of relations between innovating firms and the customers is confirmed. Science-based industries and specialized suppliers have the strongest relations with their customers. But other findings revealed that this hypothesis has to be rejected: 1) innovating firms in the supplier-dominated industries have the strongest relations with both trade organizations and suppliers; 2) whereas science-based industries were expected to have the strongest relations with the universities, our findings showed that specialized suppliers and scale-intensive industries have stronger relationships with

Eindhoven University. Although Pavitt sectors have different technological dynamics and innovation rates, we must conclude that, except for the user–producer interaction, our hypothesis cannot be considered as valid.

Hypothesis 2a is partly confirmed by our findings. The radicalism of innovations discriminated more strongly for patterns of interaction between product innovators and the actor set, than for patterns of interaction of process innovators with their actor set. Table 10.2 shows that radical innovators had stronger relations than incremental innovators: 5 for the product innovators (column 4/4a), 2 for the process innovators (column 5/5a). The actors in the value chain – customers and suppliers – in particular, developed stronger relationships with radical product innovators than with incremental product innovators. These differences were absent for radical and incremental process innovators. Radical innovators (process and product) draw more than incremental innovators on the knowledge infrastructure (Eindhoven University, Tilburg University, TNO).

Hypothesis 3a was again partly confirmed. Our findings (Table 10.2, columns 2/2a) revealed that a higher level of problematic search generates stronger relations with five regional actors; partly in the public knowledge infrastructure (Professional Secondary and Higher Professional Education, Eindhoven University) and partly in the production chain (customers, suppliers).

Hypothesis 4a was also partially confirmed (Table 10.2, column 3/3a). In 8 out of 12 bivariate relations significant differences occurred in the strength of relations between innovating firms and the actor set. Three of those (Eindhoven University, other universities and competitors) did not have the expected direction of differences between ranks and had stronger relations with firms showing intermediate levels of innovative search.

The effects of complexity of innovative activities on the strength of relationships are summarized in Table 10.3. Our findings reveal that the effects of complexity are anything but automatic. The Pavitt taxonomy, as a sectoral proxy of complexity, only affected the strength of relations with the customers in the expected direction. The other indicators for complexity of innovative activities – the radicalness of product innovations, the levels of innovative and problematic search – provide an interesting basis for developing a deeper explanation of the strength of localized relationships.

Hypothesis 1b was rejected (Table 10.4, column 1/1b). Accordingly, innovating firms from different Pavitt sectors are equal as far as the variety of regional actors involved in their innovation projects is concerned. Hypothesis 2b is also rejected. Table 10.4 (columns 5/5a and 6/6a) shows that radicalness of innovations did not affect the number of external relationships. Hypothesis 3b was confirmed (Table 10.4, column 2/2a). Our findings revealed that a higher level of problematic search induced a wider variety of external

Table 10.2 Hypotheses 1a–4a: complexity of innovative activities and strength of relationships

Actor	1 Sector	1a Rank sign.	2 Problematic search	2a Rank sign.	3 Innovative search	3a Rank sign.	4 Product innovation level	4a Rank sign.	5 Process innovation level	5a Rank sign.
Trade Organizations	Supplier	1	0	3	0	3	incremental	1	incremental	1
	Scale	2	1	2	1	2	radical	2	radical	2
	Special	4	2	1	2	1				
	Science	3								
	K-W	<0.05	K-W	ns	K-W	ns	M-W	ns	M-W	ns
Innovation Centres	Supplier	4	0	1	0	3	incremental	1	incremental	1
	Scale	3	1	3	1	2	radical	2	radical	2
	Special	1	2	2	2	1				
	Science	2								
	K-W	ns	K-W	ns	K-W	ns	M-W	ns	M-W	ns
Chambers of Commerce	Supplier	4	0	3	0	2	incremental	1	incremental	1
	Scale	1	1	2	1	3	radical	2	radical	2
	Special	2	2	1	2	1				
	Science	3								
	K-W	ns	K-W	ns	K-W	ns	M-W	ns	M-W	<0.10
TNO	Supplier	2	0	3	0	3	incremental	1	incremental	2
	Scale	1	1	2	1	2	radical	2	radical	1
	Special	3	2	1	2	1				
	Science	4								
	K-W	ns	K-W	ns	K-W	<0.10	M-W	<0.05	M-W	ns
Consultancy Firms	Supplier	1	0	3	0	3	incremental	2	incremental	1
	Scale	3	1	2	1	1	radical	1	radical	2
	Special	4	2	1	2	2				
	Science	2								
	K-W	ns	K-W	ns	K-W	ns	M-W	ns	M-W	ns
Professional Secondary Education	Supplier	4	0	3	0	3	incremental	2	incremental	2
	Scale	3	1	2	1	2	radical	1	radical	1
	Special	1	2	1	2	1				
	Science	2								
	K-W	ns	K-W	<0.01	K-W	<0.01	M-W	<0.10	M-W	ns

Table (rotated 90° on the page). Columns 2–6 report Kruskal–Wallis (K-W) rankings and significance; columns 7–9 report Mann–Whitney U (M-W) comparisons of *incremental* vs *radical* innovations.

Source		K-W	K-W	K-W	K-W	K-W	M-W (incremental / radical)	M-W (incremental / radical)
0 Higher Professional Education	Supplier	4	0	3	0	3	incremental 2	incremental 2
	Scale	2	1	2	1	2	radical 1	radical 1
	Special	1	2	1	2	1		
	Science	3						
	K-W	ns	K-W	<0.000	K-W	<0.05	M-W ns	M-W ns
Eindhoven University of Technology	Supplier	4	0	3	0	3	incremental 2	incremental 2
	Scale	2	1	2	1	1	radical 1	radical 1
	Special	1	2	1	2	2		
	Science	3						
	K-W	<0.10	K-W	<0.10	K-W	<0.05	M-W ns	M-W <0.05
Other Dutch Universities	Supplier	4	0	3	0	3	incremental 2	incremental 2
	Scale	2	1	2	1	1	radical 1	radical 1
	Special	1	2	1	2	2		
	Science	3						
	K-W	ns	K-W	ns	K-W	<0.05	M-W <0.01	M-W <0.05
Customers	Supplier	3	0	3	0	3	incremental 2	incremental 1
	Scale	4	1	2	1	2	radical 1	radical 2
	Special	2	2	1	2	1		
	Science	1						
	K-W	<0.001	K-W	<0.001	K-W	<0.05	M-W <0.05	M-W <0.01
Suppliers	Supplier	1	0	3	0	3	incremental 2	incremental 2
	Scale	3	1	2	1	2	radical 1	radical 1
	Special	4	2	1	2	1		
	Science	2						
	K-W	<0.001	K-W	<0.01	K-W	<0.01	M-W <0.10	M-W <0.05
Competitors	Supplier	1	0	3	0	3	incremental 2	incremental 2
	Scale	2	1	1	1	1	radical 1	radical 1
	Special	4	2	2	2	2		
	Science	3						
	K-W	ns	K-W	ns	K-W	<0.05	M-W ns	M-W ns

ns   not significant
K-W   Krusskal–Wallis test for k independent samples
M-W   Mann–Whitney U test for two independent samples

Table 10.3   Overview of the findings for separate hypotheses on strength of relationships

Hypotheses incl. expected rankings	Strength of relationship (incl. number of significant differences [s.d.]/number and type of actors with expected ranking)
H1a Pavitt sectors Exp.: Science based, specialized suppliers>supplier dominated, scale intensive	Partial confirmation (4 s.d./only for customers)
H2a Level of innovation Product innovation: incremental vs radical Exp.: Rad>Incr.	Partial confirmation (5 s.d./4 actors: PSE, other Dutch universities, customers, suppliers)
Process innovation: incremental vs. radical Exp.: Rad>Incr.	Partial confirmation (3 s.d./2 actors: EUT, other Dutch universities)
H3a Problematic search: low-high Exp.: low<high	Partial confirmation (5 s.d./5 actors: PSE, HPE, EUT, customers, suppliers)
H4a Innovative search: low-high Exp.: low<high	Partial confirmation (8 s.d./5 actors: TNO, PSE, HPE, customers, suppliers)

PSE: Professional Secondary Education
HPE: Higher Professional Education
EUT: Eindhoven University of Technology
TNO: National Centre for Applied Research

linkages. This also applies to Hypothesis 4b. Table 10.4 (column 3/3a) shows that higher levels of innovative search are associated with a higher variety of external relationships.

10.7   DISCUSSION AND CONCLUSIONS

Our descriptive statistics raise the issue of the utilization of the knowledge infrastructure and the intermediaries by innovating firms. The low mean scores in Figure 10.3 suggest that the innovating firms in this specific region

Table 10.4 *Hypotheses 1b–4b: complexity of innovative activities and variety of relationships*

1 Sector	1a Rank sign.	2 Problematic search	2a Rank sign.	3 Innovative search	3a Rank sign.	4 Product innovation level	4a Rank sign.	5 Process innovation level	5a Rank sign.
Supplier	2	0	3	0	3	incremental	2	incremental	2
Scale	1	1	2	1	2	radical	1	radical	1
Special	4	2	1	2	1				
Science	3								
K-W	ns	K-W	<.001	K-W	<.001	M-W	ns	M-W	ns

ns   not significant
K-W   Krusskal–Wallis test for k independent samples
M-W   Mann–Whitney U test for two independent samples

209

do not exploit external knowledge bases at all frequently and, in fact, underutilize their regional resources. However, the strength of external relationships is put in perspective by the mean scores of internal departments, which are indeed higher, but hardly exceed the score of 3, which means that the interaction frequency with this actor is 'regular'.

These findings suggest that several barriers have to be overcome before innovating firms draw on their external environment. This raises the issue as to what factors explain the existence of utilization barriers? The explanation of this phenomenon is manifold and depends on which actor's standpoint is taken. Obviously, the dependence on specific technological, organizational and economic knowledge does not necessarily generate strong links between firms and the broader knowledge infrastructure. From the perspective of firms, this can be explained by the possibilities they have for the acquisition of knowledge resources and also by the goals of their innovation. Firms can recruit personnel with the skills and qualifications necessary for innovation. If such personnel are not available or the risks of hiring new personnel are too high, firms can develop alliances with competitors, buyers or suppliers, and acquire the knowledge resources in that way.

Reasoning from the position of the universities, the problem is of a different kind. The financial structure of universities and higher education in the Netherlands is designed mainly for the production of graduates and scientific output, while it does not reward co-operation with firms. As far as the Innovation Centres are concerned, the reasons for their low innovation inputs lie in the scale of these centres. Dutch Innovation Centres have from ten to thirty employees, which puts them in the position of information brokers. Consequently, the real innovative work is done by other organizations than the ICs, which at least partly explains their low visibility in our findings. For TNO (Dutch Centre for Applied Research), there may be other reasons for the relatively low innovation inputs to innovating firms in Brabant. The majority of employees, working at the head office, are located in another province. At the time our data were gathered, TNO had only a few specific centres (logistics) in Brabant and this might have formed a utilization barrier for small and medium-sized firms. Another explanation of the weak ties with external actors is that innovation in most firms and, especially, small and medium-sized ones is often discontinuous. Since 84 per cent of our sample consists of small and medium-sized firms, this discontinuity is very likely to occur in this region. Lastly, the firms in this region may have kept their distance from the knowledge infrastructure, because the rewards of co-operation are either unknown or too small, or because the firms lack the absorptive capacity to assimilate the available external knowledge.

This finding nevertheless has profound implications for the competitiveness of this region, because empirical research has shown that stronger external relationships contribute to the innovative performance of firms in North Brabant (Oerlemans *et al.*, 1998). Accordingly, this under-utilization implies that firms in this region probably underuse their innovative capabilities. Though Brabant's regional innovation system seems to be well equipped, it did not stimulate synergism between the innovative activities. This underlines the importance of a number of regional policy initiatives taken in the early nineties. There are several projects that activate relations between small and medium-sized firms and large firms through the transfer of innovation management knowledge between SMEs and large firms (the Plato project) and the formation of networks by technology brokers from the regional Innovation Centres (the 'Vlechtwerken' - networks - project). However, neither Tilburg University, nor Eindhoven University of Technology play an important role in these projects.

The involvement of universities in firms' innovative activities is an important policy issue, which is in general addressed at a supranational level. In the Netherlands, the IORPs (Innovation Oriented Research Programmes) are aimed at intensifying the relationship between the universities and industry. Joint research programmes are prepared after extensive network research and the identification of knowledge producers and users. The implemented research programmes take user needs as a starting point (Meeus *et al.*, 1997; Oerlemans and Meeus, 1999). Our findings confirm that, in the context of these research programmes, firms recognize Dutch technical universities as the main knowledge generators. The EU and US have also initiated several programmes concentrating on stronger industry–university co-operation.

Our theoretical explanation of the strength and variety of linkages with distinct complexity indicators allows for a less speculative explanation of the phenomenon of utilization barriers and clarifies why innovating firms exploit external knowledge more or less actively. This yields new directions for future research into regional innovation systems and for the development of new policy initiatives.

The main conclusion from our exploratory analyses is that more complex innovative activities do indeed trigger stronger and more varied external relationships, but our findings also revealed that direct measures of the complexity of innovative activities (radicalness, search types) are better predictors of the strength and variety of external linkages than the indirect measures (Pavitt sectors).

Pavitt's sector classification as a proxy for complexity of innovative activities does not add directly to the explanation of the strength or variety of external relationships. Interactive learning aimed at the exploitation of external knowledge is distributed equally among sectors. From a policy perspective this finding implies that there is no need to develop a sectoral approach for the encouragement of interactive learning in this region.

The radicalness of innovations in general affects the strength, but not the variety of external relationships of innovating firms. Radicalness of product innovations intensifies links with customers and suppliers, which is not the case for the radicalness of process innovations, so our findings confirm Lundvall's hunch about the inward orientation of process innovation, as compared with a more external orientation of product innovation (Lundvall, 1992). The radicalness of both process and product innovations induces innovating firms to build stronger relations with actors in the public knowledge infrastructure. This finding, in particular, adds considerably to our speculations on the underutilization of regional knowledge bases. Radically innovating firms obviously have to draw more actively on external knowledge bases provided by the public knowledge infrastructure. Hence we infer that one of the causes of underutilization of the public knowledge base is that a majority of firms either refrain from innovation or innovate incrementally. Since there is empirical evidence that technologically inert firms show a worse innovative performance than technologically proactive firms (Meeus and Oerlemans, 1999), this once again underlines the consequences of a technologically conservative population of firms. This region has about 40 per cent of firms without any innovative activity.

The 'search' variables also added some very interesting insights. Both the level of innovative search activities and the level of problematic search activities were found to have a relatively high discriminatory value for both dependent variables. Both types of search activities were found not only to affect the strength of external relationships with both the public knowledge infrastructure and with customers and suppliers, but also to affect the variety of linkages with external regional actors.

The theoretical implications of these findings are that three out of four indicators of the complexity of innovative activities provide a sound empirical starting point for the further development of the complexity theory in explaining the connectivity within regional innovation systems. Future research should try to develop this complexity perspective further by means of more elaborate models controlling for the internal resource base, age and size, because these factors probably moderate the extent to which innovating firms draw on external knowledge bases. Another important line of research is to compare regions for their connectivity. By comparing the external linkages of innovating firms within several comparable regions, we may tease out the effects of networking on regional competitiveness. Moreover, given the low utilization of regional resources in this specific region, we suggest research focusing on the comparison of strategies for the acquisition of distinct resources and their relative contributions to innovative performance. This will allow us to support both the efficiency of network strategies and the efficacy of regional innovation systems more solidly.

Although we contend that the results of this study provide a valuable addition to the micro-foundations of the theory of innovation systems, several notes of caution are called for, firstly, because we studied a specific region, with a specific population of predominantly small and medium-sized firms and, secondly, because we did not control for differences in resource bases, size and age. A third point is that our analyses do not allow us to trace interaction effects between the independent variables.

ACKNOWLEDGEMENTS

The authors wish to thank the members of the NIAS-theme group 'The Idea-Innovation Chain' (Steve Casper, Jerald Hage, Roger Hollingsworth, Ernst Homburg, Bart Nooteboom, Birgitte Unger, Frans van Waarden and Richard Whitley), as well as Eddy Szirmai (Eindhoven Centre for Innovation Studies) for their critical comments on our paper. The usual disclaimer, of course, applies.

NOTES

1. Eindhoven Centre for Innovation Studies, Faculty of Technology Management, Eindhoven University of Technology, P.O. Box 513 Building DG 1.16, 5600 MB Eindhoven, Telephone +31 40 2473450/2640.
   E-mail: M.T.H.Meeus@TM.TUE.NL
   NIAS (Netherlands Institute for the Advanced Studies in the Humanities and Social Sciences) Royal Netherlands Academy of Arts and Sciences, Meijboomlaan 1, 2242 PR, Wassenaar, The Netherlands.
   E-mail: M.H.T.Meeus@NIAS.KNAW.NL
2. Eindhoven Centre for Innovation Studies, Faculty of Technology Management, Eindhoven University of Technology, P.O. Box 513 Building DG 1.09, 5600 MB Eindhoven, Telephone +31 40 2473450/2640.
   E-mail: L.A.G.Oerlemans@TM.TUE.NL
3. Although financial institutions like banks and venture capitalists and local and regional authorities facilitate the emergence and persistence of innovation networks they do not contribute directly to the process of interactive learning during innovation. We therefore excluded these actors from the actor set in Figure 10.1.

REFERENCES

Baldwin, W.L. and J.T. Scott (1987), *Market Structure and Technological Change*, London: Harwood Academic Publishers.

Bergman, E., G. Maier and F. Tödtling (eds) (1991), *Regions Reconsidered: Networks, Innovation and Local Development in Industrialized Countries*, London: Cassel.

Cohen, W.M. and R.C. Levin (1989), 'Empirical studies of innovation and market structure', in R. Schmalensee and R.D. Willig (eds), *Handbook of Industrial*

Organisation, Amsterdam: Elsevier Science Publishers, pp. 1060-170.
Cohendet, P., J.A. Héraud and E. Zuscovitch (1993), 'Technological learning, economic networks and innovation appropriability', in D. Foray and C. Freeman, 1993, *Technology and the Wealth of Nations. The Dynamics of Constructed Advantage*, London: Pinter Publishers, pp. 66-76.
Cooke, P., M. Gomez Uranga and G. Etxebarria (1997), 'Regional innovation systems: Institutional and organisations dimensions', *Research Policy*, (26), pp. 475-91.
Cyert, R.M. and J.G. March (1963), *A Behavioral Theory of the Firm*, Englewood Cliffs, New Jersey: Prentice Hall Inc.
Dalum, B. (1992), 'Export specialisation, structural competitiveness and national systems of innovation', in B.A. Lundvall, *National Systems of Innovation. Towards a Theory of Innovation and Interactive Learning*, London: Pinter Publishers, pp. 191-225.
DeBresson C. and E.S. Andersen (1996), *Economic Interdependence and Innovative Activity, an Input-Output Analysis*, Cheltenham: Edward Elgar Publishing.
Dierdonck, R. van (1990), 'University–industry relationships: How does the Belgian Academic community feel about it?', in *Research Policy*, (19), pp. 551-66.
Edquist, C. and B.A. Lundvall (1993), 'Comparing the Danish and Swedish systems of innovation', in R. Nelson (ed.) (1993), *National Innovation Systems. A Comparative Analysis*, New York: Oxford University Press, pp. 265-99.
Fagerberg, J. (1992), 'The home market hypothesis re-examined: the impact of domestic user-producer interaction on export specialisation', in B.A. Lundvall, *National Systems of Innovation. Towards a Theory of Innovation and Interactive Learning*, London: Pinter Publishers, pp. 226-41.
Florida, R. (1995), 'Towards the learning region', *Futures*, **27** (5), pp. 527-36.
Freeman, C. and L. Soete (1997), *The Economics of Innovation*, London: Pinter.
Foray, D. and C. Freeman (1993), *Technology and the Wealth of Nations. The Dynamics of Constructed Advantage*, London: Pinter Publishers.
Grabher, G. (1991), 'Rebuilding cathedrals in the desert: new patterns of cooperation between large and small firms in the coal, iron and steel complex of the German Ruhr area', in E.M. Bergman, G. Maier and F. Tödtling (eds), *Regions Reconsidered: Economic Networks, Innovation and Local Development in Industrialized Countries*, London: Mansell Publishing Limited, pp. 59-78.
Gregersen, B. and B. Johnson (1997), 'Learning economies, innovation systems and European integration', in *Regional Studies*, **31**, pp. 479-90.
Hage, J. and C. Alter (1994), 'A typology of interorganizational relationships and networks', in J.R. Hollingsworth and R. Boyer, *Contemporary Capitalism. The Embeddedness of Institutions*, Cambridge: Cambridge University Press, pp. 94-126.
Hagedoorn, J. and J. Schakenraad (1992), 'Leading companies and networks of strategic alliances in information technologies', in *Research Policy*, (21), pp. 163-90.
Håkansson, H. (1987), *Industrial Technological Development: A Network Approach*, London: Croom Helm.
Håkansson, H. (1989), *Corporate Technological Behavior: Co-operation and Networks*, London : Routledge.
Harabi, N. (1997), 'Channels of R&D spillovers: An empirical investigation of Swiss firms', *Technovation*, (17), pp. 627-35.
Höglund, L. and O. Persson (1987), 'Communication within a national R&D-system: A study of iron and steel in Sweden', in *Research Policy*, (16), pp. 29-37.
Illeris, S. and L. Jakobsen (1990), *Networks and Regional Development*, Copenhagen:

Akademisk Forlag, University Press Copenhagen.

Kleinknecht, A. and J.O.N. Reijnen (1992), 'Why do firms cooperate on R&D? An empirical study', in *Research Policy*, (21), pp. 347-60.

Knaap, G.A. van der and B.J.L. Tortike (1991), 'Regional economic interaction patterns between enterprises; a case study of the Northern Netherlands', in M. de Smidt and E. Wever (eds), *Complexes, Formations and Networks*, Netherlands Geographical Studies (132), Utrecht: Faculty of Geographical Sciences University of Utrecht, pp. 111-24.

Krolis, H.P. and D.J.F. Kamann (1991), 'Economic growth potential of an industrial complex: the case of the Dutch Flemish Canal', in M. de Smidt and E. Wever (eds), *Complexes, Formations and Networks,* Netherlands Geographical Studies (132), Utrecht: Faculty of Geographical Sciences University of Utrecht, pp. 53-67.

Lundvall, B.A. (1992), 'User-producer relationships, national systems of innovations and internationalisation', in D. Foray and C. Freeman (1993), *Technology and the Wealth of Nations. The Dynamics of Constructed Advantage*, London: Pinter Publishers, pp. 277-300.

Lundvall, B.A. (1993), 'User-producer relationships, national systems of innovation and internalization', in B.A. Lundvall, *National Systems of Innovation. Towards a Theory of Innovation and Interactive Learning*, London: Pinter Publishers, pp. 45-67.

Maillat, D. (1991), 'The innovation process and the role of the milieu', in E. Bergman, G. Maier and F. Tödtling (eds), *Regions Reconsidered: Economic Networks, Innovation and Local Development in Industrialized Countries*, London/New York: Mansell Publishing Limited, pp. 103-17.

Meeus, M.T.H. and L.A.G. Oerlemans (1993), 'Economic network research: a methodological state of the art', in P. Beije, J. Groenwegen and O. Nuys (eds), *Networking in Dutch Industries*, Leuven/Apeldoorn: Garant.

Meeus, M.T.H. and L.A.G. Oerlemans (1995), 'The competitiveness of firms in the region of North-Brabant', in P. Beije and O. Nuys (eds), *The Dutch Diamond. The Usefulness of Porter in Analyzing Small Countries*, Leuven/Apeldoorn: Garant/ Siswo, pp. 223-56.

Meeus, M.T.H. and L.A.G. Oerlemans (1999), *Firm Behaviour and Innovative Performance. An Empirical Exploration of the Selection-Adaptation Debate*, Research Policy (forthcoming).

Meeus, M.T.H., L.A.G. Oerlemans and E. Faber (1997), *IOP Beeldverwerking. Matchen van Kennisvraag en Kennisaanbod door Identificatie van de Doelgroepen en Netwerkanalyse* [IOP Image Processing. Matching knowledge demand and supply by means of identification of knowledge producers and users and network analysis], External report commissioned by CENTER for technology, energy and environment, Den Haag, March 1997, pp. 35.

Mezias, S.J. and T.K. Lant (1994), 'Mimetic learning and the evolution of organizational populations', in J.A.C. Baum and J.V. Singh (eds), *Evolutionary Dynamics of Organizations*, New York: Oxford University Press, pp. 179—98.

Mitchell, W. (1991) 'Using academic technology: Transfer methods and licensing incidence in the commercialization of American diagnostic imaging equipment research, 1945-1988, in *Research Policy* (20), pp. 203-16.

Morgan, K. (1997), 'The learning region: institutions, innovation and regional renewal', *Regional Studies*, **31** (5), pp. 491-503.

Nelson, R. (ed.) (1993), *National Innovation Systems. A Comparative Analysis*, New York: Oxford University Press.

Oerlemans, L.A.G. (1996), 'De ingebedde onderneming: innoveren in industriële netwerken', Tilburg: Tilburg University Press (The embedded firm. Innovation in industrial networks).

Oerlemans, L.A.G. and M.T.H. Meeus (1999), *IOP Mens Machine Interactie. Matchen van Kennisvraag en Kennisaanbod door Identificatie van de Doelgroep en Netwerkanalyse* (IOP Human Systems Interaction. Matching knowledge demand and supply by means of identification of knowledge producers and users and network analysis), external report commissioned by CENTER for technology, energy and environment, Faculty of Technology Management: Eindhoven University of Technology, April 1999, p. 41.

Oerlemans, L.A.G., M.T.H. Meeus and F. Boekema (1998), 'Do networks matter for innovation?, *Journal of Social and Economic Geography*, (3), pp. 298–309.

Pavitt, K. (1984), 'Sectoral patterns of technical change. Towards a taxonomy and a theory', *Research Policy*, (13), pp. 343–73.

Pfeffer, J. and G.R. Salançik (1978), *The External Control of Organizations: A Resource Dependence Perspective*, New York: Basic Books.

Storper, M. and B. Harrison (1991), 'Flexibility, hierarchy and regional developments: the changing structures of production systems and their forms of governance in the 1990s', *Research Policy*, (21), pp. 407–22.

Tödtling, F. (1994), 'Regional networks of high-technology firms – the case of the Greater Boston region', *Technovation*, (14), pp. 323–43.

Verspagen, B. (1997a), 'Estimating international technology spillovers using technology flow matrices', *Weltwirtschaftliches Archiv,* (133), pp. 226–48.

Verspagen, B. (1997b), 'Measuring intersectoral technology spillovers: estimates from the European and US Patent Office database', *Economic Systems Research*, (9), pp. 47–65.

Von Hippel, E. (1976), 'The dominant role of users in the scientific instrument innovation process', in *Research Policy*, (5), pp. 212–39.

Von Hippel, E. (1987), Cooperation between rivals: Informal know-how trading', in *Research Policy*, (16), pp. 291–302.

11. Innovation in Regional Supplier Networks: The Case of KIC

Roel Rutten

Firms are constantly trying to find new ways to improve their competitiveness. One such way is to redesign relations with other firms. No longer is cost reduction the prevailing motivation for firms to reconsider their patterns of collaboration. Instead they focus on added value, that is, what other firms can do to increase one's own competitiveness. Tapping into other firms' knowledge and expertise seems to be a beneficial strategy, and relations with other firms, in particular buyer–supplier relations, are increasingly being adjusted accordingly. In this chapter an effort of this kind made by Océ – a large Dutch manufacturer of copiers and printers – and several of its suppliers is discussed. Océ has, together with several selected suppliers, worked on the development of a new colour copier under the KIC project (Knowledge Industry Clustering). Much of the development for several of the modules or subassemblies for this new copier was done by the suppliers. The information on which the case study of the KIC project in this chapter is based was gathered through a series of interviews with representatives of Océ and several of the suppliers involved in the KIC project.

11.1 INTRODUCING THE CASE STUDY

A Profile of Océ

Océ is one of the leading industrial firms in the Netherlands and a world player in the market for copiers and printers. Originally started as a chemical firm in 1877, Océ entered the copying business in 1920 and has since developed into a producer of high-tech copiers and printers using state-of-the-art technology. In 1997, the turnover of Océ amounted to 2.5 billion euro (2.4 billion US dollars). Worldwide Océ employs nearly 18,000 people, 1,500 of whom work in the R&D services. The company headquarters in Venlo in the Netherlands employs 3,500 people, including 1,100 in R&D. The R&D

budget of Océ increased from 56 million euro (54 million US dollars) in 1987 to 138 million euro (133 million US dollars) in 1997.

Océ has a long tradition of working together with suppliers. One example of this is the fact that the Océ plant in Venlo is basically an R&D and assembly plant. Production is left mainly to suppliers. Océ never had a manufacturing tradition. It focused instead on the development of new concepts and products. The advantages of this way of working lie in the fact that it allows Océ more freedom in design and choice of technologies. This tradition resulted in the KIC project. At present, it is the climax of a trend towards the outsourcing of ever more complex tasks to suppliers. They are now asked to assume responsibility over parts of the product development process. KIC is, however, not the end of the line and Océ and its suppliers will continue to search for new ways to get more out of their relationship in terms of innovation, technology development and competitiveness.

Objectives of the KIC Project

For Océ the KIC project was a way to practice a new way of working together with suppliers. Instead of working on command from blueprints, Océ suppliers are now developing product engineering skills of their own.

Engineering skills and the art of collaboration on innovation are, of course, not developed overnight. They must be learned, and the KIC project was aimed at precisely that. The upgrading of suppliers from jobbers to co-developers surpassed the actual product engineering in importance, although product engineering, the material objective of KIC, was by no means forgotten, but the project offered enough slack for the participants to make it first of all a learning experience. One indication of this is the fact that Océ considers less than a third of the KIC clusters to have produced a successful output in terms of new product development.

The learning related to Océ itself as much as it did to the participating suppliers. Technically, Océ was ahead of the suppliers and it took the lead by initiating the project. In terms of actually working together with suppliers under the new paradigm, Océ had to start basically from the same position as most of its suppliers. Thus learning became a two-way process and, in this respect, both Océ and the suppliers consider the KIC project to be a success.

Objectives of the Study, and Method of Inquiry

This case study gives an in-depth look into the collaboration between Océ and its suppliers on product development under the KIC project. The objective of our research is to explain the process of innovation as it took place under the KIC project between Océ and several regionally based suppliers. Although

KIC was a project which ran for only a few years,[1] the kind of collaboration exposed during KIC is not confined to that project alone, but is part of a broader strategy of both Océ and several of the suppliers involved. We are, in other words, not talking about a specific project but rather about a new pattern of buyer–supplier relations.

The information for this case study was gathered through a series of interviews with representatives of Océ and suppliers. A total of 28 people were interviewed, 14 of whom were representatives of different suppliers. The KIC project was organized in 20 sub-projects, or clusters, each dealing with a different module or subassembly of the new colour copier. Clusters were headed by a lead supplier which assumed responsibility over the project and directed the other suppliers. A representative from Océ R&D was attached to each cluster. Of the 20 clusters, 11 were included in the inquiry. Whenever possible, the lead supplier of each cluster and the representative from Océ R&D were interviewed. In many cases, a representative from one of the other suppliers in the cluster was also interviewed. Interviews with Océ management and Océ purchasing were conducted to look at the strategy of Océ and the purchasing policy, i.e. the relationship with suppliers.

11.2 CONTEMPORARY THEORY OF INNOVATION IN REGIONAL NETWORKS

To explain and interpret our case study of the KIC network we need a theoretical framework. In Chapter 2 of this volume a broad framework on innovation, learning, networks and regions has been drafted, so we do not discuss this aspect in detail here. We shall confine ourselves to a discussion of the necessary 'bits and pieces' only.

Competitive Advantage

We start from the assumption that we now live in a knowledge-based economy where competitive advantage is derived from the creation and application of knowledge through a process of learning (Morgan, 1997). Competitive advantage based on knowledge and skills is less easy to imitate or duplicate by competitors – as opposed to competitive advantages based on low costs, economies of scale, use of technologies, and so on – and thus creates so-called higher-order advantages (Porter, 1990). Such higher-order advantages are less susceptible to ubiquitification, that is, the process by which competitive advantages are nullified because the sources on which they are based become diffused (technology), are imitated (scale economies), are surpassed (low costs), become obsolete (practices and skills), or otherwise cease to be an advantage. The globalization of the world economy is one of the main triggers behind ubiquitification of competitive advantages, as globalization leads to the diffusion of technologies to low cost countries, the internationalization of markets and the resulting erosion of scale economies. Globalization also stimulates the creation of new technologies (Best, 1990; Storper, 1992), which leaves firms that fall behind in the technology race stranded with yesterday's standards in terms of quality, efficiency and competitiveness. The way out of this trap is the creation of firm-specific competencies, that is, competencies that are not easily imitated by competitors, through the creation and use of knowledge.

We assume that readers are familiar with the differences between codified and tacit knowledge about competitive advantage. What makes tacit knowledge so important is the fact that it is meaningful only within a certain social context (Morgan, 1997). The skills, practices and know-how of a firm which are based on a substantial amount of tacit (person-embodied) knowledge can materialize in firm-specific competencies when they are embedded in an organizational context and transformed into firm-specific practices and routines (Maskell *et al.*, 1998). The creation of such firm-specific competencies – and, consequently, also their diffusion to competitors – depends on a complex process of socialization, externalization, internalization and combination of knowledge (Nonaka and Takeuchi, 1995). These processes are highly specific to the context in which they take place and only individuals who are part of that context can effectively participate in them. For outsiders to copy such firm-specific competencies takes a lot of time, as they first have to learn to understand this context. By the time they have actually copied another firm's unique competence, that particular competence may have become obsolete, as the original owner may have developed a better competence. This makes it unattractive for competitors to try to duplicate each other's unique competencies, because it only adds to the stability of competitive advantages derived from firm-specific competencies (Maskell *et al.*, 1998).

Networks and Knowledge Creation

No firm can create an advantage and be competitive in everything (Porter, 1990). Particularly in a world where the threat of ubiquitification of advantages constantly threatens their competitiveness, firms have to carefully choose the markets and sectors in which they want to compete. Successful firms, therefore, often follow a strategy of specialization (Best, 1990; van Houtum and Boekema, 1994; Porter, 1990). Firms try to create sustainable competitive advantages in those fields where they can outperform their rivals. This is a matter of competitive strategy: firms must identify their core competencies and take action to develop and strengthen their competitive advantage in these fields. They do so through the creation and use of knowledge.

Under a strategy of specialization firms depend on other firms for two reasons. First, specialization means that a firm concentrates on doing certain things better than its rivals, but it also means that it will no longer engage in certain other activities itself. Consequently, firms often depend on other firms to perform these activities for them. This creates major advantages: firms can make combinations of specialized skills and competencies and thus achieve synergies, that is, do things (develop products or applications) that were formerly beyond their reach (Best, 1990; Scott, 1988). Firms can make different combinations with different partners to seize new opportunities and thus achieve the Schumpeterian 'new combinations' at a network level. Secondly, no single firm controls all the necessary resources itself. Knowledge, too, is a resource and firms need external knowledge to further develop and upgrade their own stock of knowledge (Kogut *et al.*, 1993; Oerlemans, 1996). The Schumpeterian new combinations referred to in the previous paragraph also apply at the level of the firm. The combination of internal and external knowledge will create new knowledge that it would otherwise not have been possible to create.

It is clear now that networks are a means of creating new knowledge and that important competitive advantage can be based on this 'network knowledge'. Networks, too, are a unique context which is difficult for outsiders to understand. Firms can thus create knowledge and competencies which are unique to their network. These network-specific competencies are equally difficult to imitate, as firm-specific competencies and the competitive advantages derived from them will be resistant to ubiquitification in the same way as competitive advantages derived from firm-specific competencies.

Collaborating in networks requires trust. Since firms depend on each other for knowledge creation and competitive advantage, it is particularly important if they can trust their partner on his word. Market relations are not suited to the exchange of knowledge. Much closer and intensive communication between partners is necessary in order to convey the content and context of knowledge so that the receiver can actually use the newly acquired knowledge (Maskell *et al.*, 1998; Morgan, 1997). Successful collaboration and knowledge exchange requires a degree of openness that can never be achieved under conditions of opportunistic behaviour. Trust is essential.

Regional Embedding

A climate of trust which can be prevalent in a local business community can make collaboration even easier. Merely being a member of that community is enough to benefit from the trust that is shared within that community (Maskell *et al.*, 1998). This shared trust makes it easier for firms to switch partners without the risk of losing the trust established with other partners. The perspective looms of a constantly changing pattern of networks between the various firms in a region. It goes without saying that this will have a tremendously positive effect on the exchange of knowledge in that region.

The risk of the regional knowledge pool leaking away to other regions is small, as the knowledge is embedded in the region, in its firms and networks. It is difficult for outsiders to disentangle the relevant knowledge from its regional context. Firms that are not a part of the local business community will have difficulties in accessing the regional knowledge pool, as they do not understand the norms and social conventions that govern the interactions between firms in a particular area. The danger of local firms moving to other areas and taking the local knowledge with them is also small. The specialization of firms has spatial implications, because suppliers, the labour market and the research centres in a region will also have specialized in meeting the needs of the firms in the area. These sources of specialized knowledge are not available elsewhere, so that a firm which depends on them is not likely to move out of the area (Maskell *et al.*, 1998; Porter, 1990; Storper, 1992).

There is another process which ties firms to their home regions: the geography of knowledge. Competitive advantage is best based on competencies derived from tacit knowledge. The creation and diffusion of tacit knowledge requires intensive face-to-face communication between the owner and receiver of the knowledge. A demonstration of how something works is often the only way to transfer certain pieces of knowledge. Face-to-face communication is most effective when the individuals concerned are located close to each other. More codified forms of knowledge can be transferred over long distances fairly easily through the application of modern communication technologies, but in the case of tacit knowledge proximity is important.

Conclusion

To conclude this section we summarize the key elements of our theoretical framework:

- specialization and knowledge creation have a central place in the competitive strategy of firms;
- sustainable competitive advantage is derived from firm-specific competencies based on tacit forms of knowledge;
- collaboration with other firms is essential in order to create knowledge;

- collaboration with other firms creates new sources of competitive advantage through the use of network embedded knowledge;
- a climate of trust is essential for successful collaboration in flexible partnerships;
- regional embedding and proximity facilitate the exchange and creation of knowledge in networks.

On the basis of this theoretical exercise we expect to see a development towards knowledge creation in regional embedded networks in the practice of inter-firm collaboration, as this promises to yield sustainable competitive advantage. In the remainder of this chapter we will explore to what extent practice, in the case of KIC, behaves in accordance with theory.

11.3 KIC – EXPERIMENTS IN DEVELOPING NEW COMPETENCIES

In the early 1990s the doom scenarios of the globalization theorists seemed to be on their way to becoming a reality in the south-eastern Netherlands. Low cost producers from Eastern Europe and Asia were penetrating the European markets and the industrial sector – on which the south-eastern Netherlands is heavily dependent – did not seem to have an answer. Bankruptcies, reorganizations and mass layoffs left the region, which had only recently recovered from the economic crisis of the early 1980s, with rising unemployment figures.

The Strategy of Océ

Faced with this situation, Océ looked for a way out by exploiting its strengths. From the mid-1980s Océ had been working with suppliers under a regime of early supplier involvement. The knowledge and expertise of the suppliers was used to improve communications between Océ and the suppliers about the production of parts for Océ. The decisions which Océ took in 1993 to strengthen its competitiveness and which led to the KIC project are an extension of this policy. Océ decided to concentrate more strongly on the development of new concepts and products; it would focus on the trajectory from basic research to prototyping. The suppliers would have to play a bigger role in the final stages of the product development process, from prototyping to the actual start of production. At management level, a decision was made to reduce the number of 'first-tier' suppliers. Outsourcing to the remaining first-tier suppliers would concentrate on modules or subassemblies rather than on separate parts.

The strategy of Océ is to focus on the 'front side' of the product development process: fundamental research, feasibility studies and predevelopment. Thus Océ concentrates on technology. In the market for copiers and printers, technology is a critical success factor. Winners in this market are firms that can develop and produce new concepts, products and applications from available and new technologies more quickly than others. Océ increasingly considers this capability to be one of its core competencies. The increased R&D budget is a clear consequence of this. Océ must invest in new technologies and the development of new concepts and products. Leaving the production of these products to suppliers offers important advantages to Océ. It gives Océ more freedom in design and choice of technologies, as Océ is not confined to the limits of its own production facilities, since it has none. For every design and every product that Océ develops, a supplier will always be found to manufacture it. This relieves Océ of investing in its production facilities and the available funds can be used in R&D. In short, Océ has its hands free to concentrate on new product development, for which it has more funds and it can apply more flexibility.

Suppliers will have to assume responsibility for the engineering, the stage in the product development from the prototypes to the development of the actual product or subassembly, which can be manufactured on a large, or even mass scale. The success of this strategy depends on the availability of advanced local suppliers. The availability of advanced local suppliers, however, proved to be the weak spot in Océ's strategy. Most small and medium sized firms in the south-eastern Netherlands cannot be classified as very innovative or advanced firms. Their technologies and products are not particularly specialized. They often use efficiency rather than innovation as their key source of competitive advantage and, consequently, they are vulnerable to price competition. This was the situation in the late 1980s and early 1990s and Océ realized that if it wanted to use local suppliers, it had to help them to upgrade their performance. Here we touch on the cradle of the KIC project.

The Strategy of the Suppliers

Around 1990 most of the SMEs that participated in KIC were still jobbers. They had only limited engineering capabilities and worked basically from designs and drawings from larger firms. Where early supplier involvement was practised, the SMEs would do some re-engineering in order to make the manufacturing of the parts easier. Not many of the SMEs were specialized in particular technologies or practices. In short, their added value was limited and they were vulnerable to low cost competitors. Notwithstanding the differences between the SMEs in terms of size, market, innovation potential, and so on, important similarities can be observed in their development towards becoming stronger and more innovative firms. The key features of their strategies are the following:

Specialization

Generally the firms in our case study specialized in one or a few disciplines, depending on their size. They are on their way to becoming experts in their fields, which makes them better partners for outsourcing firms. One firm, for example, used to be a sheet metal plant that could do most kinds of sheet metalling – from 'heavy' work to precision sheet metalling – but it did not excel in any. Today, this firm is specialized in precision sheet metalling and has a very good reputation in this field. Specialized suppliers can advise outsourcing firms much better on the manufacturability of their designs, which makes them much more valuable for these larger firms. Consequently, their competitiveness has improved.

Product development

Firms realize that they have to offer more added value. They do so by specializing in activities in which they have a competitive advantage (doing things better) and by investing in product development (doing new things). All the suppliers in our case study have invested in product development skills, although in varying degrees. Most suppliers are too small to have products of their own. A typical SME in our case study has two to four persons working in its engineering department. These firms, however, have significantly improved their product engineering skills, which enables them to assist the product development efforts of larger firms much better. This is a result of the policy of outsourcing firms to involve suppliers in more complex tasks in product development. While limited product engineering skills used to be sufficient, SMEs are now required to think at a more conceptual level. They have to go beyond the stage where their prime focus is on how to manufacture a given part as well and efficiently (process engineering) as possible. Things like the optimum measurements, weight, choice of materials, design, etc. of a part are now determined by suppliers to a much larger degree. This gives suppliers the opportunity to exploit more fully their knowledge of materials and production technologies and processes.

Collaboration

The firms in our case study were well aware of the fact that collaboration in the field of product development is a must. Starting from their own discipline(s), firms look for partners specialized in complementary disciplines and skills, so that, together, they can manufacture multidisciplinary subassemblies. Firms make partnerships in various ways. Sometimes a group of firms formalize their partnership in an alliance, for example, the VDL Group and the Van Geel Group. The individual firms in such an alliance remain independent, but they always have an infrastructure for collaboration at hand. In most cases, however, firms have a set of preferred partners with whom they form changing networks for different assignments. The composition of these networks varies, depending on the kind of specializations and disciplines needed for a particular assignment. As one of our respondents said: 'knowing things is important, but knowing people who know things is equally important. It is crucial that you are part of the right network'.

Knowledge and learning

Specialization and product development require knowledge and skills. The firms in our case study were all trying to increase their stock of knowledge, mainly through collaboration with relevant partners, which enabled them to learn from each other. It is important to note that we are not talking about advanced or high technology know-how. The smaller firms, in particular, operate on a much more down-to-earth level of knowledge, which is focused on application. They use tried and proven off-the-shelf knowledge and technology which they combine in inventive new ways, such as connecting glass to synthetic materials, a particularly difficult technique. These firms may not be 'high tech', but they are certainly very knowledge-intensive and, in their respective fields of expertise, they work hard to acquire and develop state-of-the-art technologies and skills. Another kind of knowledge which the firms in our case study had to learn were managerial skills. Working closely together with other firms on product development is a process which must be learned. It was new to most firms involved in the KIC project and the relevant managerial skills still had to be developed and learned. As in all learning processes, the lack of relevant skills gave rise to some difficulties in the early stages of the KIC project.

Outsourcing

Some of the firms in our case study, such as Nebato and Te Strake, are developing towards becoming main suppliers. Their engineering capabilities are developed (and are developing further) and they are working together more closely with outsourcing firms on product development and engineering. Some of the parts which these larger suppliers have engineered are produced by smaller subcontractors, which is leading to the emergence of a pattern of layered supplier networks.

What the region has witnessed is a process of upgrading of SMEs. Some of the firms in our case study needed the KIC project to trigger this upgrading, while other firms were already working on it. The elements of the strategy discussed above that we found in the SMEs have been responsible for the development from jobber to something more innovative and competitive. Such a process of upgrading is necessary to safeguard the long-term survival of firms and, indeed, of manufacturing industry in the south-eastern Netherlands. KIC proved to be an important accelerator of this process. In the following sections we will take a closer look inside the KIC network and explain how it worked and created innovation.

Participation in KIC

The suppliers had several motives for participating in the KIC project. For most firms in our case study the KIC project fitted their strategy. We need to make a distinction here between the more advanced firms, that is, those firms already engaged in a process of upgrading before KIC, and firms that used KIC to initiate a process of upgrading. To the former group of firms KIC was a strategic choice, this is the way they wanted to work and KIC was a welcome opportunity to advance their skills with respect to working in multidisciplinary teams. Learning is another motive for participating in KIC, mentioned frequently by the more advanced firms. About half of the firms in our case study saw KIC in this way: it presented a strategic opportunity. The other firms did not initially see KIC as an important strategic opportunity, but they had good motives for going along anyway. Their motives were related to the firm's strategy in general rather than to innovation strategy: their relation with Océ and turnover. These motives also played a role, of course, for the first category of firms.

Suppliers were asked by Océ to participate in the KIC project. Most of the firms have worked for Océ for a considerable number of years and, because of the good relationship they have with Océ, they decided to participate in KIC. Some firms felt they could not refuse to participate, as Océ is one of their largest customers and firms will go a long way to keep such customers happy. One supplier even admitted that they agreed to take part in the KIC project before they knew what the project was about and what was expected of them. Océ did not put pressure on any of the firms to make them participate in KIC. On the other hand, particularly in the first years of the project, no assessment was made of the candidate suppliers. Basically, the only criterion that Océ used was whether the technologies used by a candidate supplier were appropriate for the project for which it was selected. An assessment of the candidates' strategies became common practice only after a year or two. Consequently, in the first few years a number of firms which were not ready for this kind of responsibility became involved in the KIC project. These firms learned a lot during their involvement in the KIC project. Although the projects they worked on are not textbook examples of efficient product development in multidisciplinary teams. It took a lot of effort from both sides to bring these projects to a satisfactory conclusion.

The biggest worry of suppliers is that of filling their production capacity and they assumed that working on the KIC project would lead, if not immediately, in the longer term to more work being offered to them by Océ, but the KIC project did not work in quite that way. KIC was concerned with engineering, not with production. Put simply (too simply as the reality is more complicated), the Océ R&D department ran the KIC project – the engineering – and the Océ Purchasing department ran the outsourcing of work to suppliers. Basically, if a supplier, or a group of suppliers, had successfully completed the engineering of a certain subassembly for Océ R&D, the Océ Purchasing department could decide to have that particular subassembly manufactured by a different supplier or group of suppliers. Suppliers knew this when they started with the KIC project, yet all of them gave extra work from Océ as a motive for participating in KIC. On the other hand, suppliers were not wrong in assuming that Océ would become more dependent on them if they played a bigger role in Océ's product development. Once a supplier has certain skills and knowledge which are important for a particular subassembly, it is difficult not to use that supplier for the production of that subassembly.

The Place of KIC in Product Development

The KIC project was the materialization of a new product development strategy. Under this strategy suppliers work together with other suppliers and with representatives from Océ, where they assume a larger responsibility for product development. In this section we will discuss the role of the suppliers under the KIC project.

Product development is basically a three-step route. In the first step, the research is carried out. Here, new concepts are invented and developed into rudimentary models of products. The second step is the stage at which the functions of the new product and its various parts are worked out. The final step is the engineering, where the parts undergo a final process of modification to make them fit for mass production. In traditional situations where suppliers are involved in product development, such as early supplier involvement, they are involved towards the end of the engineering phase. Under the KIC project, the suppliers were involved throughout the engineering phase and even played a role in the development phase. Moreover, under a regime of early supplier involvement, Océ has contacts with many suppliers. Basically, a supplier is acquired for each separate part. The idea of KIC is that outsourcing and engineering no longer take place at the level of separate parts, but at a higher level: that of modules or subassemblies. Suppliers have to work together in multidisciplinary teams.

Each of the teams has a main contractor which is responsible for the relationship with Océ. The involvement of the suppliers earlier in the product development process has the following advantages.

Quality
Involving suppliers in product development at an early stage allows Océ to benefit from the knowledge and skills of its suppliers. For example, Océ uses synthetic materials in its products, but Océ is not an expert in the field of synthetics. Formerly, Océ would design the synthetic parts of its products, such as the exterior of a control panel, itself, a job that a supplier specialized in synthetic materials could do much better. Also Océ would have the interior of the control panel, the electronics and related information technology, manufactured by another supplier and Océ would itself fit the interior and exterior to each other in order to make the required control panel. The new way of working, advocated by KIC, takes a different approach to the development and engineering of, in this example, the control panel. Océ specifies the conditions and requirements that a control panel must meet in terms of performance, communication with the rest of the copier it is made for, macro geometry (the control panel must fit in its designed location on the copier) and so on. Océ then assigns one supplier to the task of developing and engineering this control panel. The supplier, in this case an IT firm, is responsible for the entire control panel, including the exterior, for which it hires other suppliers. Should the main contractor have wanted to make the exterior out of metal instead of synthetics, it would have been free to do so, provided the conditions specified by Océ were met. This is, of course, a hypothetical option, but in other projects choices had to be made between various production technologies such as various types of welding or moulding. Because the suppliers were given responsibility for the engineering of complete subassemblies, they could choose the best options based on their experiences, skills and knowledge.

So, under a system of early supplier involvement Océ largely determines the production technologies to be used, as Océ largely determines how the parts and subassemblies are designed. Under the new way of working, Océ determines the functions of a subassembly. The design of this subassembly and its various parts is left to the responsible supplier(s). This enables the suppliers to use all their relevant skills and knowledge and not just those they are hired for. Moreover, by working together in teams on subassemblies, suppliers find solutions that they could never have conceived by working alone on individual parts. Suppliers now oversee a larger part of the engineering process and, consequently, can see things (difficulties and opportunities) as a whole. As a team, they can develop an integrated solution for a complete subassembly. In short, they can offer more added value.

Efficiency

Working on this higher level also generates significant efficiency advantages. In themselves the changes worked out by suppliers, such as fixing a piece of metal with three bolts instead of four, may sometimes look unimportant. Under a regime of early supplier involvement, a supplier would just have thought of a way to produce the four bolts and the piece of metal as efficiently as possible and perhaps suggest some changes to the design of the piece of metal. Now, however, a supplier is told what these four bolts and the piece of metal are for. Based on his experience, the supplier can now argue that a less strong design, with three instead of four bolts, would still be strong enough for this particular part to perform its designed function flawlessly. This one bolt may save perhaps only a few cents, but over a series of several thousand copiers, that is important. Moreover, Océ has designed the piece of metal with the bolts in a certain place on the subassembly. Knowing the function of that subassembly and working together with other suppliers, our supplier can suggest that the piece of metal should be fitted at a different place. This could make the subassembly much easier to manufacture and might lead to further improvements elsewhere in the design.

Efficiency gains are also achieved because the various stages in the engineering process are now integrated. Formerly, Océ would do the initial engineering of a subassembly and then leave the engineering of the various parts of the subassembly to different suppliers. The various parts, once finished, had to be assembled into one subassembly, which then required some further engineering by Océ. The new way of working makes most of this engineering and re-engineering superfluous, as the engineering is now an integrated process in which all the parties concerned participate. It also means less work for Océ's engineers, as the coordination of the engineering is now the responsibility of a main contractor and Océ's engineers have their hands free to do other things, which was one of the reasons for Océ to start the KIC project.

In practice, however, this has not occurred. Océ engineers had to devote a lot of time and energy to the various projects. The reason for this is obvious: KIC was a completely new experience for all the partners involved. They still had to learn how to manage engineering in multidisciplinary teams. Moreover, some of the suppliers were not ready for this new way of working and, in yet other cases, the tasks assigned to the suppliers were simply too difficult. They did not have the technology and skills necessary to do the things Océ had in mind for them, while sometimes Océ did not even know exactly what it wanted the suppliers to do. It had a concept, an idea of a function that a certain subassembly had to perform, but often suppliers need more than that to base a project on. Careful definition of projects is one important lesson that Océ learned from KIC.

Time economies

From the efficiencies discussed above, one would expect the engineering to proceed more quickly, but our respondents' views on this are contradictory. Potentially, working in multidisciplinary teams could speed up the engineering, but according to Océ engineers, this was not the case in the KIC project. Some suppliers were of the same opinion, while others actually said that the engineering had indeed been speeded up. The explanation for this set of contradictions lies, we believe, in the nature of KIC as a learning process. It was new to everybody so, logically, there were few time economies. The fact that suppliers now did parts of the engineering that Océ used to do itself left some of Océ's engineers somewhat frustrated at seeing the suppliers coping with considerable difficulties which they could have solved quite easily. On the other hand, most of the suppliers were happy finally to have a chance to show that their practical approach to engineering could lead to a better result than Océ's conceptual approach. Suppliers start engineering with the possibilities and limitations of their machinery and equipment in mind. From there they work towards the functions that a certain part or subassembly has to perform. Océ engineers start from the functions and then work their way downward to a design which can be manufactured. Both work from the right point of view in relation to their own position and somewhere in these multidisciplinary engineering teams a balance had to be found between these viewpoints. That, however, proved to be difficult and made it impossible to economize on time in the KIC project.

Finding the right balance between the suppliers' practical approach and the Océ engineers' conceptual approach is perhaps the key to the successful engineering of subassemblies in multidisciplinary teams. It is also the most difficult part, not in the least because the balance is different for every project. Moreover, the technical and managerial skills of the suppliers involved is crucial. Some suppliers, usually the larger ones, are more capable of thinking and working at a more abstract level than others. A good project definition is also of crucial importance. All this had to be learned by the KIC partners. We would like to share the optimism of many of our respondents that time economies will be obtained once the partners have learned how to play the game.

Innovation at the inter-firm level

By working together on product development and engineering in multidisciplinary teams the boundaries between individual firms fall away. The co-ordination of the required resources (knowledge, money, time, capital, and so on) is now performed at an inter-firm, or network level. In the past, innovation was largely the product of a single firm's efforts. In the age of multidisciplinary projects, firms must pool their efforts. This means that decisions, too, must be made at an inter-firm level. Under the KIC project the decisions that mattered most – those concerning the day-to-day operations – were taken at the engineering level. Here engineers, representatives from sales and quality departments and directors or deputy directors of the firms involved in the project would decide on what actually would happen, that is, which technologies and materials would be used and developed, time schedules, necessary manpower, and so forth. These decisions – taken on a network level – had, of course, far-reaching consequences for the individual firms in the project. The blurring of boundaries between firms was further encouraged by the fact that the individuals working on the project developed strong personal relations across organization boundaries.

The Management of Multidisciplinary Projects

The management of multidisciplinary teams was something the firms in our case study had to learn. For most KIC projects a group of firms was brought together in a network, a multidisciplinary team. In some cases, however, only one supplier was involved in the project, which created, of course, a bilateral collaboration between Océ and the supplier. In the projects where more than one supplier was involved, one of the suppliers was always the 'lead partner' which meant it was responsible for the project and the co-ordination of activities with the other partners in the project (Océ and the other suppliers).

Each KIC project had basically two sides: the formal and the technical side, the actual engineering part of the project. In a typical KIC project these two sides were separated. The formal side, the contracts, budgets, responsibilities and so on, were negotiated at management level. This allowed the engineers to concentrate on the technical content of the project without having to worry about formalities. The engineers of the firms involved in the project would work on the project without interference from the management, although the latter would be kept informed of the progress of the project. Any obstacles related to time, money, or other formalities that arose during the project would be dealt with by the management. Although not all KIC projects worked with this organizational structure, the general feeling is that the separation of management responsibilities from engineering responsibilities was an effective way of working, certainly more effective than when these aspects were entangled with each other.

Working together in multidisciplinary teams means that the lines of communication have become much shorter. Engineers from the firms involved in a project now communicate directly with each other. On other levels, too (management, sales, etc.), direct lines of communication have been established. Combined with the separation of the management and engineering parts of the project this greatly helped to build trust. Trust is essential in the kind of intimate collaboration portrayed in the KIC project – a fact that our respondents acknowledged wholeheartedly. After the initial phase of each project in which the partners got to know each other, collaboration improved and trust grew in the mutual relations between the suppliers and Océ. There were, of course, variations in trust building towards both extremes. In one case, the partners had finished the engineering part of the project before the contracts were signed, whereas in other cases the conflicting views of conflicting personalities on how to manage the project prevented trust from flourishing as much as in the other projects. But on the whole we found a remarkable level of trust between the firms on the KIC project. This, we believe, can be explained as follows:

- *Openness and equality.* Although Océ was officially in charge of the project, not in order to put the blame a supplier should something go wrong, but in order to give the suppliers, who traditionally play a subordinate role, the chance to use their knowledge and experience. Océ deliberately stayed in the background, although of course it had the final word when decisions were made and human nature made the suppliers attribute more value to the opinions and suggestions put forward by Océ than to opinions and suggestions from their own circle. Nevertheless, all the suppliers in our case study explicitly stated they felt very comfortable with the relations with Océ during the project and that they in no way felt restrained. This helped to create an atmosphere of trust where creativity flourished.
- *Mutual interest and dependence.* The partners involved in a KIC project had a strong mutual interest in finishing the project. They depended on each other to make the project a success. In such a situation the partners have to rely on each other and opportunistic behaviour would only harm them. The success of the project would be jeopardized and this would surely backfire on them in future relations. Although this interpretation may explain the effort put into the project by each of the partners, it does not do justice to the degree of openness that we have found in virtually all the firms in our case study. This leads us to our third explanation.
- *A culture of openness and trust* seems to be present among the firms in our case study. Collaboration is common practice for these firms, although not usually to the degree portrayed in the KIC project. Firms report that, in general, their survival depends on working together with their partners. This may have led to the openness found in our research. From our findings we cannot be conclusive about the level on which this culture of trust is present; in manufacturing industry, in the region (the south-eastern Netherlands), or on the national level. Other research

does not provide us with definite answers either, but we believe that a combination of sectoral and regional influences form an important part of the explanation.

The direct lines of communication between the engineers of the firms involved in the projects proved to be a good move for two reasons. First, it made communication and exchange of information much easier. A question was almost always followed by an immediate response. This not only makes the engineering more effective, but it also helps to create an atmosphere of co-operation. People can actually see that their partners are as dedicated to the project as they are. Secondly, engineers can relate to each other quite easily. They are like colleagues, even though they are from different firms. A manager from one of the suppliers confessed that it was almost 'touching' to see a group of engineers working together with such dedication. Engineers speak the common language of the profession. There is no need to explain the effect this has on trust-building and collaboration between firms.

Trust and collaboration, however, ultimately depend on people. A multidisciplinary team will lead to nothing if the individuals composing the team do not 'gel'. This is an issue often overlooked by economists and technicians in their explanations of inter-firm collaboration. The human factor plays a decisive role in group processes of this kind, and organization sociology and group psychology are at least as important as traditional economic theory.

The Regional Dimension

An important aspect of the KIC project is its regional dimension. It is a strategic choice of Océ to collaborate with regional suppliers. One of the motives that Océ had for initiating the KIC project in the first place was their wish to upgrade regional suppliers, so that Océ could fall back on a more advanced regional network of partners for future engineering projects. Océ has connections with suppliers worldwide, of course, including the engineering field, and KIC is by no means an attempt to concentrate all engineering efforts in the south-eastern Netherlands. The most important ground on which suppliers are selected for participation in engineering projects is their skills, not their location. However, a regional network has important advantages, which we will discuss below, and, to make things easier for Océ, a very significant part of the Dutch manufacturing industry is located in the south-eastern Netherlands. The chances of finding a skilled partner in this region are therefore very good. This allows Océ to benefit both from skills and proximity.

As Table 11.1 shows, the share of regional suppliers in total purchasing increased from 34 per cent in 1988 to 45 per cent in 1996, whereas the share of suppliers located elsewhere in the Netherlands dropped from 27 per cent to 10 per cent. This must be seen in relation to the increase of the value of purchasing from 77 million euro (74 million US dollars) in 1988 to 235 million euro (226 million US dollars) in 1996. This clearly shows the regional strategy followed by Océ. The moderate increase in the share of total purchasing for Europe and the rest of the world is an indication of the search for the best available partners on a global scale. The supplying firms in our case study also showed a strong regional focus – as is common with SMEs throughout the western world. Most business partners (approximately 75 per cent on average), such as suppliers and customers, of the SMEs in our case study were located within a 75 km radius.

Table 11.1   Purchasing for assembly by Océ

	1988	1993	1996
Total amount of purchasing in million euro	77	123	235
– of which in the region (%)	34	41	45
– of which in the rest of the Netherlands (%)	27	20	10
– of which in the rest of Europe (%)	32	31	35
– of which in the rest of the world (%)	7	8	10
– total	100	100	100

Source: Océ (presentation by Dr. H. Knibbe at Tilburg University on March 27, 1998)

Spatial proximity is important for reasons of communication. The answers from respondents from both Océ and the suppliers agreed with respect to this issue. Working in multidisciplinary teams requires intensive communication between firms. The content of this communication is often highly person-embedded knowledge. The nature of an engineering project, that is, exploring new grounds and finding new solutions, implies that little of the knowledge in the project is codified. As always, the less codified the knowledge, the more important personal, face-to-face communication becomes for transferring the knowledge. Our respondents mentioned several examples where face-to-face communication, in their experience, was the most effective form of communication.

● Different organizations have different customs and different ways of doing and saying things. When Océ engineers speak of a prototype, they do not mean exactly the same thing as when a particular supplier speaks of a prototype. Organizations – or better, people – have to learn to know each other if they want to co-operate effectively in a team. Face-to-face communication is essential for this.

● Engineering in multidisciplinary teams is a team effort. This means that the members of such a team have to meet each other and discuss the problems they are faced with and the solutions they have in mind for solving them. Each member of the team has specific knowledge of the technologies and skills that his firm possesses. This knowledge is highly firm-specific and to a large extent tacit. The possibilities and solutions that they can offer in favour of the team effort must be explained to the other team members before they can be used. Other team members have at least to understand how a technique works before they can relate it to their own technologies and skills. Only in this way can the combination of various technologies (disciplines) lead to synergy.

● Engineering is to a certain degree a process of trial and error. Engineers construct new prototypes and find out through experiments if they meet the specifications. Engineering on a prototype often means that the engineers involved have actually to work on the prototype, that is, they have to be in the same location as the prototype.

Face-to-face communication is necessary for performing the activities described above. As engineering is a creative process, it requires a lot of communication. Modern communication technologies are of a great help, but they cannot undo the advantages of proximity. Partners in the team have to meet each other frequently – as a team or on a bilateral basis – to discuss the project and to find solutions. Moreover, the trust which is necessary for effective, intimate co-operation in teams cannot be achieved through electronic communication.

11.4   CONCLUSIONS

In this final section we discuss the findings of our case study of the KIC project. First, we argue that KIC was a success. Then we make a link between the theoretical framework and the results of the case study. We conclude with a discussion on the prospects for innovation in regional supplier networks.

The Success of KIC

Was KIC as success? If we look at the technical side of the project the results are modest. Basically, two factors are responsible for this. First, in several cases, the projects were too difficult. The shortcomings in the project definition discussed earlier contributed to the already high level of difficulty of many of the projects. Engineering projects have to be challenging, of course, but Océ admitted that they had overestimated the engineering capabilities of the suppliers. Most of the firms had yet to learn how to engineer.

Secondly, several of the projects dealt with technologies and knowledge that were very specific to copiers. A control panel, for example, can be found on a variety of machines, including copiers, but modules dealing with toner, for example, are very specific to copiers. These copier-specific projects complicated the engineering in two ways. In the first place, these technologies are at the heart of Océ's competitive advantage. As much as Océ wanted to share relevant knowledge with its suppliers, it could not let the suppliers in on the details of this highly sensitive knowledge. This put serious constraints on several of the projects. One of the suppliers, for example, was working on a system to transport toner through a copier and to a sheet of paper to make a copy. In order to develop such a system it is important to know the characteristics of the kind of toner you are working with, e.g. how it behaves at certain temperatures. However, this supplier was not even allowed to touch the toner, let alone study it. The lesson learned from this is that certain engineering projects which deal with sensitive technologies cannot be effectively executed by multidisciplinary teams.

The second constraint of copier-specific projects is felt in the longer term. To return to the example of the control panel, a control panel can be developed for several firms, not just for Océ. Firms involved in this project can quite easily apply their engineering skills for other firms as well. Océ took the view that, if a supplier works on engineering projects for several larger firms, it becomes a more skilled engineer and, thus, a better partner for Océ. On the other hand, engineering skills related to copier-specific technologies cannot be used for other firms. In the Netherlands Océ is the only developer of copiers and printers. Investing in engineering skills is attractive for suppliers only if they can work for several larger firms. In the end, their main concern is obtaining enough orders to keep their business going. This means that company-specific technologies are not very appropriate and that more than one large firm has to be willing to work with suppliers on product engineering in multidisciplinary teams.[2] Océ does not have enough projects to make engineering departments of several suppliers profitable. Nor does it want to have them.

Yet, KIC stirred an enormous amount of enthusiasm and energy. Both among the suppliers and Océ. For all involved, KIC was a learning process and it should be judged as such. Océ and the suppliers have learned vital skills that will enable them to complete future KIC-type projects much more easily. These skills are not only technical, but also managerial. Not only have the partners involved learned how to engineer a subassembly that no one could have engineered on its own, they have also learned how to manage a team effort. This leads us to conclude that KIC has paid off as a learning process and will continue to do so. Considering the increasing international competition in the manufacturing industries, one can be certain that the firms involved in KIC will put their newly acquired skills and knowledge into practice, as it will help them to stay ahead of the competition.

Theory and Practice

In the theoretical section of this chapter we presented a theoretical framework to study collaboration in supplier networks. This framework had six key elements which we will compare with the findings of our case study in order to discover how far the practice of the KIC project supports some of the basic theoretical assumptions of the learning paradigm.

The first key element was that specialization and knowledge creation have a central place in the competitive strategy of firms. This we can confirm from the findings of our case study. The firms in the project were driven by their desire to protect and strengthen their competitiveness for the future. The suppliers do so by concentrating on high value activities, that is, they play a larger role in product engineering and then produce the parts (or subassemblies) they have helped to develop. This requires the suppliers to specialize in one or a few disciplines (technologies and techniques) and to develop specialized skills. That, of course, is a process of knowledge creation. As discussed earlier, Océ's strategy, too, is aimed at strengthening competitiveness through specialization and knowledge creation. Leaving much of the engineering to suppliers gives Océ the opportunity to concentrate more of its resources on the earlier stages of the product development, which is where Océ creates its added value in the race with its competitors.

Our second key element – sustainable competitive advantage is derived from firm-specific competencies based on tacit forms of knowledge – was not directly investigated in our case study. We did not look at the specific competencies of the individual firms in our case study, although these were either present or were being created as a result of KIC. After all, the reason for a supplier to be admitted to a multidisciplinary team is that it has specific skills and competencies that are valuable to the task of the team. Having specific skills and competencies is therefore a must for a firm that wants to collaborate with other firms on product engineering, and that is very important for competitiveness.

Our third key element – collaboration with other firms is essential in order to create knowledge – was also confirmed in our case study. Product engineering in multidisciplinary teams is a highly interactive process, where the participants constantly exchange and absorb knowledge. In this way, several firms which are each specialized in only one or a few disciplines can develop a multidisciplinary module or subassembly. This subassembly is the materialization of the knowledge created in a team, a product of collaboration.

Our fourth key element - collaboration with other firms creates new sources of competitive advantage through the use of network embedded knowledge – points to a phenomenon which is related to the firm-specific competencies of the previous key element: network-specific competencies. In their collaboration and mutual problem-solving efforts, the firms in a multidisciplinary team create skills, competencies and knowledge which are specific to their network. This gives them the ability to do things that are unique; no other group of firms can do exactly the same thing, at least not in the short term. Provided these skills are valuable (in this case) for Océ, they provide the partners in the network with an important competitive advantage. Océ becomes dependent on their specific network competencies and, if Océ decided to change partners, it would be faced with considerable costs. Network-specific competencies, if they can be developed, are important tools for suppliers to strengthen their competitive position, as the KIC case proves.

The fifth key element of our theoretical framework was that a climate of trust is essential for successful collaboration in flexible partnerships. Our case study gave more than enough proof in support of this. Trust develops over time, but it helps if the partners have a common background. We feel that, in the case of KIC, the common background was related to a combination of industry, regional and national characteristics. The fact that the partners shared these characteristics enhanced the building of trust in network relations. Our analyses, however, do not allow us to be more specific about this.

The sixth and final key element – regional embedding and proximity facilitate the exchange and creation of knowledge in networks – was also easily recognizable in our case study. All our respondents stated that proximity was very important for the kind of projects they were involved in. We conclude from our findings that, when significant amounts of tacit knowledge have to be transferred between people and organizations, spatial proximity is of tremendous help.

The case study of the KIC project has provided us with enough material for several more contributions. We have by no means finished discussing the wealth of facts derived from our research, but this contribution already confirms the theoretical assumptions we made in the first part of this chapter. The case study of the KIC project must therefore be regarded as a contribution to the body of empirical data in support of the learning region paradigm.

Innovation in Regional Supplier Networks

The KIC project has shown that innovation in regional supplier networks can work, but that it comes at a cost. Both Océ and the suppliers involved have made considerable investments, which have so far yielded little reward. Yet the potential for product and process innovation, from the very simple to the highly complex, evoked in the networks is enormous. If experience enables the engineering to be done more quickly, the regional supplier networks will prove very effective in the field of innovation.

Are the regional supplier networks therefore the magic tool that will make innovation work? For the SME sector in general they most certainly are not. It takes advanced firms to participate effectively in such regional supplier networks, particularly as far as the lead partner is concerned. These firms must have product development capacity of their own and only a small number of SMEs are large enough to afford an engineering department. For those who can, however, regional supplier networks are indeed an important tool for innovation, though not a magic one. Smaller suppliers are also needed in regional supplier networks, but they must be sufficiently specialized to be of value in a multidisciplinary team. As it is, not many SMEs are particularly specialized. Even in the KIC project – which involved, in general, the better than average SMEs – many SMEs were on the way to becoming specialized suppliers. Consequently, only a relatively small number of suppliers will be able to benefit directly from participating in regional supplier networks. Another reason is that the amount of engineering projects that large firms have for suppliers is finite. When the above-mentioned conditions are met, however, we believe that innovation in regional supplier networks is an essential tool. The future of the manufacturing industry lies in initiatives like KIC.

NOTES

1. This is caused by the fact that KIC was partially funded from support schemes from the European Commission. These schemes run for a number of years only.
2. Océ and several other actors in the region are now trying to involve more large firms in KIC-like projects.

REFERENCES

Best, M. (1990), *The New Competition: Institutions of Industrial Restructuring*, Cambridge: Polity Press.
Buijel, C. and H. Burks (1996), *Handboek KIC (KIC Handbook)*, Venlo: Drukkerij Knoops.

Van Houtum, H. and F. Boekema (1994), 'Regions seen as laboratories for a new Europe: the applicability of the flexible specialisation model', in J. Van Dijck and J. Groenewegen (eds), *Changing Business Systems in Europe: an Institutional Approach*, Brussels: VUB Press.

Kogut, B. *et al.* (1993), 'Knowledge in the network and the network as knowledge: the structuring of new industries', in G. Grabher (ed.), *The Embedded Firm: on the Socio-economics of Industrial Networks*, London: Routledge.

Maskell, P., E. Heikki, H. Ingjaldur, A. Malmber and E. Vatne (1998), *Competitiveness, Localised Learning and Regional Development: Specialisation and Prosperity in Small Open Economies*, London: Routledge.

Morgan, K. (1997), 'The learning region: institutions, innovation and regional renewal', *Regional Studies*, **31** (5), pp. 491–503.

Nonaka, I. and H. Takeuchi (1995), *The Knowledge-Creating Company: How Japanese Companies Create the Dynamics of Innovation*, Oxford: Oxford University Press.

Oerlemans, L. (1996), *De Ingebedde Onderneming: Innoveren in Industriële Netwerken [The Embedded Firm: Innovation in Industrial Networks]*, Tilburg: Tilburg University Press.

Porter, M. (1990), *The Competitive Advantage of Nations*, London: The Macmillan Press.

Scott, A. (1988), 'Flexible production systems and regional development: the rise of new industrial spaces in North America and Western Europe', *International Journal of Urban and Regional Research*, **12** (2), pp. 171–85.

Storper, M. (1992), 'The limits to globalisation: technology districts and international trade', *Economic Geography*, **68**, pp. 60–93.

PART FOUR

Conclusions

12. The Analysis of Learning Regions: Conclusions and Research Agenda

Roel Rutten, Silvia Bakkers and Frans Boekema

The final chapter of this volume looks at where we stand in the analysis and understanding of the phenomenon of the learning region. In this chapter we try to place the learning region paradigm in a broader perspective. In other words, we will reflect on what we, as scholars and practitioners, are doing, what we have achieved and where we should go. Because of the diversity of the issues raised in this volume, the reader may be left with a sense of confusion. This volume promised a better understanding of the learning region paradigm, but it may seem that the dust has yet to settle after the storm of discussions unleashed in the preceding pages. This final chapter will show that everything can be set against a coherent common background; that of the learning region paradigm.

THE OBJECTIVE OF ANALYSIS: TO CREATE A BROADER PERSPECTIVE

Three principal questions need to be answered in the light of the objective of this book. Firstly, what are learning regions; in what way is the learning region paradigm important to scientific research and, finally, how can the learning region paradigm contribute to economic and social development? In each of the chapters of this volume answers can be found to each of these questions. It is not proposed to present 'the best of the answers' here. Rather, this section will elaborate on them from a more general angle of inquiry.

What are Learning Regions?

This question employs the plural 'regions', rather than the singular 'region'. One of the most important conclusions is that the features of the various examples of innovation and regional learning discussed in this volume cannot be narrowed down to a single set of characteristics of 'the learning region'.

The manifestations of the concept are simply too diverse. Hence also the use of the term 'learning region paradigm' in the introductory chapter. In other words, searching for 'the learning region' is to miss the point. This has important consequences, not just for scientific inquiry into the learning region paradigm, but for the practice of regional learning as well.

The reader will have noticed the variable use of the terms 'regional learning' and 'learning regions'. This does not mean that both these terms refer to the same thing. On the contrary, to separate these two things at an analytical level is an important step towards understanding the phenomenon of learning regions. Regional learning is an activity, in other words a complex and dynamic process. It means that actors who are connected to a certain geographical space in one form or another engage in a process of mutual and sometimes interactive learning. This is a necessary condition to being able to talk about learning regions, but it is by no means a sufficient condition. This brings us back to our initial question: what are learning regions? It becomes clear from the views discussed in this volume that learning regions are a metaphor. This does not mean that there are no learning regions. On the contrary, regions such as the Third Italy and Silicon Valley have every right to label themselves learning regions. The point is that the characteristics of these regions cannot be generalized at an analytical level to define what constitutes learning regions. For it is not the characteristics that matter, but the processes that constitute the regional learning within these regions. What characterizes economically successful regions today is a high level of mutual learning between regional actors and the vast amount of knowledge that is exchanged between them. In other words, these regions are breeding grounds for innovation. Most scholars agree that innovation is the trigger for economic development.

As we have already said, it is more than just the process of regional learning that ultimately creates learning regions. Actors are embedded in social and regional structures that differ from region to region. In order to understand regional learning, it is necessary to understand the relations of the actors with their environment and the institutional context of these regions. Using the vocabulary of Whitley (1993), the analysis must focus on the business system of a region. Whitley uses the concept of business systems to refer to different paths of development at a national level. 'Business systems are particular arrangements of hierarchy–market relations which become institutionalized and relatively successful in particular contexts. They combine differences in the kinds of economic activities and skills ... with variations in market organization and differences in how activities are authoritatively directed' (Whitley, 1993, p. 6). The particular contexts in this definition can be applied to regions as well as nations and even municipalities. In fact, the particular context must be understood to include both regions and nations, because each influences developments in the other in various ways.

The merit of redefining the analysis of learning regions in terms of the analysis of regional business systems is that it does justice to the complexity of the analysis of the learning region paradigm. Levels of analysis, for example, include those of individual actors (e.g. firms, knowledge centres and authorities), groups of actors collaborating in networks (e.g. the knowledge infrastructure and buyer–supplier collaboration), and the region (e.g. the institutional dynamics and regional economic development). These and other issues are addressed in the next section, where a research agenda for the analysis of learning regions is presented. Although it is possible to study the various subjects in isolation – in fact, that is what most studies do, as they address only the role of the knowledge infrastructure, for example – the result will be a study of regional learning rather than learning regions. As long as scholars take the time to consider the relations and interdependencies between the various subjects and levels of analysis, this is not a problem. On the contrary, it will only add to our understanding of learning regions. Hence also this volume.

The Importance of the Learning Region Paradigm to Scientific Research

The answer to the second question – what is the importance of the learning region paradigm to scientific research? – lies in the theoretical background to the learning region paradigm. According to Morgan (1997, p. 494), the learning region paradigm has emerged from an attempt to marry two disciplines of economic study, that is, the evolutionary economic theory (for an overview see Nelson, 1994) and the related Schumpeterian innovation theory, on the one hand, and economic geography (for a contemporary publication, see Scott, 1998), on the other. The new paradigm has been advocated by Morgan (1997), Storper (1997) and Cook and Morgan (1998), among others. The core of their argument is the 'association between organizational and technological learning within agglomeration' (Morgan, 1997, p. 495). This association, according to Storper, has two roots.

> The first concerns localized input–output relations, or traded interdependencies, which constitute webs of user–producer relations essential to information exchange. The second, and more important factor, concerns the role of untraded interdependencies (like labour markets, regional conventions, norms and values, public or semi-public institutions) which attach to the process of economic and organizational learning and coordination (Morgan, 1997, p. 495).

It is precisely these untraded interdependencies that, in the language of Maskell *et al.* (1998), create firm-specific and region-specific competencies. These competencies are difficult, if not impossible, for competitors to imitate and are therefore responsible for the creation of sustainable competitive advantage.

Competitive advantage is the pivot around which the learning region paradigm turns in terms of theoretical development. Learning regions ultimately seek, through a process of regional learning, to create better conditions for firms to exchange knowledge, to learn and create a competitive advantage. Although the word 'regional' may suggest otherwise, the learning region paradigm does not ignore the global context of competition. On the contrary, globalization and localization are in fact two sides of the same coin (Thrift and Amin, 1993). Learning often extends far beyond the boundaries of the region in which an actor is located. But it is the regional context, the regional business system, that, to a large extent, determines how successful that firm is in the global competition. Herein lies the theoretical value of the learning region paradigm. The nature of our economy has changed fundamentally during the past two decades and continues to change at a rapid pace. Traditional economic theory has proved to be poorly adapted to explaining the behaviour of firms and the process of economic development in the new global economy (cf. Best, 1990). New paths of theoretical inquiry are necessary to understand the nature of our economy. This understanding is fundamental for the public and private sectors alike to devise their policies and strategies that will shape our world in the 21st century. This volume is proof that the learning region paradigm is capable of delivering such understanding.

The Learning Region Paradigm and Economic and Social Development

The last question that needs to be answered is how the learning region paradigm can contribute to economic and social development. The learning region paradigm can be accused of ignoring the social consequences of the kind of economic growth it advocates. Sceptics have also argued that national governments can use the learning region paradigm to withdraw completely from the field of regional economic development and leave it to the regions themselves. Considering the enormous differences in economic development that still exist between Europe's regions, such a move would yield potentially dangerous consequences for cohesion within the European Union (Morgan, 1998). However, the learning region paradigm is not a playground for the strong and wealthy regions only, but it is true that most publications on learning regions, including this volume, that have been published so far, have paid little attention to social development.

It is widely accepted today that learning generates innovation and that innovation is the key to competitiveness and economic development (OECD, 1992). This knowledge has trickled down to public policy at various levels (EC, 1996). The promotion of regional learning gathered momentum throughout Europe during the 1990s, as shown in this volume, and these regional innovation policies have contributed to economic development in the regions concerned. What has yet to be addressed, however, is the danger that is sometimes referred to as jobless growth (Massey and Meegan, 1992). To put it differently, the evolutionary perspective of the learning region paradigm is a long-term perspective. Innovations do not create jobs in the short term, nor do they tackle complex social issues (such as the position of weaker groups in society). There is no getting around that fact. But this does not mean that the learning region paradigm is completely devoid of social connotations.

The introductory chapter to this volume discusses the knowledge-based economy, a condition towards which our economy is rapidly transforming itself. The learning region paradigm can be seen as a concept that fits into the wider context of the knowledge-based economy. The way in which our economy functions under the knowledge-based economy is radically different from that of the post-war era, and so is the position of workers and of people in general (cf. Best, 1990; Reich, 1991; Nonaka and Takeuchi, 1995). As for firms, the success of people in the knowledge-based economy depends on their ability to access, process, develop, and use knowledge. Thus the social challenge of the learning region paradigm is to create the right conditions for people to learn. The traditional dispute on the boundaries between the public and private spheres, that is, which are the fields for public policy, becomes irrelevant in the knowledge-based economy. The public and private spheres both benefit from people learning and both share the responsibility for creating the necessary conditions. The conditions will differ, of course, between regional business systems. Exactly how these conditions are to be created is an issue that lies beyond the scope of this volume. What matters here is the perspective. In the knowledge-based economy economic and social development alike are the result of learning. In fact, one cannot thrive without the other. A region suffering from social distress is not a good place for companies to invest in that depend on knowledge and innovation for their competitiveness rather than on cheap labour, for example. And these companies, in turn, create better jobs and pay higher wages than those which depend on cheap labour (cf. Jacobs, 1996).

The learning region paradigm is applicable to all types of regions and not just to the more advanced and prosperous ones. As the use of the business systems concept implies, the learning region paradigm is not a plea for some kind of political autonomy for regions, nor is it an excuse for national governments to withdraw from regional development policy. The region is a very effective level for certain interventions, but is less suited for others. The advantage that regional actors possess is that they can target their interventions more specifically to their target groups and objectives, because they are familiar with the 'couleur locale'. SME policy, for example, is best implemented at a regional level, but the regional level lacks the scale needed to sustain, for example, a knowledge infastructure, that is, a collection of research and education centres that can support learning in firms. For this kind of intervention, the national and European levels are much more appropriate. In terms of policy, the learning region paradigm is a plea for co-operation between the various levels of government. This does, however, require regions to be sufficiently empowered to play their new role. In other words, the learning region paradigm is also an attempt to put flesh on the bones of additionality, that is, the concept used by the European Commission to implement policy along the lines discussed above (cf. EC, 1998; Morgan, 1998).

To summarize, the learning region paradigm is a proponent of the knowledge-based economy. It offers a long-term perspective on economic and social development that is based on a combination of learning and the unique characteristics of each region. If regional actors achieve a productive mode of co-operation among themselves and with national actors, the learning and regional characteristics create the conditions through the regional business systems for sustainable economic and social development.

ISSUES FOR ANALYSIS: PROPOSALS FOR A RESEARCH AGENDA

In this section, attention shifts to the issues in need of analysis to further our understanding of the learning region paradigm. This section distinguishes five such issues. Each is broadly defined so as to include different aspects of the issues. There are, of course, overlaps between the issues, as they are inter-connected. Before turning to them, however, we must comment on the different levels of analysis of the learning region paradigm.

Levels of Analysis

Basically, the learning region paradigm can be explored along three levels of analysis. Each of the issues for analysis discussed below can be studied at these three levels. The first level of analysis is the actors. Actors possess, acquire, process, exchange and create knowledge through learning. This makes actors the basic level of analysis. Under the learning region paradigm, four types of actor are relevant: firms, authorities, organizations in the knowledge infrastructure (research and education centres and intermediary organizations), and networks. In the context of the learning region paradigm, networks must be regarded as actors, because, as argued in this volume, knowledge is increasingly embedded in networks instead of individual organizations. Actors are connected to and embedded in the other levels of analysis, that is, factors and regional business systems. But where this background is not the main concern of an inquiry, actors can be studied in isolation. The process of learning that takes place in and between actors is therefore the main concern of the analysis.

The second level of analysis is that of factors. Factors can be seen as the learning region version of supply-side economics. The availability of factors differs from region to region both in quantity and quality. Examples of factors include the geographical location of a region, the availability of physical infrastructure, the regional knowledge infrastructure, and the level of education of the labour force (cf. Jacquemin and Wright, 1993). These factors are the conditions that influence the success of actors to a significant degree. Advanced regions, in general, have a more advanced stock of factors and the regional actors have closer relations with these factors.

The third level of analysis, the regional business system, concerns the analysis of institutions, values, norms, labour relations, modes of government intervention, and so on. This level connects actors and factors and shows the patterns behind regional development. These patterns are often stable over time and are responsible for the fact that regional development is to a substantial degree path-dependent (cf. Maskell *et al.*, 1998). Even more than factors, regional business systems are responsible for the differences in economic development between regions, because whether or not actors will engage in a process of mutual learning and make an effort to expand and strengthen the factors in their region is to a large degree dependent on the characteristics of the regional business system. The variations between regional business systems are also responsible for the fact that there is no one best way of promoting regional learning and for the fact that there is no single list of characteristics of 'the learning region'. In other words, a blueprint is not available.

1. Knowledge, Innovation, and Learning

Knowledge, innovation, and learning are the core of the learning region paradigm. The need to analyse these issues from a learning region perspective becomes even clearer against the background of the emerging knowledge-based economy. Several questions stand out in the analysis of knowledge and innovation.

In the knowledge-based economy, knowledge is the most strategic resource and learning the most important process. But what are the other characteristics of the knowledge-based economy? How do the 'rules of the game' differ from those of the post-war era? What are the implications of the knowledge-based economy for firm structure and hierarchy, for example? Do organizations become flatter in order to respond more quickly to rapidly changing environments? In that context, the back-to-core-competencies debate seems to fit into the framework of the knowledge-based economy. Because firms do not have sufficient knowledge to be experts in everything, they have to specialize in certain activities. The question is, what knowledge is strategic to firms, what can they outsource and what can they not? These and other questions need to be answered. The typology of Best (1990), where he distinguishes between 'big business' and 'the new competition' may offer a good starting point for analysis here.

The purpose of learning is to produce innovations in terms of new product development, new processes and organizational renewal. In view of the fact that the rules of the game are different in the knowledge-based economy, it seems perfectly logical to assume that a theory of innovation must be developed that takes these new rules into account. This new theory must start with the basic building block of the innovation process: knowledge. Knowledge comes in many different forms, such as technical knowledge, managerial knowledge, knowledge of markets and customer preferences (Jacobs, 1996). And it is not just the high-tech knowledge that makes the difference. 'Pedestrian forms of knowledge' are responsible for many innovations (Morgan, 1997). Moreover, the difference between tacit (embedded) and codified forms of knowledge has an enormous impact on learning processes (Nonaka and Takeuchi, 1995). In the introductory chapter we argued that innovation in the knowledge-based economy could be explained in terms of Schumpeter's new combinations. Innovation, therefore, is the product of making new combinations of knowledge through learning.

Knowledge is generated from many different sources, and knowledge transfer is necessary to bring knowledge from the supplier to the demander. Traditionally, this transfer has been effected in a market. The knowledge market, however, suffers like other markets from imperfections and this explains why knowledge demand and knowledge supply do not adequately match. The idea of a knowledge market, however, is counter-productive. Since most knowledge is tacit, there can never be a situation in which actors are perfectly informed about knowledge, not even on a hypothetical level, as in neoclassical economics. Consequently, there can never be a knowledge market and that is precisely why knowledge is such a strategic resource. In order for knowledge to be traded on a knowledge market, it must be codified. But codified knowledge can never be a source of durable competitive advantage, which means that the whole idea of a knowledge market is alien to the knowledge-based economy. Other transfer mechanisms apply in the knowledge-based economy. Nonaka and Takeuchi (1995) propose a knowledge spiral to explain the transfer and creation of knowledge within firms, but given the fact that organizations depend on each other for their knowledge supply, it is fruitful to expand the notion of the knowledge spiral to an inter-organizational level.

2. Global, Local Interplay

Over the past decade it has become clear that globalization does not mean the end of geography (cf. Storper, 1997 and Scott, 1998). What is not clear, however, is which activities require proximity and which do not. Questions remain, such as do suppliers have a future in the western countries or will their work flow to low-cost countries? Or is there a future for knowledge-intensive manufacturing in western countries? On another level the convergence-divergence debate continues. Will regions become more alike, or will differences in their institutional structure remain and continue to 'dictate' different paths of development? Evidence from Maskell *et al.* (1998) suggest the latter may be the case. But more analysis and comparison of regional business systems are needed to learn the answer. As for the question of where activities are best performed, given the conditions of the knowledge-based economy, the concept of the geography of knowledge (Storper, 1997) offers a good starting point for analysis. The geography of knowledge suggests that innovation is tied to certain geographical areas because it involves the exchange of large amounts of tacit knowledge. This requires face-to-face communication over a considerable period of time, in which case, proximity will facilitate communication tremendously. On the other hand, codified knowledge can be transferred easily on a global scale through the use of modern information and communication technologies. Consequently, activities that depend largely on codified knowledge are not tied to certain areas.

Many questions remain unanswered, such as the role of research and education centres. Some of these centres are strongly embedded in their own regions, whereas others have few or no relations with other actors in their region. Perhaps a distinction between fundamental, new knowledge and Morgan's 'pedestrian forms of knowledge' may be helpful. The assumption here is that fundamental knowledge operates on a global scale and pedestrian forms of knowledge, such as vocational education and applied research, operate on a national or regional scale. Centres for vocational education and applied research would specialize in those activities demanded by regional firms. This would create unique regional conditions as the source of a region's competitive strength (cf. Maskell *et al.*, 1998). It would also explain persistent differences in the institutional structures (business systems) of regions.

3. New Governance Structures

By their nature, knowledge and learning extend beyond the boundaries of organizations, making the knowledge-based economy a network economy. This raises questions about the dynamics of inter-firm collaboration in the knowledge-based economy and the regional embedding of these dynamics. The knowledge-based economy calls for an entrepreneurial firm (cf. Best, 1990; Nonaka and Takeuchi, 1995) which has less hierarchy and gives employees more responsibility in their work. Best (1990) argues that a reintegration of thinking and doing is necessary in order to achieve the best results. An entrepreneurial firm capitalizes on all its sources of knowledge, including the pedestrian forms of knowledge. Moreover, in the services sectors the main means of production are the workers. They are referred to as knowledge workers or symbolic analysts (Reich, 1991). An entrepreneurial firm creates the conditions that allow knowledge to flow through the organization and facilitates the process of learning. The entrepreneurial firm has been studied at length, following a tradition that began with Penrose (1959). More analysis in this tradition, but centred on the role of knowledge, will provide new insights. Another promising line of analysis seems to come from the socio-technical tradition (for example, Taylor and Felten, 1993). The latter looks at the optimal design of work within an organization from an organizational design perspective, and ensuring a free flow of knowledge through the organization and facilitating learning are certainly design issues.

To return to the inter-firm, or network, level of analysis, here too, exchange of knowledge and learning calls for different structures governing inter-firm relations. It was argued above that knowledge is not a good that can be exchanged on a market. One way of illustrating this clearly is to compare a candle and a fire. One can light someone else's candle and still have one's own fire.[1] Moreover, innovations increasingly become a network product, as they are the result of a combination of different 'pieces of knowledge' from different organizations. Consequently, traditional Williamsonian transaction cost economics may not be appropriate for explaining transactions involving knowledge and learning. Moreover, transactions economics does not take space into account in its explanations. A new approach to governance structures seems necessary and, as firms become more dependent on each other, opportunistic behaviour becomes increasingly counter-productive. Trust is the glue that binds firms and organizations together in networks (cf. Morgan, 1997 and Maskell *et al.*, 1998). Analysis of the role of trust and reputation in networks is necessary to help explain the inter-firm dynamics in the knowledge-based economy. Trust may also be connected to space, as it can be institutionalized in regionally-based networks (cf. Maskell *et al.*, 1998).

It is also interesting to learn what the effect of learning is on the balance of power in networks. Does the fact that firms depend on each other for knowledge mean that traditionally weaker partners, such as suppliers, can suddenly find themselves in a much more powerful position? Evidence from this volume points in that direction, but more research is needed. Finally, the role of new information and communication technologies in the process of knowledge exchange and learning must be addressed. How does it affect relations within and between organizations, and how does it affect the factor of space?

4. The Role of Government

It was argued earlier that the public–private debate is irrelevant in the knowledge-based economy, as both sectors are responsible for knowledge and learning. This places public–private partnership in a whole new perspective. As this volume has explained, the role of government has changed from that of traditional rule-maker to animateur. The 'new regional policy' has been discussed in great detail in this volume. It aims at the promotion of innovation through knowledge and learning in order to improve the competitiveness of the firms in a region. This is the practice of the learning region paradigm and it is well understood by now, although scientific analysis is never finished. But two important questions remain open: the level of policy intervention and the validation of regional policy.

It is clear from experience that SME policy is most effective on a regional level, while the knowledge infrastructure operates at the national or supranational (e.g. European) level. But more research is needed into the appropriate level of various kinds of policy interventions. In other words, the concept of subsidiarity needs to be given a scientific basis. Regional and national authorities and, in the case of the EU, the European authorities, must find a balance between their respective competencies. Another question is whether more powerful regional authorities make more effective regional innovation policies. Power, here, does not necessarily mean political power. The role of regional authorities is that of animateur and a good animateur does not rely solely on formal power, although a certain degree of the latter will be necessary. The 'toolkit' of this animateur is also a question that has not been answered satisfactorily. We need to know which interventions are most effective under which conditions? Moreover, the collaboration between authorities, both horizontally and vertically, must be addressed. In short, although the last decade has produced much research into the role of government, many questions remain open.

When the subject of 'policy' is raised, the inevitable question of its effectiveness always follows. Validation and evaluation of the new regional policy is difficult for a number of reasons. Firstly, its effects are felt only in the longer term. A firm does not establish a stronger competitive position overnight and the possible increase in jobs may take even longer. Secondly, the direct results of the new regional policy are often tacit. A better co-ordination between regional actors is difficult to express in money, while the amount of knowledge which is transferred to SMEs, for example, is equally difficult to measure. Traditional indicators, such as increased employment, increase in gross national or regional product, investments, number of new research centres, number of trainees in a programme, and so on, are not sufficient in the area of knowledge exchange and learning. Researchers here have the difficult task of providing new indicators to capture the significant processes in the knowledge-based economy.

5. The Social Dimension of the Learning Region Paradigm

It was argued earlier that the social dimension of the learning region paradigm has so far received little attention in scientific analysis. A good starting point for such an analysis is perhaps the position of the individual worker or unemployed person in the knowledge-based economy. How can the conditions be created for these persons to learn? On a higher level of analysis, it is important to look at job creation. Optimists say that the knowledge-based economy creates better jobs. Employers become more dependent on the skills of their employees and are therefore willing to pay higher wages and provide better working conditions. Pessimists, on the other hand, argue that innovation leads to the loss of jobs. Both are partly right (cf. EC, 1996 and Morgan, 1998). More research is needed to find out how many jobs are created and lost as a result of the shift of the economy towards knowledge-based production. It is also important to learn what kind of jobs are created and lost. Is it only 'good' jobs that are created and 'bad' jobs that are lost? A related question is how does this affect the population in a region? Do new jobs go to inhabitants of that region or do they lose their jobs, while new jobs go to newcomers from outside? And, on a more fundamental level: can a region afford not to use the potential of knowledge and skills of a considerable part of its population because they do not actively participate in the economy? And if not, what can be done to activate them? The answers to these questions must be found to help shape the new regional innovation policies.

At the turn of the millennium, the knowledge-based economy is becoming a reality and the learning region paradigm a looming perspective. There is much that we know about this perspective and it has been put into practice in many regions in varying degrees. Many questions remain, however. Hence this research agenda. Our future depends more than ever on our ability to create better products and services than our competitors. This ability is based on knowledge. Knowledge is a characteristic of people first of all, and is therefore not subject to organizational boundaries, if only because people can change jobs and disperse knowledge through the Internet. This makes networks, rather than individual actors, become the focus of the action. Because of various processes these networks are tied to regions, which means that globalization and localization are complementary rather than in conflict. Consequently, understanding the dynamics that shape our global economy must start with an analysis of the dynamics of our regional world. It is perhaps ironical that, now that we have the ability to operate on a global scale, we are confronted again with our regional context. On the other hand, it also means that all the world's regions have a chance of success in the global economy.

NOTE

1. Based on a remark by Mikel Landabaso during the conference on learning regions of March 27, 1998 in Tilburg, the Netherlands that was at the basis of this volume.

REFERENCES

Best, M. (1990), *The New Competition: Institutions of Industrial Renewal*, Cambridge: Polity Press.

Cooke, Ph. and K. Morgan (1998), *The Associational Economy: Firms, Regions, and Innovation*, Oxford: Oxford University Press.

EC (European Commission) (1996), *Green paper on innovation*, Brussels: EC.

EC (European Commission) (1998), *Reinforcing cohesion and competitiveness through RTD and innovation policies*, Brussels: EC.

Jacobs, D. (1996), *Het Kennisoffensief* [the knowledge offensive], Alphen aan den Rijn: Samson.

Jacquemin, A. and D. Wright (1993), *The European Challenges post-1992: Shaping Factors, Shaping Actors*, Aldershot: Edward Elgar.

Maskell P., E. Heikki, H. Ingjaldur, A. Malmber and E. Vatne (1998), *Competitiveness, Localised Learning and Regional Development: Specialisation and Prosperity in Small Open Economies*, London: Routledge.

Massey, D. and R. Meegan (1992), *The Anatomy of Job-loss*, London, New York: Methuen.

Morgan, K. (1997), 'The learning region: institutions, innovation and regional renewal', *Regional Studies*, **31** (5), pp. 491–503.

Morgan, K. (1998), *Balancing cohesion and innovation*, paper presented at the Intelligent Region European Conference, Cardiff, 18–19 May.

Nelson, R. (1994), 'Evolutionary theory about economic change', in N. Smelser and R. Swedberg (eds), *The Handbook of Economic Sociology*, Princeton, N.J.: Princeton University Press, pp. 108–36.

Nonaka, I. and H. Takeuchi (1995), *The Knowledge-Creating Company: how Japanese Companies Create the Dynamics of Innovation*, Oxford: Oxford University Press.

OECD (Organisation for Economic Co-operation and Development) (1992), *Technology and the Economy: the Key Relationships*, Paris: OECD.

Penrose, E. (1959), *The Theory of the Growth of the Firm*, Oxford: Oxford University Press.

Reich, R. (1991), *The Work of Nations: Preparing Ourselves for 21st-century Capitalism*, New York: Vintage Books.

Scott, A. (1998), *Regions and the World Economy: the Coming Shape of Global Production, Competition and Political Order*, Oxford: Oxford University Press.

Storper, M. (1997), *The Regional World, Territorial Development in a Global Economy*, New York: The Guildford Press.

Taylor, J. and F. Felten (1993), *Performance by Design: Sociotechnical Systems in North America*, Englewood Cliffs, N.J.: Prentice Hall.

Thrift, N. and A. Amin (1993), 'Globalisation, institutional thickness and local prospects', in *Revue d'economie regionale et urbaine*, (3), pp. 405-27.

Whitley, R. (1993), 'Societies, firms and markets: the social structuring of business systems', in R. Whitley (ed.), *European Business Systems: Firms and Markets in their National Context*, London: Sage, pp. 5-45.

Index

259